Sport in the global society

General Editors: J.A. Mangan and Boria Majumdar

The interest in sports studies around the world is growing and will continue to do so. This unique series combines aspects of the expanding study of *sport in the global society*, providing comprehensiveness and comparison under one editorial umbrella. It is particularly timely, with studies in the aesthetic elements of sport proliferating in institutions of higher education.

Eric Hobsbawm once called sport one of the most significant practices of the late nineteenth century. Its significance was even more marked in the late twentieth century and will continue to grow in importance into the new millennium as the world develops into a 'global village' sharing the English language, technology and sport.

Other Titles in the Series

Matters of Sport

Essays in Honour of Eric Dunning

Edited by
Dominic Malcolm and Ivan Waddington

Routledge
Taylor & Francis Group

LONDON AND NEW YORK

First published 2008 by Routledge
2 Park Square, Milton Park, Abingdon, Oxon OX14 4RN

Simultaneously published in the USA and Canada by Routledge
270 Madison Avenue, New York, NY 10016

Routledge is an imprint of the Taylor & Francis Group, an informa business

© 2008 Dominic Malcolm and Ivan Waddington

Typeset in Minion 10.5/13pt by the Alden Group, OxfordShire
Printed and bound in Great Britain by MPG Books Ltd, Bodmin, Cornwall

British Library Cataloguing in Publication Data
A catalogue record for this book is available from the British Library

ISBN 10: 0-415-34833-1 hbk
ISBN 10: 0-7146-8282-9 pbk

ISBN 13: 978-0-415-34833-1 hbk
ISBN 13: 978-0-7146-8282-2 pbk

CONTENTS

Series Editors' Foreword

SPORT IN THE GLOBAL SOCIETY was launched in the late nineties. It now has over one hundred volumes. Until recently an odd myopia characterised academia with regard to sport. The global *groves of academe* remained essentially Cartesian in inclination. They favoured a mind/body dichotomy: thus the study of ideas was acceptable; the study of sport was not. All that has now changed. Sport is now incorporated, intelligently, within debate about *inter alia* ideologies, power, stratification, mobility and inequality. The reason is simple. In the modern world sport is everywhere: it is as ubiquitous as war. E.J. Hobsbawm, the Marxist historian, once called it one of the most significant of the new manifestations of late nineteenth century Europe. Today it is one of the most significant manifestations of the twenty-first century world. Such is its power, politically, culturally, economically, spiritually and aesthetically, that sport beckons the academic more persuasively than ever- to borrow, and refocus, an expression of the radical historian Peter Gay- 'to explore its familiar terrain and to wrest new interpretations from its inexhaustible materials'. As a subject for inquiry, it is replete, as he remarked of history, with profound 'questions unanswered and for that matter questions unasked'.

Sport seduces the teeming 'global village'; it is the new opiate of the masses; it is one of the great modern experiences; its attraction astonishes only the recluse; its appeal spans the globe. Without exaggeration, sport is a mirror in which nations, communities, men and women now see themselves. That reflection is sometimes bright, sometimes dark, sometimes distorted, sometimes magnified. This metaphorical mirror is a source of mass exhilaration and depression, security and insecurity, pride and humiliation, bonding and alienation. Sport, for many, has replaced religion as a source of emotional catharsis and spiritual passion, and for many, since it is among the earliest of memorable childhood experiences, it infiltrates memory, shapes enthusiasms, serves fantasies. To co-opt Gay again: it blends memory and desire.

Sport, in addition, can be a lens through which to scrutinise major themes in the political and social sciences: democracy and despotism and the great associated movements of socialism, fascism, communism and capitalism as well as political cohesion and confrontation, social reform and social stability.

The story of modern sport is the story of the modern world-in microcosm; a modern global tapestry permanently being woven. Furthermore, nationalist and imperialist, philosopher and politician, radical and conservative have all sought in sport a manifestation of national identity, status and superiority.

Finally, for countless millions sport is the personal pursuit of ambition, assertion, well-being and enjoyment.

For all the above reasons, sport demands the attention of the academic. *Sport in the Global Society* is a response.

J.A. Mangan
Boria Majumdar

Series Editors
Sport in the Global Society

Eric Dunning: This Sporting Life
Ivan Waddington & Dominic Malcolm

Eric Dunning's first publication in the sociology of sport was an article entitled 'Football in its Early Stages', which was based on his MA thesis and which was published in *History Today* in 1963.[1] This was followed a year later by an article on 'The Evolution of Football', which was published in *New Society*.[2] It is important to note the dates of these publications, for they were among the earliest, and in Britain were probably the very first, published pieces of research to examine sport from a properly sociological perspective. Writing many years later, Dunning recalled how he had become involved in the sociological study of sport and how his postgraduate supervisor, Norbert Elias, had suggested that his first task as a young graduate student was to construct a relevant bibliography. Dunning recalls that 'even the most exhaustive literature search came up with only one unambiguously sociological item', Gregory P. Stone's classic 'American Sports: Play and Display'.[3] Dunning noted that in addition there was, of course, Huizinga's *Homo Ludens*, plus 'a handful of useful items by psychologists and some extremely valuable work by physical educationalists such as Peter McIntosh'.[4] But, he continued, 'little of that was really sociological in the sense of being oriented around sociological and sociologically relevant concepts and theories so I decided – this really was my idea rather than Norbert's – to orientate my research around his work on "civilizing processes".[5] Dunning's decision to apply Elias's theoretical framework to sport marked the beginning of a long and very productive relationship between Dunning and Elias, and a significant point in the genesis of a theoretically informed sociology of sport.

It is important to locate Dunning's work in its proper historical context, and more specifically in the context of the development of the sociology of sport, if we are to appreciate fully his contribution to the development of what is now a major sub-discipline within sociology. When Dunning began his research in this area in 1959, the sociology of sport did not exist as a sub-discipline. At that time there were no organized academic groups concerned specifically with the sociology of sport, and no specialist journals in the field; indeed, as Dunning has noted, there was among some sociologists at that time a 'contemptuous dismissal of sport as an area of sociological enquiry'.[6] It was not until 1964 that the International Sociological Association established an International Committee for the Sociology of Sport, which later became the International Sociology of Sport Association. The International Committee held its first symposium in Cologne in 1966, and in the same year the first specialist journal, the *International Review of Sport Sociology* (relaunched as the *International Review for the Sociology of Sport* in 1984, with Dunning as an associate editor) began publication in Warsaw. Even after the establishment of the *IRSS*, however, the development of the sociology of sport as a sub-discipline was, for many years, a slow and difficult process.

A second specialist journal, the *Journal of Sport and Social Issues*, began publication in 1977. By this time, Dunning had already published his first book in the area, *The Sociology of Sport: A Selection of Readings* (1971). [7] But the continued slow development of the field is indicated by the fact that, in a paper on sport and violence which was published in the second issue of the new journal, Harry Edwards and Van Rackages noted that 'In the new International Encyclopedia of the Social Sciences, neither "sport" nor "violence" rates entry as a subject worthy of social scientific investigation in its own right'.[8] Both areas have, of course, subsequently become the focus of a great deal of sociological research and the relationship between sport and violence is an area to which Dunning has made an outstanding contribution, as Mennell, Bairner and Maguire point out in their essays in this volume.

One year after the *Journal of Sport and Social Issues* began publication, the North American Society for the Sociology of Sport (NASSS) was established with 21 founding members. The NASSS website indicates that a small group of North American sociologists felt a growing need at that time to establish a specialist study group in what it describes as this 'newly emerging field'.[9] It might be noted that, by that time, Dunning had already been working and publishing in this 'newly emerging field' for almost two decades.

A third major journal in the area, the *Sociology of Sport Journal*, did not begin publication until 1984, just two years before the publication of Elias and Dunning's seminal *Quest for Excitement*,[10] which has since been translated into Italian,

Spanish, Portuguese, French, Japanese and Greek editions. Even at this time, however, the sociology of sport was not fully accepted within the parent discipline. In the first issue of the *SSJ*, the editor (Jay Coakley) noted that, 'Although the field has grown considerably over the past 15 years, it still does not enjoy a "critical mass" of scholars as large as that associated with other subfields within sociology'. Moreover, while the 'contemptuous dismissal' of work in the sociology of sport, which Dunning had encountered in the 1960s, may have been less evident in the early 1980s, the *SSJ* editor still felt it necessary to point out that 'a number of sociologists remain sceptical about the significance of work on sport'.[11]

Enough has been said to indicate that Eric Dunning was a genuine pioneer in developing what, in the 1960s, was not only an unfashionable field of enquiry, but one which was then considered by many sociologists as a field not worthy of serious academic study. In this regard, Dunning has a strong claim to be considered as a genuine 'founding father' of the sociology of sport.

In addition to his contribution to the sociology of sport, Dunning has, as Mennell points out in his essay in this book, also made significant contributions to several other areas of sociology (friends and colleagues who have played sport with, and perhaps more particularly against, Dunning will smile at Mennell's mischievous sub-heading, 'The Unsporting Dunning'). However, and notwithstanding his contributions to other areas – most notably, sociological theory, the sociology of development and race relations, as well as his translations of some of Elias's major works into English – Dunning is without doubt best known for his work in the sociology of sport. Indeed, in many ways, Dunning's own career has developed co-relatively with the development of the sub-discipline to which he has made such a distinguished contribution over a period of some 40 years.

However, as Mennell notes, Dunning himself accepts the label 'sociologist of sport' only as a matter of convenience, for he has always seen research on sport only as a means of contributing theoretically and empirically to the development of the discipline of sociology as a whole. In this regard, the central object of Dunning's work has been not merely to add to our knowledge of sport but, more particularly, to test, extend and develop, through its application to the specific field of sport, the more general theoretical approach initially developed by Norbert Elias, that is figurational or process-sociology. In this regard, it might be said that Dunning's writings, together of course with those of Elias, have helped to establish figurational sociology as a particularly influential theoretical framework within the sociological study of sport.

The prominence of figurational sociology within the sociology of sport is a matter to which Dunning himself has drawn attention. Writing in 1992, he noted that:

> When he died in August 1990 at the age of 93, Elias had come to be a widely respected, if still in some ways controversial figure, in the sociological world. Nevertheless, recognition of his work remains patchy and his influence has penetrated less widely and deeply into the world of Anglo-American sociology than those of such continental countries as The Netherlands, Germany, France and Italy. There is, however, one exception to this pattern. It involves not a national

sociological community but a particular sub-discipline. I am referring, of course, to
the sociology of sport. In this field Elias is a well-known name, even in Britain and
America, so much so that some people seem erroneously to think that figurational
or process-sociology, the type of sociology for which he sought to lay the
foundations, is concerned solely with the study of sport!

He continued:

> An interesting question is posed in this connection. Why, in countries where Elias's
> contributions are widely ignored in 'mainstream' sociology, should they have been
> granted a degree of recognition in what is, in my view wrongly, generally defined by
> the 'guardians' of the currently dominant paradigms as one of the subject's marginal
> byways? A friend once suggested that I might have had something to do with it. It is
> not modesty that leads me to reject such an idea. It is rather that a sociologically
> more plausible explanation is ready to hand, one that does not involve according too
> much weight to the contributions of a single individual. This more plausible
> explanation relates to the fact that, as Horne and Jary . . . have rightly noted, Norbert
> Elias and I were among the first to enter the field. A consequence of this was that,
> when the sociology of sport started to expand in the 1970s and 1980s, and
> particularly when, in that connection, Marxists began to develop an interest in the
> problems that it poses, they found themselves entering a terrain already occupied by
> a paradigm in some ways similar to but in others different from their own. They
> responded with critical gusto and it was in such a context that the figurational
> sociology of sport, and with it Norbert Elias, began to gain a degree of recognition if
> not acceptance.[12]

We agree with much of this analysis. It is certainly the case that, although sociologists
in general have shown a growing interest in the figurational or process-sociological
approach in recent years, and although we believe this interest is likely to continue to
grow, it is nevertheless clearly the case that figurational sociology remains a much
more influential theoretical framework within the sociology of sport than within the
broader discipline of sociology more generally. We also agree with Dunning's
suggestion that a major reason for its relative prominence within the study of sport is
because he and Elias were among the first to enter the field. However, we believe that
Dunning's unnamed friend who suggested that perhaps Dunning had something to do
with the prominence of figurational sociology within the sociology of sport was in fact
correct and that, in rejecting this suggestion, Dunning was being unduly modest.

Of course, the development of science – like the development of sport – is, as Elias
pointed out, a social process and, as such, it cannot be explained in terms of the
actions of a single individual. In this regard, Dunning is correct to be sceptical about
explanations of developments which, as he puts it, accord 'too much weight to the
contributions of a single individual'. In this regard, one can no more explain scientific
developments in individualistic terms than one can explain the origins of rugby in
terms of the individualistic William Webb Ellis myth, as Dunning and Sheard have
persuasively argued.[13]

However, while Elias and figurational sociologists more generally rightly insist
that processes of social development – for example the development of sport
or science – must be explained in terms of *social* processes, this does not mean that

they can be understood without reference to the actions of concrete individuals. Indeed, Elias acknowledged the role – albeit a limited role – that individual people sometimes play in processes of development. Thus he argued that, while the belief 'in the unlimited power of individual people over the course of history is wishful thinking', it is similarly unrealistic to believe 'that all people are of equal importance for the course of history'.[14] We would argue that the work of Dunning has played a very important part in establishing figurational sociology as a major framework within the sociology of sport; indeed, we would suggest that, notwithstanding the widespread recognition that his work has received, it has still been undervalued in this respect. We believe it is time for a reconsideration of Dunning's part in this development.

As we noted earlier, Dunning has pointed out that he and Elias were among the first sociologists to write about sport. In this context we would wish to suggest that, because Elias undoubtedly started out as the senior partner, and because of Elias and Dunning's close personal, and academically very fruitful, relationship, Dunning's own contribution has perhaps been overshadowed because of the tendency within the sub-discipline to subsume the work of Dunning under the umbrella of Norbert Elias's theoretical contribution. As a consequence, commentators have sometimes failed to recognize the very real significance of Dunning's own contribution. Let us explore this argument further.

In his highly regarded book on Elias, Stephen Mennell points out that, although he was a keen sportsman, Elias 'came to sport as a topic for sociological investigation relatively late in his career'.[15] To be more precise, Elias appears to have come to sport as a topic for sociological investigation only after he began to supervise Dunning as a postgraduate student for, apart from one passing mention of boxing, of just two pages, in *The Civilizing Process*, Elias wrote nothing on sport until the mid-1960s. As Mennell puts it, 'it seems to have been Eric Dunning's interest in pursuing the sociology of sport which spurred Elias in the same direction'.[16] And although Elias wrote some hugely insightful essays on sport, this area of study appears never to have been as central to his own academic interests as it was to Dunning's. It is, for example, not without significance that in their co-edited *The Norbert Elias Reader*, Johan Goudsblom and Stephen Mennell, both of whom are thoroughly familiar with all aspects of Elias's work, included just one essay by Elias on sport.[17]

There are, too, other indications that Elias may have been unusually reliant on Dunning when it came to writing about sport. The vast majority of Elias's very considerable published work (he published 19 books in total) was sole authored; indeed, the bibliography of Elias's work which is included in Mennell's book indicates that Elias only ever had two co-authors. One of these was John Scotson, with whom Elias co-authored just one publication, *The Established and the Outsiders*.[18] The other author with whom Elias wrote was Eric Dunning, with whom Elias wrote several works; significantly, all were on sport, for Elias never published jointly with Dunning on any other subject. Elias's first publication in the sociology of sport was the essay, 'Dynamics of Sport Groups with Special Reference to Football',[19] which was co-authored with Dunning and which appeared in 1966, three years after Dunning's first, and sole authored, paper on sport had been published. It is also of interest to note that, of Elias's many books, just two were on sport and these – *Sport im Zivilisationsprozess*,[20] published in Germany in 1983, and *Quest for Excitement* (1986) – were both co-authored with Dunning. Indeed, Elias wrote only a handful of essays on sport without the collaboration of Dunning. The first two of these did not appear until 1971 and, again significantly, they consisted of a brief Forward to Dunning's first edited book, *The Sociology of Sport*, and the essay, 'The Genesis of Sport as a Sociological Problem', which was also included in the same book. Mennell's bibliography of the works of Elias, and that included in Goudsblom and Mennell's Elias reader, indicate that Elias only published two other essays on sport without the co-authorship of Dunning – 'An Essay on Sport and Violence', which was published in *Quest for Excitement*, and an essay on football and the civilizing process, which was published in German in 1983.[21] It is also striking that almost all of Elias's writings on sport, both sole authored and co-authored with Dunning, were written in a relatively short period of time from the mid-1960s to the early 1970s (although *Quest for Excitement* was not published until 1986, most of the essays by Elias had been drafted some years before). That the study of sport was not perhaps a central or continuing concern of his work is also suggested by the fact that, although he continued writing until the very end of his long life, and although he produced several major works in the last years of his life – including *Involvement and Detachment* (1987),[22] *Die Gesellschaft der Individuen* (1987),[23] *The Symbol Theory* (1991)[24] and, perhaps most notably, *Studien über die Deutschen* (1989),[25] which was described by Mennell and Dunning in their English translation of the book as 'the most important book by Elias since *The Civilizing Process*'[26] – he appears not to have written anything on sport after he left Leicester in the 1970s, other than the work published in Germany, referred to above, which clearly drew on his own and Dunning's work which had been done at Leicester many years before. Whilst Dunning clearly owes much to the theoretical insights of Elias, it is not unreasonable to suggest that, without Dunning's contribution, Elias's own work on sport – assuming that he would have written about sport without the stimulus of Dunning's interest, which is itself perhaps doubtful – may not have had the critical mass necessary to become a significant theoretical perspective in the sub-discipline and, consequently, the sociology of sport may have developed in a radically different direction over the last 40 years.

In marked contrast to the work of Elias, the study of sport has been the most central and continuing theme of Dunning's research and publications for more than 40 years. To date, Dunning has authored and edited, either alone or with others, a total of 17 books, of which no fewer than 14 have been on sport. He has also written, alone or with others, in the region of 80 papers on sport, which have been published as journal articles or chapters in books. There can be no doubt about the influence which his writings have had. As we noted earlier, *Quest for Excitement*, which was co-authored with Elias, has been translated into six foreign languages, but many of Dunning's other works have had hardly less impact. For example, between 1984 and 1990 Dunning and his Leicester colleagues produced three books on football hooliganism and, as Alan

Bairner points out in his essay in this collection, the work of the 'Leicester School' 'has been more substantial and more influential than that which has been produced by any other individuals or research groups' (p. 595). Of the books on football hooliganism, *Hooligans Abroad* was translated into German in 1988,[27] while a Portuguese edition of *Football on Trial* was published in 1994.[28]

Of Dunning's other books, *Barbarians, Gentlemen and Players,* his study with Ken Sheard of the development of Rugby football, is arguably the best sociological study of the development of any sport. Originally published in 1979, it was translated into Japanese in 1983 and a new, updated edition has recently been published by Routledge. Dunning's outstanding contribution to the sociology of sport was recognized when his book, *Sport Matters,*[29] was awarded the prize of the North American Society for the Sociology of Sport as the outstanding book published in the field in 1999. The title of this *Festschrift, Matters of Sport,* clearly echoes the title of that award-winning book.

The impact of Dunning's work on the sociology of sport in general, and the figurational approach to sport in particular, is perhaps most clearly indicated by the central focus in many figurational studies of sport on civilizing processes and associated issues of violence and violence control. In one sense, it might seem odd to suggest that this is evidence of the impact of Dunning's work, for the theory of civilizing processes was, of course, initially developed by Elias. However, as we saw earlier, it was Dunning's idea to apply the theory of civilizing processes to sport. Since then, figurational sociologists have made such a sustained contribution to the study of civilizing processes and sport that some critics have suggested that figurational sociologists are preoccupied with issues of violence and its control. Stokvis, for example, has criticized figurational sociologists for what he sees – quite wrongly in our view – as an over-concentration on violence; this approach, he claims, is 'too limited' and has led them to neglect other important areas of research.[30] We have responded to this criticism elsewhere[31] and will not repeat those arguments here.

Whilst we might dispute Stokvis's idea that figurational sociology of sport is too narrowly focused on violence, it remains the case that, as Dunning, Malcolm and Waddington have recently noted, 'a substantial proportion of the work produced by figurational sociologists of sport has focused on sports in which forms of controlled violence are socially tolerated and/or which attract violence-prone spectators'.[32] That figurational sociologists have made such a major contribution to this area cannot, of course, be explained simply in terms of Dunning's work. In his initial decision to apply Elias's theory of civilizing processes to sport, Dunning was encouraged and supported by Elias, and Elias himself subsequently wrote about civilizing processes and sport. In addition, some of Dunning's postgraduate students have also contributed highly original work in this area; particularly worthy of note in this regard is the work of Sheard on boxing, Malcolm on cricket and Smith on shooting.[33] However, there can be no doubt that, of all the people working in this field, Dunning has made by far the largest and most significant contribution. Indeed, it may well be the case that, without Dunning's work, Elias's theory of civilizing processes would have had relatively little impact on the sociology of sport.

But it would be a mistake to end this introduction by focussing solely on violence and civilizing processes. As some of the contributors to this book indicate, and as the work of Malcolm on race/ethnicity, of Waddington on sport, health and drugs, of Waddington, Roderick, Malcolm, Sheard and Smith on pain and injury in sport, of Maguire and van Bottenburg on globalization, of Tuck, Malcolm and Parry on national identity, of Green on physical education and of Maguire, Mansfield, Colwell and Smith on sport and gender indicate,[34] figurational and figurationally-informed work on sport has contributed to the study of many areas within the sociology of sport. Dunning's contributions to these areas, as a researcher and as a teacher and colleague, has also been of major importance.

We would like to end this introduction by adding our own tribute to Dunning, to sit alongside those of the other contributors to this *Festschrift*. Both of us initially encountered Eric when we were students at the University of Leicester, albeit some 25 years apart. Both of us have collaborated with Eric on research and publishing projects, though interestingly neither of us particularly did so at the outset of our careers. Our respective work has at times focussed on violence but at others has not. At times we write with a more explicitly figurational tone, whilst at others the impact of Elias and Dunning's ideas is more implicit. We have over the years worked increasingly closely with Eric; we have learnt a great deal from him, have argued with, and on occasions been infuriated by, him, but have always greatly valued his advice and support and, above all, his friendship. Eric has been a source of inspiration and a supportive, diligent and constructive critic. To his colleagues, and to his students, he has always given unstintingly of his time and his advice. We believe Eric's unnamed friend was not mistaken: Eric has had something – indeed, not a little – to do with the prominence of figurational sociology within the sociology of sport and this *Festschrift* provides both an appropriate marker and a celebration of this influence.

Notes

[1] Dunning, 'Football in its Early Stages'.
[2] Dunning, 'The Evolution of Football'.
[3] Stone, 'American Sports'.
[4] Huizinga, *Homo Ludens*; McIntosh, *Physical Education in England since 1800.*
[5] Dunning, 'Figurational Sociology and the Sociology of Sport', 224.
[6] Ibid.
[7] Dunning, *The Sociology of Sport.*
[8] Edwards and Rackages, 'The Dynamics of Violence in American Sport', 3.
[9] http://issa.fr.fm/ accessed 19 Aug. 2004.
[10] Elias and Dunning, *Quest for Excitement.*
[11] Coakley, 'Editor's note'.
[12] Dunning, 'Figurational Sociology and the Sociology of Sport', 223.
[13] Dunning and Sheard, *Barbarians, Gentlemen and Players.*
[14] Elias, *The Society of Individuals*, 54.
[15] Mennell, *Norbert Elias*, 140.
[16] Ibid.
[17] Goudsblom and Mennell, *The Norbert Elias Reader.*

[18] Elias and Scotson, *The Established and the Outsiders*.
[19] Elias and Dunning, 'Dynamics of Sport Groups'.
[20] Elias and Dunning, *Sport im Zivilisationsprozess*.
[21] Elias, 'Der Fussballsport im Prozess der Zivilisation'.
[22] Elias, *Involvement and Detachment*.
[23] Elias, *Die Gesellschaft der Individuen*.
[24] Elias, *The Symbol Theory*.
[25] Elias, *Studien über die Deutschen*.
[26] Dunning and Mennell, 'Preface', *The Germans*, vii.
[27] Williams, Dunning and Murphy, *Hooligans Abroad*.
[28] Murphy, Williams and Dunning, *Football on Trial*.
[29] Dunning, *Sport Matters*.
[30] Stokvis, 'Sport and Civilization'.
[31] Dunning, 'Figurational Sociology of Sport'. Murphy, Sheard and Waddington, 'Figurational Sociology'. Malcolm, 'Cricket and Civilizing Processes'.
[32] Dunning, Malcolm and Waddington, 'Conclusion', 203.
[33] Sheard, 'Boxing in the Western Civilizing Process'. Malcolm, 'Cricket: Civilizing and De-civilizing Processes'. Smith, 'Clay Shooting'.
[34] Malcolm, 'Stacking in Cricket'. Malcolm, '"It's not Cricket"'. Malcolm, '"Clean Bowled"'. Waddington, *Sport, Health and Drugs*. Waddington and Roderick, 'Management of Medical Confidentiality'. Roderick, Waddington and Parker, 'Playing Hurt'. Malcolm and Sheard, '"Pain in the Assets"'. Malcolm, Sheard and Smith, 'Protected Research'. Maguire, 'Sport, Identity Politics and Globalization'. Maguire, *Global Sport*. van Bottenburg, 'The Popularity of Sports in Continental Europe'. Tuck, 'The Men in White'. Parry and Malcolm, 'England's Barmy Army'. Green, 'Physical Education Teachers in their Figurations'. Green, *Physical Education Teachers on Physical Education*. Green, 'Physical Education, Lifelong Participation and the "Couch Potato Society"'. Maguire and Mansfield, '"No-body's Perfect"'. Colwell, 'Feminisms and Figurational Sociology'. Smith, 'British Non-elite Road Running and Masculinity'.

References

Coakley, Jay. "Editors note". *Sociology of Sport Journal*, 1, no. 1 (1984): 1–2.
Colwell, Sharon. "Feminisms and Figurational Sociology: Contributions to Understanding of Sports, Physical Education and Sex/gender." *European Physical Education Review* 5, no. 3 (1999): 219–40.
Dunning, Eric. "Football in its Early Stages." *History Today* (Dec. 1963).
Dunning, Eric. "The Evolution of Football." *New Society* 83 (April 1964).
Dunning, Eric. *The Sociology of Sport: A Selection of Readings*. London: Frank Cass, 1971.
Dunning, Eric. "Figurational Sociology and the Sociology of Sport: Some Concluding Remarks." In *Sport and Leisure in the Civilizing Process: Critique and Counter-Critique*, edited by E. Dunning and C. Rojek. Basingstoke and London: Macmillan, 1992.
Dunning, Eric. *Sport Matters: Sociological Studies of Sport, Violence and Civilization*. London: Routledge, 1999.
Dunning, E. and K. Sheard. *Barbarians, Gentlemen and Players: A Study of the Development of Rugby Football*. 2nd edn. London: Routledge, 2005.
Dunning E., D. Malcolm, and I. Waddington. "Conclusion: Figurational Sociology and the Development of Modern Sport." In *Sport Histories: Figurational Studies of the Development of Modern Sports*, edited by E. Dunning, D. Malcolm, and I. Waddington. London: Routledge, 2004.
Edwards, H. and V. Rackages. "The Dynamics of Violence in American Sport: Some Promising Structural and Social Considerations." *Journal of Sport and Social Issues* 1, no. 2 (1997): 3–31.

Elias, Norbert. *The Society of Individuals*. Oxford: Basil Blackwell, 1991.

Elias, Norbert. *Die Gesellschaft der Individuen*. Frankfurt: Suhrkamp, 1987. Published in English as *The Society of Individuals* Oxford: Blackwell, 1991.

Elias, Norbert. *Involvement and Detachment*. Oxford: Blackwell, 1987.

Elias, Norbert. "Der Fussballsport im Prozess der Zivilisation." In *Der Satz 'Der Ball ist rund' hat eine gewisse philosophische Tiefe. Sport, Kultur, Zivilisation*, edited by Modellversuch Journalistenweiterbildung an der FU Berlin. Berlin, 1983.

Elias, Norbert. *Involvement and Detachment*. Oxford: Blackwell, 1987.

Elias, Norbert. *The Symbol Theory*. London: Sage, 1991.

Elias, Norbert. *Studien über die Deutschen*. Published in English as *The Germans*, translated by E. Dunning and S. Mennell. Cambridge: Polity Press, 1996. Frankfurt: Suhrkamp Verlag, 1989.

Elias, N. and E. Dunning. *Quest for Excitement: Sport and Leisure in the Civilising Process*. Oxford: Blackwell, 1986.

Elias, N. and E. Dunning. *Sport im Zivilisationsprozess*. Munster: Lit Verlag, 1983.

Elias, N. and E. Dunning. "Dynamics of Sport Groups with Special Reference to Football." *British Journal of Sociology* 17, no. 4 (1966): 388–402. Reprinted in Elias and Dunning, *Quest for Excitement*: 191–204.

Elias, N. and J. L. Scotson. *The Established and the Outsiders*. 2nd edn. London: Sage, 1994.

Goudsblom, J and Mennell, S., eds. *The Norbert Elias Reader*. Oxford: Blackwell, 1998.

Green, K. "Physical Education Teachers in their Figurations: A Sociological Analysis of Everyday "Philosophies" in Physical Education." *Sport, Education and Society* 7, no. 1 (2002): 65–83.

Green, K. *Physical Education Teachers on Physical Education*. Chester: Chester Academic Press, 2003.

Green, K. "Physical Education, Lifelong Participation and the "Couch Potato Society"." *Physical Education and Sport Pedagogy* 9, no. 1 (2004): 73–86.

Huizinga, J. *Homo Ludens: A Study of the Play Element in Culture*. London: Routledge and Kegan Paul, 1955.

McIntosh, Peter. *Physical Education in England since 1800*. London: Bell, 1968.

Maguire, Joseph. "Sport, Identity Politics and Globalization: Diminishing Contrasts and Increasing Varieties." *Sociology of Sport Journal* 11, no. 4 (1994): 263–82.

———. *Global Sport: Identities, Societies, Civilizations*. Cambridge: Polity, 1999.

Maguire, J. and L. Mansfield. ""No-body's Perfect": Women, Aerobics and the Body Beautiful." *Sociology of Sport Journal* 14, no. 3 (1998): 109–37.

Malcolm, Dominic. "Cricket and Civilizing Processes: a Response to Stokvis." *International Review for the Sociology of Sport* 37, no. 1 (2002): 37–57.

Malcolm, Dominic. "Cricket: Civilizing and De-civilizing Processes in the Imperial Game." In *Sport Histories: Figurational Studies of the Development of Modern Sports*, edited by E. Dunning, D. Malcolm, and I. Waddington. London: Routledge, 2004, pp. 71–87.

Malcolm, Dominic. "Stacking in Cricket: a Figurational Sociological Reappraisal of Centrality." *Sociology of Sport Journal* 14, no. 3 (1997): 263–82.

Malcolm, Dominic. ""It's not Cricket": Colonial Legacies and Contemporary Inequalities." *Journal of Historical Sociology* 14, no. 3 (2001): 253–75.

Malcolm, Dominic. ""Clean Bowled?" Cricket, Racism and Equal Opportunities." *Journal of Ethnic and Migration Studies* 28, no. 2 (2002): 307–25.

Malcolm, D. and K. Sheard. ""Pain in the Assets": The Effects of Commercialization and Professionalization on the Management of Injury in English Rugby Union." *Sociology of Sport Journal* 19, no. 2 (2002): 146–69.

Malcolm, D., K. Sheard, and S Smith. "Protected Research: Sports Medicine and Rugby Injuries." *Sport in Society* 7, no. 1 (2004): 97–110.

Mennell, Stephen. *Norbert Elias: An Introduction*. Oxford: Blackwell, 1992.

Murphy, P., J. Williams, and E. Dunning. *Football on Trial*. London: Routledge, 1990.

Murphy, P., K. Sheard, and I. Waddington. "Figurational Sociology and its Application to Sport." In *Handbook of Sports Studies*, edited by J. Coakley and E. Dunning. London: Sage, 2000: 92–105.

Parry, M. and D. Malcolm. "England's Barmy Army: Commercialization, Masculinity and Nationalism." *International Review for the Sociology of Sport* 39, no. 1 (2004): 73–92.

Roderick, M., I. Waddington, and G. Parker. "Playing Hurt: Managing Injuries in English Professional Football." *International Review for the Sociology of Sport* 35, no. 2 (2000): 165–80.

Sheard, Kenneth. "Boxing in the Western Civilizing Process." In *Sport Histories: Figurational Studies of the Development of Modern Sports*, edited by E. Dunning, D. Malcolm, and I. Waddington. London: Routledge, 2004: 15–30.

Smith, Stuart. "Clay Shooting: Civilization in the Line of Fire." In *Sport Histories: Figurational Studies of the Development of Modern Sports*, edited by E. Dunning, D. Malcolm, and I. Waddington. London: Routledge, 2004: 137–52.

Smith, Stuart. "British Non-elite Road Running and Masculinity: a Case of "Running Repairs"?" *Men and Masculinities* 3, no. 2 (2000): 187–208.

Stokvis, Ruud. "Sport and Civilization: is Violence the Central Problem?" In *Sport and Leisure in the Civilizing Process*, edited by E. Dunning and C. Rojek. London: Macmillan, 1992.

Stone, Gregory P. "American Sports: Play and Display." *Chicago Review* IX (Fall 1955): 83–100.

Tuck, J. "The Men in White: Reflections on Rugby Union, the Media and Englishness." *International Review for the Sociology of Sport* 38, no. 2 (2004): 177–99.

van Bottenburg, Maarten. "The Popularity of Sports in Continental Europe." *The Netherlands Journal of Social Sciences* 28 (1992): 3–30.

Waddington, Ivan. *Sport, Health and Drugs*. London: Spon, 2000.

Waddington, I. and M. Roderick. "Management of Medical Confidentiality in English Professional Football Clubs: Some Ethical Problems and Issues." *British Journal of Sports Medicine* 36, no. 2 (2002): 118–23.

Williams, J., E. Dunning, and P. Murphy. *Hooligans Abroad*. London: Routledge, 1984.

The Contribution of Eric Dunning to the Sociology of Sport: The Foundations

Stephen Mennell

From his schooldays, Eric Dunning was always a sportsman. But it was his encounter with Norbert Elias at the University of Leicester in 1956 that eventually turned him into a sociologist of sport. Arguably, it was the encounter with Eric that turned Elias into a sociologist of sport too.

Eric had arrived as an undergraduate with the intention of specializing in economics, but Elias's introductory lectures made such an impression on him that he switched to sociology. He had the advantage (unusual among British students then as now) of reading and speaking German, and was thus able to follow up Elias's vague reference to having written 'something on civilization' by borrowing Ilya Neustadt's copy of the original 1939 edition of *Über den Prozeß der Zivilisation*. After taking his first degree, Eric enrolled for an MA under the supervision of Elias. He recalls walking across Victoria Park one day, watching boys playing soccer, and very hesitantly asking, 'Dr Elias, do you think it would be a good idea to study the sociology of football for my thesis?' Somewhat to his surprise, Elias was enthusiastic. But that was characteristic of Elias. Just as in his Frankfurt days, when he had for example encouraged Gisèle Freund to study photography and Ilse Seglow the theatre from a sociological point of view, so in Leicester Elias continued to encourage students to work on topics of which they had personal knowledge. Thus in a way Elias's response was predictable. But, given the then prevailing mood of British sociology more widely, Eric was right to be apprehensive. I well remember, in the late 1960s right at the start of my own academic career and before I had met Eric in person, hearing it said mockingly that 'Ah, Eric Dunning, he's interested in the sociology of football, ha ha!'. The clear implication was that *real men*, or real sociologists, study important things like social stratification, not frivolous things like football. That in itself is some measure of the extent to which Eric became the founding father of the entire burgeoning sub-discipline of the sociology of sport.

As for Elias himself, he had been a keen sportsman, losing the sight in his right eye in a skiing accident in his youth, and remaining a strong swimmer until the last years of his life. Yet he came late to sport as a topic for sociological investigation. He had made some passing mention in *The Civilizing Process*[1] of how the modern boxing match represented a strongly tempered form of aggressiveness compared with the bloodier spectacles often enjoyed in earlier days. But it was only in the 1960s, after Eric had joined the staff of the Department of Sociology at Leicester, that Elias began to write at length – alone and in collaboration with Eric – about sport, and only in 1986 that a good proportion of their essays were collected in book form as *Quest for Excitement*. Although some of the chapters appear under both names, some under Elias's alone, and some under Dunning's with or without other collaborators, the book essentially represents a single joint corpus of thinking and writing about sport, and so in the sketch that follows I shall make no attempt to disentangle Dunning's contributions from Elias's.

The Quest for Excitement in Unexciting Societies

The problem that Dunning and Elias – and a very few other pioneers – faced in persuading fellow sociologists to take sport seriously as a subject for sociological research was that games and sports are too stubbornly familiar a part of life in contemporary societies. They are too easily taken for granted. Moreover, though enjoyed by so many people, they are often regarded as a trivial aspect of life – or were a few decades ago. It was necessary to make an effort to stand back and view them in a more detached way in order to see their peculiarities and the important sociological questions that need to be asked about them.

The common characteristic of games and sports is that they involve competition: in them, people as individuals or as teams use bodily strength or other skills in competing against each others, or perhaps – as in mountaineering – against dangerous forces of nature. Beyond that, Elias and Dunning make a threefold distinction between 'sports', 'games', and 'sport-games'. In their usage, 'games' are activities in which the competition between players is *not physical*: games like chess and draughts for example. 'Sports', on the other hand, always involve *physical* competition but they are not games and are not exactly 'played': boxing and athletics are examples here. 'Sport-games' involve physical competition but *are* 'played': examples are soccer, rugby, baseball, and both the words 'sport' and 'game' apply to them.

One peculiarity of many sports and sport-games is that there are rules constraining contestants with the aim of reducing the risk of physical injury to a minimum. In some, such as boxing or American football, violence is intrinsic to the activity, yet even there rules are designed to keep such practices under control. In spite of this minimization of physical danger, sports are *exciting*, and across the world vast numbers of people give up part of their leisure time to sport, either as spectators or as participants themselves. What kind of society must it be, for people so much to enjoy the excitement and tensions engendered by physical contests where no blood flows and contestants do no serious harm to each other? This is the question underlying Elias and Dunning's investigations into sport.[2]

An answer to this question necessitates comparisons with other kinds of society, past or present, where sports in quite this form are not found, or not to the same degree. An answer to this question, moreover, leads beyond a better understanding merely of sports themselves: Elias and Dunning contended that it also makes a contribution towards a sociology of the emotions.[3]

Elias had sought to show in *The Civilising Process* that people in contemporary 'advanced' societies have to be able to maintain a fairly even and stable control over their more spontaneous libidinal, affective and emotional impulses and over their fluctuating moods. Social survival and success depend on 'a reliable armour, not too strong and not too weak, of individual self-restraint'.[4] This applies both to occupational roles and to many private relationships and activities. Indeed, they give satisfaction, both from the standpoint of each individual and from that of the others with whom he or she associates, only subject to such a pattern of restraints. In these societies, there is relatively small scope for showing strong feelings, strong dislikes of people, let alone 'hot anger, wild hatred, or the urge to hit someone over the head'.

People strongly agitated, in the grip of feelings they cannot control, are cases for hospital or prison. Conditions of high excitement are regarded as abnormal in a person, as a dangerous prelude to violence in a crowd.[5]

One of Elias and Dunning's first papers was originally entitled 'The Quest for Excitement in Unexciting Societies'; they were being ironic when they spoke of 'unexciting societies'. Life in constantly changing complex modern societies is very often 'exciting' in most senses of the word. It is, for instance, intellectually stimulating. What they meant was that opportunities for a more unreflected expression of excitement are, in many spheres of social life, severely limited.[6] Yet containing strong feelings and maintaining an even control of drives throughout life is likely to lead to emotional staleness in most people (the extent varies between individuals). How is this to be handled socially?

Other sociologists theorizing about leisure had often viewed it as simply providing opportunities for the *relaxation* of tensions generated in the work sphere of life. Polarizing work and leisure as opposites, they had implicitly used a scale of values in which work was rated the most important part of life, and leisure viewed in effect as a means to an end, in terms of its functions for work. Tensions were viewed as something bad, something to be got rid of.[7]

Elias and Dunning's view is different. In modern societies, there is a historically unparalleled variety of leisure activities and an important class of them – including sports – serve not simply to dissipate tensions generated in other spheres of life, but to provide opportunities for pleasurable excitement. They meet a socially conditioned psychological need in their own right, and if they also relax the tensions arising from work, it is an indirect result of the *generation* and resolution of exciting tensions in leisure. More exactly, argue Elias and Dunning, the leisure sphere in modern societies provides an enclave within which *a controlled and enjoyable decontrolling of restraints on emotions is permitted.*[8] Leisure activities generally allow the emotions to flow more freely in a specially constructed setting in some ways reminiscent of non-leisure reality. Sports are an especially clear illustration of this: they always consist of a controlled struggle in an imaginary setting.[9]

Apart from sports and games, many other kinds of leisure activity are also designed to appeal directly to people's feelings and arouse them in various ways, eliciting excitement resembling that produced in 'real-life' situations, but without its risks and dangers. Concerts, opera, plays, films, dancing, paintings, card games, novels, detective stories, thrillers – all these can perform a similar function. Elias and Dunning use the term *mimetic* for this class of activities. Literally, that means 'imitative', and Elias explains the use of the term as follows:

> If one asks how feelings are aroused and excitement elicited by leisure pursuits, one discovers that it is usually done by the creation of tensions. Imaginary danger, mimetic fear and pleasure, sadness and joy are produced and perhaps resolved by the setting of pastimes. Different moods are evoked and perhaps contrasted, such as sorrow and elation, agitation and peace of mind. Thus the feelings aroused in the imaginary situation of a human leisure activity are the siblings of those aroused in real-life situations – that is what the expression 'mimetic' means – but the latter are linked to the never-ending risks and perils of fragile human life, while the former momentarily lift the burden of risks and threats, great or small, surrounding human existence.[10]

Thus, as Aristotle first argued in the *Poetics*, a tragedy enacted in the theatre may evoke in the audience mimetic tension, feelings of fear and pity closely related to those experienced in witnessing the predicaments ensnaring people in real life – feelings lightened in the situation of a theatrical setting by music, movement, poetry and other mimetic symbols. In the concert hall, too, the music plays upon the audience's emotions, building up tensions which are finally relieved in applause. In the same way, at a football match spectators savour the mimetic excitement of a battle swaying to and fro on the field, knowing that in this battle little real harm is likely to befall either the players or themselves. Torn between hopes of success and fears of defeat, they openly manifest their feelings in the company of many other people, something which is all the more enjoyable and liberating because in society at large people are more isolated and have few opportunities for collective manifestations of strong feelings.[11] For participants as opposed to spectators, however, it should not be forgotten that some sports and sport-games differ from other activities of the mimetic type in that that they do involve real, *not* imaginary, danger to life or limb.

The Spare Time Spectrum

To appreciate the full significance of the mimetic class of activities, the argument continued, it was necessary to make a thorough break with the misleading static polarity of work versus leisure. It was a mistake to imagine that there are only *two* strongly contrasted categories of activity: on the one hand 'work', socially highly subject to rigid time discipline and where the function for others or for impersonal social units is paramount; and on the other hand 'leisure', meaning everything we freely choose to do, primarily with ourselves in mind, in our pursuit of the excitement and pleasure absent in work. Not all forms of work are always entirely devoid of excitement and pleasure, and there are many other intermediate kinds of activities. Elias and Dunning conceptualize them in a 'spare-time spectrum'. Many domestic activities – financial transactions, household maintenance, housework and so on – have to be performed like work whether one likes it or not, and this category of 'private work and family management' tends to take up more time as the standard of living rises. Then biological needs have to be catered for – sleeping, eating, drinking, washing and caring for one's body, making love. These needs recur, and satisfying them is pleasurable. Eating, cooking and making love shade into the pleasures of general sociability. But they also become highly routinized and not particularly pleasurable. They

> can all be, and usually are, routinized up to a point, but they can also be de-routinized from time to time in a more deliberate manner than is often the case. At the same time, they all have this in common with the mimetic class of activities: they can provide heightened enjoyment provided one is able to cater for them in a non-routine manner, such as eating out for a change.[12]

Routinization recurrently afflicts leisure activities of the mimetic type too. Concerts, plays, football matches may sometimes be found unexciting and boring. The perpetual tension between routinization and deroutinization *within* leisure activities is a principal source of their dynamics; it is seen, for instance, in 'going to the brink', which Elias and Dunning see as an intrinsic feature of them.

It can thus be seen that the connections between activities across the spare-time spectrum are fairly complex. Moreover, the forms of activity in which excitement is found change in the course of social development.

Pressures and restraints have existed in all human societies, and so, it would appear, have leisure activities as a social enclave within which restraints may be loosened. The Dionysian festivals of the ancient Greeks – times of religious excitement or 'enthusiasm' – and the carnivals of medieval Christendom are examples of religious activities with functions analogous to the mimetic class of modern leisure activities. Here, as in other aspects of civilizing processes, there is a no zero-point. However, argues Elias, the character of leisure pursuits changes in the course of the process, along with the balance between external constraints and learned self-restraints. Close analysis of the long-term civilizing process indicates that as restraints on people's behaviour become more all-embracing, more even, and internalized as a more or less automatically operating self-control, counter currents appear towards a balancing loosening of social and personal restraints.[13]

New forms of relatively uninhibited music and dancing are symptoms, and so perhaps is the more active spectator participation in sports events seen in many countries.

At the same time, the overall trend of the long-term civilizing process is reflected in ways that, in order to provide a *pleasurable* excitement, modern leisure activities have to conform with the comparative sensitivity to physical violence which is characteristic of people's social habitus in the later stages of a civilizing process. Gladiators fighting to the death, Christians fending off hungry lions, public hangings, or the burning alive of cats[14] would produce not enjoyment but severe revulsion in nearly all modern spectators. So the rules of modern sports always more or less curb the use of physical violence by participants against each other. At the same time the tension of the contest has to be kept up, both for players and spectators: the rules are usually adjusted in an attempt to ensure reasonable equality between, say, boxers of similar weight, between attacking and defensive functions in soccer (for example, the offside rule) or between batsmen and bowlers in cricket (for example, the lbw rule), in order to achieve relatively unpredictable contests.

A contest may also be *too* exciting – perhaps not so much because the rules maintain too high a tension as because of developments in society at large:

> if tensions arise in the wider society, if restraints on strong feelings become weakened there and the level of hostility and hatred between different groups rises in good earnest, the dividing line separating play and non-play, mimetic and real battles may become blurred. In such cases a defeat on the playing field may evoke the bitter feeling of a defeat in real life and a call for vengeance. A mimetic victory may call for a continuation of the triumph in a battle outside the playing field.[15]

These hypotheses arose out of, and in turn led to further testing in, comparative and developmental investigations of many particular forms of sport.

Earlier Forms of Games

Game contests and forms of competitive physical exercise are ubiquitous in human societies. They were found in many small-scale tribal societies. They were found in the ancient world. Are not the modern Olympic Games a conscious 'revival' of those of ancient Greece? Was not football, albeit of a cruder kind, played between rival villages or rival guilds in the Middle Ages? Yes. But were they quite the same thing as what today we call 'sports'? The ancient Greek equivalents of boxing and the form of wrestling called the pancration, which was among the most popular of the contests, would scarcely qualify. The level of violence was much higher than permitted today. Modes of attack forbidden in the modern forms of contest – such as head-butting, the use of legs and dangerous holds – were allowed. There were no time limits and contestants were not necessarily evenly matched in weight and strength. Deaths and permanent injuries were far from uncommon. Limbs were broken, eyes gouged out, people strangled. In one instance a boxing match ended when one fighter struck his opponent with his outstretched and leather-armoured fingers below the ribs, penetrated his abdomen and proceeded to disembowel him.[16] Baron Coubertin did not revive this form of contest!

These contests were not in fact totally unregulated. There was a judge, and people were not actually encouraged to gouge out each other's eyes. But these things happened in the heat of battle. Moreover, the contestant who killed or maimed his opponent went unpunished. It sometimes happened that the dead man's corpse was crowned as victor if he died especially valiantly, but loss of the crown was the most the killer would suffer. There is no evidence that the spectators or participants felt the horror and repugnance that we would feel today at such 'brutalities' (as we would consider them).

In fact people today might easily find it difficult to reconcile these seemingly brutal facets of the Greeks with the much-admired literature, philosophy and art of the same people. The contradiction stems entirely from the standpoint of our own values. For them there was no contradiction. The skills, physical and temperamental, used in the game contest were closely related to skills necessary in 'real life'; the mimetic distance, so to speak, was relatively small. In Greek society, if murder was committed, it was the *duty* of the victim's kin – not of the state, for the state monopoly of violence was little developed – to exact revenge. Greek citizens also fought for their city in hoplite armies; it was not exceptional for all the males of a vanquished city to be slaughtered *en masse* and the women and children sold into slavery. Such instances of genocide did not, any more than deaths and maimings in the games, bring forth the moral revulsion they would today. Greek literature affords plentiful evidence of the pity and compassion which could be felt for the victims, but very little of feelings of horror and indignation towards the perpetrators. All this, Elias points out, is very much in line with what the theory of civilizing processes would lead one to expect. The level of physical insecurity was much higher, and both state-formation and conscience-formation were much less well advanced. The level of internalized inhibitions against physical violence was lower, and the associated feelings of shame and guilt weaker, than in the relatively developed nation-states of the twentieth century.

Unlike the Greek games, the folk football of medieval and early modern Britain was not very directly related to any military skills, although certain other early pastimes such as archery very obviously were. While the authorities sought to encourage the latter, they repeatedly issued edicts – which had little or no effect – making football illegal, because from their standpoint it was inherently riotous and destructive. The modern reader, thinking of football hooliganism, may be tempted to remark, '*plus ça change* ...'; but in fact the game itself, in spite of the continuity in the name, was very different from its modern successor.[17]

Games with some generic resemblance to football were widespread in Britain, and indeed in Europe. They were much less highly regulated than their modern descendants, but not completely anarchic. They were governed by local custom and tradition. It was common, for instance, for a game to be played on certain holidays, such as Shrove Tuesday. The games themselves varied a good deal from place to place. According to local custom, the game could involve at one and the same time elements which to modern eyes are reminiscent of soccer, rugby, hurling, hockey, even polo (if some participants rode on horseback). Above all, however, the games were much more violent: they seem always to have involved fighting between the players, and not necessarily in the immediate vicinity of the ball! Often the struggle was pursued over several miles of terrain, with an indeterminate number of participants, and its very loose structure afforded plentiful opportunities to settle private scores. Such as they were, restraints were imposed not by highly elaborate formal regulations, which require a high degree of training and self-control,[18] but by custom. A high level of violence was customarily accepted. Injuries were sustained, blood flowed, and the people – often with the connivance of the local gentry – persisted in playing their games in the face of sporadic attempts by ineffective authority to suppress them. If the state apparatus was insufficiently developed to enforce a ban, how much less likely was it that common national codes of detailed rules, written down and subject to criticism and revision, could be developed and observed? Such codes, now taken for granted, were then inconceivable.

Just as the violence of the Greek games seems to modern eyes at odds with Greek art and literature, so the violence of medieval and early modern folk games may be at odds with the nostalgic image of a harmonious folk society shared by many laymen and some social scientists. Elias and Dunning[19] take the opportunity to criticize the once-influential model of 'folk society' developed by Robert Redfield on the basis (among other things) of Tönnies's notion of *Gemeinschaft*, and of Durkheim's idea of mechanical solidarity. The country people and townsfolk who took part in these semi-institutionalized fights between local groups lived for the most part in settlements that, by twentieth-century standards, were no more than villages and small towns, strong candidates for inclusion in the list of 'folk' or 'traditional' societies. It has often been said that such societies were permeated by feelings of great 'solidarity', which can easily be taken to mean that tensions and conflicts were less strong and feelings of friendship and unity greater than in the large-scale mass societies of today. 'As they intimately communicate with each other, every member claims the sympathy of the others', wrote Redfield.[20] But the term 'solidarity' is misleading, for this social closeness may foster inescapable enmities and hatreds as well as friendships.

One can, indeed, often observe expressions of strong and spontaneous 'fellow feeling' in traditional societies. But such expressions of what we might conceptualize as 'strong solidarity' were perfectly compatible with equally strong and spontaneous enmities and hatreds. What was really characteristic, at least of the traditional peasant societies of our own Middle Ages, was the much greater fluctuation of feeling of which people were then capable and, in connection with this, the relatively greater instability of human relationships in general. In connection with the lesser stability of internalized restraints, the strength of passions, the warmth and the spontaneity of emotional actions were greater in both directions: in the direction of kindness and readiness to help as well as in that of unkindness, callousness and readiness to hurt.[21]

The folk games of medieval and early modern times were thus one manifestation of people in an earlier stage of the civilizing process. They were indeed *game* contests. But were they *sport* contests in the modern sense? If not, how did the latter develop out of the former? The word *sport* acquired its modern meaning, and many of the activities to which it has applied took shape, in England during the eighteenth century. Elias regards England as having played an especially important part in what he calls the *sportization* of leisure as we know it today.

The Significance of England

Why is English the international language of sport, in much the same sense that French is the language of cookery and Italian of music? That was one of the questions which led Elias and Dunning to examine closely the part Britain played in the sociogenesis of so many sports which are now widely played in more or less identical ways in many parts of the world.[22] The list of sports which first assumed their modern, internationally recognizable form in England is impressive: soccer, rugby, horse-racing, wrestling, boxing, lawn tennis, fox-hunting, rowing, cricket, athletics and (from Scotland) golf. The very word *sport* is English, and though recorded as early as 1440, only in the eighteenth century did it acquire its specific modern connotations of a pleasurable pastime involving competitive physical exertion and skill, but with a relatively moderated use of violence.

Why should it have come about that 'the civilizing of game-contests and the restraint on violence to others through social rules which require a good deal of individual self-control developed first in England'?[23] There is no suggestion that the need for pastimes of this kind was unique to England. The speed with which, mainly from the mid-nineteenth century onwards, other countries adopted many of the English models of sport (sometimes then further adapting them for their own tastes, as in for instance American football) suggests that they corresponded to some human social requirement by then more widespread. Nevertheless, why was it that highly regulated contests requiring physical exertion and skill, and known both in performer and spectator forms as 'sport', first appear among the landed aristocracy and gentry of eighteenth-century England?

An answer can be found in the link between 'sportization' to 'parliamentarization'. The parallel has often been noted between, on the one hand, political conflicts played out according to agreed parliamentary rules and on the other hand, sporting contests played according to the rules of the game. But this commonplace idea is only at the level of analogy. *Quest for Excitement* gives it a specific historical context and explanatory weight. The parliamentarization of political conflict in eighteenth-century England was a relatively rare route out of a cycle of violence. Whigs and Tories peacefully relinquishing office to each other, the use of debating skills in place of force, the gradually increasing level of mutual trust, depended on the two sides being essentially members of a single dominant class of landowners. The argument is not that parliamentarization *caused* sportization, still less that the sportization of pastimes caused parliamentarization of politics! Rather the explanation is that the *same people* were caught up in two aspects of a broader process of development. This is an illustration of the principle that figurational sociology is concerned with *people in the round*; they are not separate political, economic and sporting beings.

> It was simply that the same class of people who participated in the pacification and greater regularization of factional contests in Parliament were instrumental in the greater pacification and regularization of their pastimes... Sport and Parliament

as they emerged in the eighteenth century were both characteristic of the same change in the power structure of England and in the social habitus of that class of people which emerged from the antecedent struggles as the ruling group.[24]

There were other respects in which social and political circumstances in eighteenth-century England favoured sportization. One was the relatively early establishment there of freedom of association. Political clubs began to be formed during the Commonwealth and Restoration periods, but it was only as the cycle of violence gradually subsided that they came to be seen as a normal and legitimate part of political life rather than as subversive; sociologists from Alexis de Tocqueville to Jürgen Habermas[25] have emphasized the role of clubs (another English word which has spread internationally) in political development. The same social device was readily employed in the emerging organization of sport.

Another aspect of English society facilitated the involvement of the landowning class in sports. The free English peasantry as a class had been all but broken by enclosures. Landowners no longer had any great fear of revolt by the agrarian lower classes. By and large, their employees knew their place. That made for easier relationships, and helps to explain how noblemen and gentry came to be involved in organizing both participant and spectator sports. Cricket matches were organized between retainers of two gentlemen, and younger gentlemen might join in with no fear of social derogation. The first cricket clubs were also formed in the eighteenth century. Similar involvement can be seen in other sports too. Often the customary rules of folk sports and sport-games were modified in accordance with the needs of gentlemen. Boxing is an example. Tighter sets of rules were developed, eliminating among other things the use of the legs; later, gloves were introduced and competitors matched according to weight. The new rules both conformed with a higher sensitivity to violence *and* made for a more even and exciting contest. Gentlemen promoted contests between lower-class professional fighters, when betting enhanced their excitement as spectators, as in horseracing and other sports. At the same time, however, boxing also became the 'gentlemanly art of self-defence', gradually used in place of the duel in settling disputes between at least younger males of the gentry class.

The involvement of members of the upper classes had one other consequence. When contests in whatever sport began to be arranged between parties at a greater distance than the neighbouring villages which had been the usual range of folk games, purely local, widely varying, customary rules were no longer adequate. Gentlemen's clubs (for example in cricket) and the public schools and universities (in soccer and rugby) came to lay down standard sets of rules which made possible competition among individuals or clubs no matter from where they came. Later came county and national associations.

Foxhunting, so peculiarly English a pastime and so prominent a part of the lives of the landowning classes in the eighteenth and nineteenth centuries, is an especially clear illustration of sportization as a civilizing spurt.[26] That may seem strange. Foxhunting is today somewhat marginal to most people's conception of 'sport', and indeed many people regard it as barbarous rather than civilized. Other subsequent civilizing spurts have intervened to change our perception of it, and today it is the subject of political controversy in England. Nevertheless, when compared with *earlier* forms of hunting, foxhunting as it became codified in the eighteenth century is a good example of what sportization involves.

The puzzlement of foreigners at foxhunting is a long-standing joke. Elias relates the story of the Frenchman who heard an Englishman exclaim 'How admirable! the sport which the fox has shown in this charming run of two hours and a quarter'. The Frenchman replied: '*Ma foi*, he must be worth catching when you take so much trouble. *Est-il bon pour un fricandeau?*'.[27] There are several other distinctive features, apart from the prey not being eaten. Why, if during their pursuit of the fox the hounds disturb some other animal – such as a hare, which *is* eatable – are they whipped away from it, back on to the scent of the fox? Why, as far as possible, do huntsmen try not to 'switch foxes', keeping the hounds on the track of the first fox detected? Why was it such a severe breach of the gentlemanly code to shoot a fox? Why, indeed, do the humans take no direct part in killing the fox? And why, above all and increasingly in the course of time, have huntsmen dwelt more on the pleasures of the chase than on the killing itself?

These things were not always so. Earlier forms of hunting imposed fewer restraints:

> People enjoyed the pleasure of hunting and killing animals in whatever way they could and ate as many of them as they liked. Sometimes masses of animals were driven near the hunters so that they could enjoy the pleasures of killing without too much exertion. For the higher-ranking social cadres, the excitement of hunting and killing animals had always been to some extent the peacetime equivalent of the excitement connected with killing humans in times of war. As a matter of course people used for both purposes the most suitable weapons at their disposal. After firearms had been invented, foxes were shot just like other animals.[28]

The fox was not even considered absolutely inedible, at least among the poor in times of dearth. By the eighteenth century, however, not only did members of the nobility and gentry never eat foxes, but they even killed them by proxy, delegating the function to their hounds. 'It corresponded better to the sensitivity of civilized gentlemen to let the hounds do the killing and confine their own activity to assisting them, to the anticipatory excitement and to watching the killing.'[29] Their sensitivity was lower than that of many people nowadays, but already higher than that of their forebears. It already represented an example of the long-term shift towards visual pleasures to which Elias referred in *The Civilizing Process*. Today, for many people – probably *most* non-hunters – there is no pleasure even in watching the kill.

Furthermore, a shift from even visual pleasure in the kill towards the pleasures of the chase is evident among eighteenth-century foxhunters, and still more in the nineteenth. The emphasis is more and more on the fore-pleasure and less on the consummation. Killing foxes is actually rather easy, and if it were only a matter of protecting farmers' poultry they would certainly be shot. The various rules of hunting are all designed to make it *less* easy, at some cost in mortality among poultry, but with considerable gain in the excitement, the competition, and even the danger to life and limb among the riders making up 'the field'.

Foxhunting demonstrates a general principle in sports: rules are developed which serve to generate and prolong a tension-equilibrium that is pleasurably exciting for participants, and with a good chance of a culmination in pleasurable catharsis – release from tensions. That is why most sports, like good wines, need time to mature. Basketball is an example of a sport which was simply invented by a particular person[30] but that is rare. 'As a rule, sports have gone through a period of trial and error before reaching a form which secured sufficient tension for sufficient time without fostering tendencies towards stalemate.'[31]

That can be seen in the history of rugby football. In *Barbarians, Gentlemen and Players* (1979), Dunning and Sheard provide another demonstration of this process of development through trial and error, of the civilizing and sportization of older and more violent folk-games, and of England's peculiar role as a seedbed of modern sports.

They show how rugby was one of the less violent codes which emerged in the nineteenth century out of the common matrix of traditionally more violent folk-games; how the bifurcation took place between rugby and soccer (a still less violent and more restrained code); how later in the century, when rugby had come to be played by many working-class men, the tension between middle-class players and their social inferiors – and, as an expression of this tension, the conflict over amateurism and incipient professionalism – led to the split between the Union and League forms of rugby; and how both codes have continued to modify their rules in order to achieve the optimum tension-equilibrium both for spectators and players.

Dunning and Sheard are especially interesting on the part played in this story by the English public schools, and how the development of the games cult there was linked to broader developments in English social structure.[32] Rugby, of course, took its name from one of those schools. Many of the public schools had their own variants on traditional folk games, and in the first quarter of the nineteenth century they seem to have been played with great ferocity: 'hacking', or kicking on the shins with iron-tipped boots was commonly an essential part of the game. Indeed some resisted eliminating this, on the grounds that anything gentler was less 'manly'.

How, nevertheless, did violence in play come to diminish? Little credence need be given to the story of how rugby was invented one day in 1823 in Rugby when an individual boy, William Webb Ellis, picked up the ball and ran with it. The process was much more gradual, though it is true that a set of rules for the game was for the first time written down and published at Rugby in 1845. Nor is it quite adequate to depict Dr Thomas Arnold, headmaster of Rugby 1828–42, as the 'inventor' of the games cult generally.

Dunning and Sheard's explanation in summary is as follows. The public schools had during the eighteenth century become extremely disorderly places. Out and out rebellions by the boys were quite frequent – sometimes they even had to be put down by soldiers. One reason seems to have been that sons of the aristocracy had come to constitute a large proportion of the pupils, and they despised the masters as social inferiors. Effective control tended to pass to the older and stronger students; bullying and 'fagging' were rife. Dr Arnold was one of several headmasters in the 1820s and 1830s who attempted to come to grips with the problem, setting out to reform and, quite literally, pacify the schools. He reached in effect a compromise settlement through the prefectorial system: the dominance of the older boys in matters outside the classroom was legitimized, the authority of the masters in class accepted. Circumstances at Rugby were especially favourable. It was not then one of the most prestigious public schools, and had a relatively low percentage of aristocratic pupils.

Moreover, in the wider society, the process of embourgeoisement had by now proceeded to a point where the power-ratio between the landed upper class and the commercial and industrial middle class was much more nearly even than formerly. The aristocracy was less able to treat the middle class with such unqualified contempt, while on the other hand the middle classes still deferentially sought to emulate the aristocracy.

In this context, Dr Arnold's principal direct contribution to the growth of the games cult lay in his effective suppression of *field-sports* among the pupils – forbidding them to keep the guns and packs of hounds characteristic of the pastimes of the gentry. Once this had been achieved, games of the football type proved acceptable functional equivalents for enough of the boys.

Football nevertheless began to change markedly. Several innovations characteristic of rugby, notably the oval ball and the H-shaped goal posts, were made by the boys over a period of time. And various restrictions on violence were embodied in the rules, the observance of which required they be learned and internalized with a considerable measure of restraint. (For this process of the growth of rules and their internalization – in contexts besides sport too – Elias uses the term *regularization*.) These innovations possibly arose because by now the violent traditions of folk-football had lower class connotations: to play according to those codes was ungentlemanly. In turn, when the rules of what was to become soccer were first codified, notably at Eton a few years later, the wish to differentiate a still more restrained, *gentle*manly, code from the rugby code associated with relative *parvenus* seems to have played some part.

Even if circumstances there favoured the development of the game which bears its name, Rugby School was not unique. The sportization of games proceeded in several other schools. And what was happening in the schools was part of a more general civilizing spurt in nineteenth-century England, now affecting many strata of society; the social historian Harold Perkin remarked, somewhat colourfully, that between 1780 and 1850 'the English ceased to be one of the most aggressive, brutal, rowdy, outspoken, riotous, cruel and bloodthirsty nations in the world, and became one of the most inhibited, polite, orderly, tender-minded, prudish and hypocritical'.[33] England was not unique. Not all modern sports originated there. Ruud Stokvis pointed out that in Germany an ideology of 'keep fit' and gymnastics was developed, with a much more directly nationalist and military flavour, in rivalry with the English ideology of sport as increasingly a non-military end in itself.[34] But sports and games in many other countries were probably moving in the same direction as in England,[35] and, where regularization was first achieved in England, it may simply have been convenient to impose the English codes on diverse native variants in order to facilitate competition at national and international level. In other words, there is an element of path-dependency here. Thus the French variety of boxing gave way to the standardized English form, as did the Italian *calcio* variant of football. England's political and economic position as a world power at the time also had some bearing on the spread of sport and, as Stokvis argues, on the ideology of amateurism.

> Amateurism is originally an English phenomenon. At the end of the nineteenth century Great Britain was the most influential and powerful country in the world … England's worldwide prestige heightened the esteem in which her sportsmen were held. As a consequence of this the English were in a position to demand that amateur conditions be introduced in other countries also. If this was not done, the English refused to come to these countries for competitions, and sportsmen from these countries were not granted admission to competitions in England.[36]

The Unsporting Dunning

In the 1980s and 1990s, Eric Dunning became especially well known for his research – alone and in collaboration with colleagues in Leicester – on sports-related violence, and notably on football hooliganism. Because other contributors to this *Festschrift* discuss that corpus of work in detail, I shall not – at the risk of this essay presenting *Hamlet* without the Prince of Denmark. What I have done is sketch the foundations of Eric's contributions to the sociology of sport, stressing especially his early work with Norbert Elias. By extension, I have emphasized how closely those contributions are bound up with the wider intellectual project of the theory of civilizing processes and of 'figurational sociology'.

The figurational sociology of sport is itself controversial – witness for instance the volume of critiques and counter-critiques of *Sport and Leisure in the Civilizing Process*[37] – but debates centring on sport are only part of the much wider-ranging controversies about the theory of civilizing processes. That is very apparent in the essays collected in Eric's book *Sport Matters*.[38] Indeed Eric accepts the label 'sociologist of sport' only as a matter of convenience; he has always seen research on sport only as a means of contributing theoretically and empirically to the development of the discipline of sociology as a whole. It would be easy for readers of this collection of essays to overlook the fact that Eric has written extensively on subjects other than the sociology of sport.

In fact the first time that I, as an undergraduate in Cambridge, heard the name of Eric Dunning, was when he and Earl Hopper published their article 'Industrialisation and the Problem of Convergence',[39] a hard-hitting critique of John Goldthorpe's then-recent (1964) and celebrated dismissal of the notion that the USA and USSR must necessarily converge under the impact of economic development.[40] (Both Goldthorpe and Hopper were former colleagues of Eric's at Leicester and were jointly responsible in 1965–66 for delivering the main final-year sociology lecture course to my cohort of students; Eric's involvement in this debate with Goldthorpe and Hopper imprinted the name of Dunning on my mind several years before I actually met him.) Subsequent history appears to have vindicated Dunning and Hopper rather than Goldthorpe.

I did not know it at the time, but since around 1960 Eric and John had been locked in intellectual combat in the debates within the Department of Sociology at Leicester about the whole nature of the sociological enterprise. Central to these debates was what Elias[41] was later to call 'the retreat of sociologists into the present' and Goudsblom to criticize as the discipline's tendency towards 'hodiecentrism' or today-centredness.[42] On the one side were functionalists like the anthropologist Percy Cohen and, especially, Popperians like John Goldthorpe who, though originally a historian himself, has throughout his career maintained a sceptical stance towards historical sociology. On the other side were developmentalists like Elias, Ilya Neustadt and the young Eric Dunning. Eric recalls how, in British sociology at the time, the very term 'development' was anathema through its historical (but not logically inevitable) connection with 'progress theories' of the Victorian kind – at one conference, his use of the word was enough to provoke shouts from the audience of 'Hobhouse! Hobhouse!' So some of Eric's earliest essays were concerned with defending the concept of development.[43] Eric's paper, 'In Defence of Developmental Sociology'[44] is a notably ambitious demolition job on Karl Popper's *The Poverty of Historicism*,[45] a book which, throwing out the developmental baby with the bathwater of 'inexorable laws of historical destiny', helped to impress hodiecentrism on a generation. But, as Elias once commented, 'Es gibt Fortschritten, aber kein Fortschritt' [there are progressions, but no progress]. At a minimum, Elias, Dunning and other figurational sociologists would contend that time is always one axis in any sociological explanation. In that sense, the Dunning and Hopper critique of Goldthorpe on convergence belongs in the same category: basically they argued that future trends could not be predicted from the study of two functional systems at one point in time. As a reminder that there are continuities as well as developmental trends over time, Eric's debate with John Goldthorpe has continued until as recently as 2000, when he reviewed the latter's book *On Sociology*.[46]

These early battles in which Eric championed a developmental sociology have been continued in his various defences of Elias against what he (and I) see as misunderstandings of Elias's work. Thus we jointly wrote a critique of Zygmunt Bauman's work on Elias,[47] while elsewhere Eric defended Elias's theory of state formation against misunderstanding in the pages of *Sociology*[48] and, more recently, fended off the charge of Eurocentrism levelled at Elias by one of Britain's most distinguished anthropologists.[49] Easier to overlook, but at least as important, is Eric's essay 'Some Comments on Norbert Elias's "Scenes from the Life of a Knight"'[50] which – though its title does not reveal this – is Eric's critique of the attempt by Tony Giddens (another former colleague in Leicester) to create a 'social theory' purged of all elements of development and evolution.

More of Eric's time off the sports field (so to speak) has been taken up in translating and editing Elias's work. With Robert van Krieken he translated the essay 'Towards a Theory of Social Processes'[51] and with me 'On the Sociology of German Anti-Semitism'.[52] Much greater labours were our translation of *The Germans*[53] and revised version of *The Civilising Process*. As a result of our work on *The Germans*, Eric has in recent years read deeply in the history of the Holocaust. Although he has lectured on the subject, his planned book on the subject is still on the stocks. I hope I am not giving away secrets if I reveal that Eric's distinctive insight into the puzzle of how ordinary civilized Germans were able to participate in genocide is through a connection he forges with a darker side of play and the quest for excitement.

One other area in which Eric has had a longstanding research and teaching interest is race relations.[54] This dates back to the year he spent in the 1960s at Washington University, St Louis, when the battle for civil rights in the South was at its height, and when he married his first wife – a scion of what, following E. Franklin Frazier, he always refers to as the 'black bourgeoisie'. But readers of this *Festschrift* can be expected to be familiar with Eric's interest in race relations because, like his writings on violence in Britain[55] and his fine essay on 'Power and Authority in the English Public Schools',[56] they crosscut with his writings on sport.

What are the underlying links between the sporting and the unsporting Dunning? One of them certainly lies in the sociology of emotions. The picture of human emotions that emerges from the work on sports and leisure by Elias, Dunning and their associates is not especially attractive:

> I have not *chosen* to discover that struggle and the enjoyable excitement produced by it provide an indispensable complement to the equally indispensable restraints of life. If I were free to choose my world, I would probably not have chosen a world where struggles between humans are found exciting and enjoyable … I would probably have chosen to say: avoid struggle. Let us all live in peace with each other.[57] (my italics)

But they present the world as they find it. Quite apart from the enjoyable excitement of sex, human beings also need other forms of enjoyable excitement, including the excitement of battle. In relatively highly pacified societies, the need has come to be met – in a quite unplanned way – by the provision of mimetic struggles, enacted in a specially constructed context with a minimum of injury to human beings. And that is the context for the 'controlled decontrolling of emotional controls', not only for routinization but also for deroutinization.

A final point: that memorable phrase – the controlled decontrolling of emotional controls – first formulated in the context of the sociology of sport and leisure, has been taken up and developed as a conceptual tool in understanding many other aspects of modern life. A notable instance is Cas Wouters's influential work on the so-called 'permissive revolution', or more exactly the waves of informalization and reformalization that have washed over and transformed manners, sexual mores and emotional habitus in contemporary societies.[58] Eric Dunning is a key founding father of the sociology of sport but, precisely because he has never been *only* a sociologist of sport, through his broader interests and writings he has helped to ensure that the still fairly new sub-discipline has had a wider influence, and has indeed moved steadily from the periphery towards the centre of sociology itself.

Notes

[1] Elias, *The Civilizing Process*, 170–1.
[2] Elias and Dunning, *Quest for Excitement*, 1.
[3] Ibid., 59ff.
[4] Ibid., 41.
[5] Ibid., 41.

[6]   Ibid., 71.

[7]   Ibid., 92–3.

[8]   Ibid., 65ff., 96.

[9]   Ibid., 50–1.

[10] Ibid., 42.

[11] Ibid., 43.

[12] Ibid., 69.

[13] Ibid., 66

[14] Elias, *The Civilizing Process*, 171.

[15] Elias and Dunning, *Quest for Excitement*, 43.

[16] Ibid., 140.

[17] Ibid., 175–90; Dunning and Sheard, *Barbarians, Gentlemen and Players*, 21–45.

[18] Elias and Dunning, *Quest for Excitement*, 183.

[19] Ibid., 179–81.

[20] Redfield, 'The Folk Society'.

[21] Elias and Dunning, *Quest for Excitement*, 180.

[22] That question was, at any rate, the way in which Elias broached the issue with me in one of our earliest meetings in the early 1970s.

[23] Elias and Dunning, *Quest for Excitement*, 24.

[24] Ibid., 40.

[25] de Tocqueville, *Democracy in America*; Habermas, *The Structural Transformation of the Public Sphere*.

[26] Elias and Dunning, *Quest for Excitement*, 150–74.

[27] Ibid., 160.

[28] Ibid., 161.

[29] Ibid., 163.

[30] Ibid., 297*n*.

[31] Ibid., 157.

[32] See also Dunning, 'Power and Authority in the Public Schools'.

[33] Perkin, *The Origins of Modern English Society*, 280.

[34] Stokvis, *Strijd over Sport*; R. Stokvis, 'Debates on Sport', 95–8.

[35] Even the Spanish bullfight, now regarded by many people as still less civilized – in the colloquial sense – than foxhunting, has shown long-term civilizing tendencies, according to Driessen ('Civiliseringstendensen in het Spaanse Stierevecht'). Driessen argues that besides civilizing pressures, the cultural mechanism of ritualization also played a part. Nevertheless, he says that since the eighteenth century bullfighting has developed increasingly towards professionalization, specialization, differentiation, sequestration in permanent bullrings, and more restrictive regulation. All of these developments, he says, can be interpreted as part of the civilizing and state-formation processes. The present stylized form in which the bullfighter allows the bull's horns to pass close to his almost motionless body demands very great self-control.

[36] Stokvis, 'Debates on Sport', 96.

[37] Dunning and Rojek, eds. *Sport and Leisure in the Civilizing Process*.

[38] So much is Eric Dunning a team player that *Sport Matters* was his first – and so far only – sole-authored book.

[39] Dunning and Hopper, 'Industrialisation and the Problem of Convergence', 163–86.

[40] Goldthorpe, 'Social Stratification in Industrial Society', 97–122.

[41] Elias, 'The Retreat of Sociologists into the Present'.

[42] Goudsblom, *Sociology in the Balance*.

[43] Dunning, 'The Concept of Development'.

[44]   Dunning, 'In Defence of Developmental Sociology'.

[45]   Popper, *The Poverty of Historicism*.

[46]   Goldthorpe, *On Sociology*. Dunning, 'Goldthorpe's View of Sociology'.

[47]   Dunning and Mennell, '"Figurational Sociology": Some Critical Comments on Zygmunt Bauman's: "The Phenomenon of Norbert Elias"'.

[48]   Dunning, 'A Response to J.R. Robinson's "The Civilising Process"'.

[49]   Dunning, 'Some Comments on Jack Goody's "Elias and the Anthropological Tradition"'.

[50]   Dunning, 'Some Comments on Norbert Elias's "Scenes from the Life of a Knight"'.

[51]   Elias, 'Towards a Theory of Social Processes'.

[52]   Elias, 'On the Sociology of German Anti-Semitism'.

[53]   Elias, *The Germans*.

[54]   Dunning, 'Dynamics of Racial Stratification'; 'Race Relations'; 'The Figurational Dynamics of Racial Stratification'.

[55]   Dunning *et al.*, 'Violent Disorders in Twentieth Century Britain'; E. Dunning *et al.*, 'Violence in the British Civilizing Process'.

[56]   Dunning, 'Power and Authority in the Public Schools'.

[57]   Elias and Dunning, *Quest for Excitement*, 59.

[58]   See for example C. Wouters, 'Formalization and Informalization: Changing Tension Balances in Civilizing Processes', and 'Developments in Behavioural Codes between the Sexes'.

References

de Tocqueville, A. *Democracy in America*. Chicago: University of Chicago Press, 2000: 1835–40.

Driessen, H. "Civiliseringstendensen in het Spaanse Stierevecht [Civilizing Tendencies in the Spanish bull-fight]." *Sociologische Gids* 29, no. 3–4 (1982): 326–41.

Dunning, E. "The Concept of Development: Two Illustrative Case Studies." In *The Study of Society*, edited by P. Rose. New York: Random House, 1967: 879–93.

Dunning, E. "Dynamics of Racial Stratification: Some Preliminary Observations." *Race* 13, no. 4 (1972): 415–34.

Dunning, E. "Race Relations." In *Human Societies*, edited by G. Hurd., revised ed. 1973. London: Routledge & Kegan Paul, 1986: 110–33.

Dunning, E. "In Defence of Developmental Sociology: A Critique of Popper's *Poverty of Historicism* with Special Reference to the Theory of Auguste Comte." *Amsterdams Sociologisch Tijdschrift* 4, no. 3 (1977): 327–49.

Dunning, E. "Power and Authority in the Public Schools: a Case Study and Conceptual Discussion." In *Human Figurations: Essays for Norbert Elias*, edited by P. Gleichmann, J. Goudsblom, and H. Korte. Amsterdam: Stuchting Amsterdams Sociologisch Tijdscrift, 1977: 225–57.

Dunning, E. "Some Comments on Norbert Elias's 'Scenes from the Life of a Knight'." *Theory, Culture and Society* 4, no. 2–3 (1987): 366–71.

Dunning, E. "A Response to J.R. Robinson's 'The Civilising Process': Some Remarks on Elias's Social History." *Sociology* 23, no. 2 (1988): 289–307.

Dunning, E. *Sport Matters: Sociological Studies of Sport, Violence and Civilization*. London: Routledge, 1999.

Dunning, E. "Goldthorpe's View of Sociology." *Figurations* 15 (2000): 3–5.

Dunning, E. "Some Comments on Jack Goody's 'Elias and the Anthropological Tradition.'" *Anthropological Theory* 2, no. 4 (2002): 413–20.

Dunning, E. "The Figurational Dynamics of Racial Stratification: A Conceptual Discussion and Development Analysis of Black-white Relations in the United States." In *Norbert Elias*, edited by E. Dunning and S. Mennell. 4 vols, Vol.II, London: Sage, 2003: 387–406.

Dunning, E. and E. Hopper. "Industrialisation and the Problem of Convergence." *Sociological Review* 14, no. 2 (1966): 163–86.

Dunning, E. and S. Mennell. "'Figurational Sociology': Some Critical Comments on Zygmunt Bauman's: 'The Phenomenon of Norbert Elias'." *Sociology* 14, no. 2 (1979): 497–501.

Dunning, E. and Rojek, C., eds. *Sport and Leisure in the Civilizing Process: Critiques and Counter-Critiques*. London: Macmillan, 1992.

Dunning, E. and K. Sheard. *Barbarians, Gentlemen and Players: A Sociological Study of the Development of Rugby Football*. Oxford: Martin Robertson, 1979. Second edition with a new introduction, London: Frank Cass, 2004.

Dunning, E., P. Murphy, and I. Waddington. "Violence in the British Civilizing Process." In *Norbert Elias*, edited by E. Dunning and S. Mennell. Vol II, London: Sage, 2003: 5–34.

Dunning, E., P. Murphy, T. Newburn, and I. Waddington. "Violent Disorders in Twentieth Century Britain." In *The Crowd in Contemporary Britain*, edited by G. Gaskell and R. Benewick. London: Sage, 1987: 19–75.

Elias, N. "The Retreat of Sociologists into the Present." *Theory, Culture and Society* 4, no. 2–3 (1987): 223–49.

Elias, N. *The Germans: Power Struggles and the Development of Habitus in the Nineteenth and Twentieth Centuries*. (Translated by E. Dunning and S. Mennell) Cambridge: Polity Press, 1996.

Elias, N. "Towards a Theory of Social Processes." *British Journal of Sociology* (translated by R. van Krieken and E. Dunning) 48, no. 3 (1997): 355–83.

Elias, N. *The Civilizing Process*. New edition, translation revised by E. Dunning, J. Goudsblom and S. Mennell. Oxford: Blackwell, 2000.

Elias, N. "On the Sociology of German Anti-Semitism." (translated by E. Dunning and S. Mennell)[originally 1929] *Journal of Classical Sociology* 1, no. 2 (2001): 219–225.

Elias, N. and E. Dunning. *Quest for Excitement: Sport and Leisure in the Civilizing Process*. Oxford: Blackwell, 1986.

Goldthorpe, J. H. "Social Stratification in Industrial Society." In *The Development of Industrial Societies*, edited by P. Halmos. *Sociological Review Monograph No. 8*. Keele: University of Keele, 1964: 97–122.

Goldthorpe, J.H. *On Sociology: Numbers, Narratives, and the Integration of Research and Theory*. Oxford: Oxford University Press, 2000.

Goudsblom, J. *Sociology in the Balance*. Oxford: Blackwell, 1977.

Habermas, J. *The Structural Transformation of the Public Sphere: An Inquiry into a Category of Bourgeois Society*. Cambridge: Polity Press, 1989.

Perkin, H., *The Origins of Modern English Society, 1780–1880*. London: Routledge & Kegan Paul, 1969.

Popper, K. *The Poverty of Historicism*. London: Routledge & Kegan Paul, 1977.

Redfield, R. "The Folk Society." *American Journal of Sociology* 52, no. 4 (1947): 292–308.

Stokvis, R. *Strijd over Sport: Organisatorisch en Ideologisch Ontwikkelingen*. Deventer: Van Loghum Slaterus, 1979.

Stokvis, R. "Debates on Sport: Organisational and Ideological Developments." *Netherlands Journal of Sociology* 18, no. 1 (1982): 95–8.

Wouters, C. "Formalization and Informalization: Changing Tension Balances in Civilizing Processes." *Theory, Culture and Society* 3, no. 2 (1986): 1–8.

Wouters, C. "Developments in Behavioural Codes between the Sexes: Formalization of Informalization in the Netherlands, 1930–85." *Theory, Culture and Society* 4, no. 2–3 (1987): 405–27.

Civilized Mayhem: Origins and Early Development of American Football

Allen Guttmann

That American football is a violent sport is not exactly news. George Stade, an admirer of the game, proclaimed that football is a sport 'whose mode is violence and whose violence is its special glory'.[1] There is no dearth of evidence to support Stade's claim. The rules of the game allow players to block and tackle one another in ways that are clearly intended not only to intimidate their opponents, but also to inflict severe physical pain.[2] Players boast of their ability to injure and even to cripple their opponents. Asked how he felt after an unusually rough play, a San Diego Charger replied, 'It felt warm all over'.[3]

Coaches preach what players practice. They routinely instruct their teams in the techniques of physical violence. At Ohio State University, Woodrow 'Woody' Hayes was a master of his trade. 'We teach our boys to spear and gore', he bragged, 'We want them to plant that helmet right under a guy's chin... I want them to stick that mask right in the opponent's neck.'[4] Coaches are candid about the mayhem committed by their teams. Vincent Lombardi, of the Green Bay Packers, condensed his apologia – if one can call it that – to five words: 'Football', he explained, 'is a violent game'.[5]

The names of the teams tell us something about the nature of the game. While English football supporters cheer for Sheffield Wednesday, Manchester United, or Bolton Wanderers or – with a hint of violence – Arsenal or Spurs, American fans roar their approval of the Chicago Bears, the Carolina Panthers, the Detroit Lions, the Los Angeles Rams. Local tradition accounts for exceptions such as the New England Patriots or the New Orleans Saints (from the jazz musicians' rendition of 'The Saints Go Marching In'), but most NFL names suggest feral or barbaric behaviour.

And yet, despite the gory talk, American football is much less violent than it was a century ago. The injuries are probably *more* frequent, but they are almost certainly less severe. In the sense used by figurational sociologists, the game has become more civilized. In their classic study, *Barbarians, Gentlemen and Players* (1979), Eric Dunning and Kenneth Sheard traced the processes that transformed the rough-and-tumble of medieval folk-football into the more-or-less civilized modern game of Rugby Union Football.[6] My modest emulation of their extraordinary achievement is an attempt to describe the transformation of English rugby into American 'gridiron' football, a sport that is more rationalized (Max Weber) and more civilized (Norbert Elias) than the game of folk-football that is the ancestor of all modern football codes.

I

When rugby football arrived in the United States, in 1874, Americans had been playing one or another form of folk-football for over 200 years. Like their British cousins, the colonists were in constant conflict with political authorities fearful of the disorder that accompanied the game. In 1657, for instance, Boston's magistrates imposed a 20-shilling fine for 'playing at foot-ball in the streets'.[7] Eighteenth-century Harvard students engaged in informal kicking and running games that their teachers tried vainly to forbid. New Haven was also a venue for football. 'An engraving of Yale College in 1807 showed students in beaver hats and swallow-tailed coats playing football on New Haven Common, while an elder who closely resembled college president Timothy Dwight looked on with an air of disapproval.'[8] At Harvard and Yale, as at other antebellum colleges, the president and the faculty did their best to encourage studious piety and to discourage boisterous play. In the short run, the president and the faculty prevailed. On 2 July 1860, on the eve of the Civil War, students at Harvard College, with mock solemnity, buried 'Football Fightum', whose age at the time of his decease was given as 'LX Years'.[9] In the long run, however, the students were victorious. Tender piety made room – at least on Saturday afternoons – for rough play. Compulsory chapel attendance disappeared along with required courses in Christian morals. The pagan festivities of the 'football weekend' assumed the status of a secular ritual, 'the most vitally folkloristic event in our culture'.[10]

Historians of American sports sometimes assert that the first intercollegiate football game was the Princeton-Rutgers contest of 6 November 1869, won by the latter with a score of six goals to four, but that historic contest was an approximation of association football (soccer). Something akin to modern rugby was brought to the United States on 15 May 1874, when students from Montreal's McGill University competed in the first of a pair of games against Harvard. (The rules for the second game were more or less those of soccer.) This contest, which occurred only two years after Oxford and Cambridge inaugurated their rugby rivalry, ended in a scoreless tie.[11]

The new game was immensely attractive to privileged upper-class youths in need of some way to demonstrate the manly courage that their fathers and older brothers had recently proved on the bloody battlefields of the Civil War. Football spread rapidly within what later came to be called the 'Ivy League'. On 26 November 1876, representatives from Harvard, Columbia, Princeton and Yale met at Springfield, Massachusetts, and formally adopted the rules of Rugby Football Union, an organization that was then, of course, only five years old.[12]

II

In a deservedly famous essay entitled 'Football in America: A Study in Culture Diffusion',[13] sociologists David Riesman and Reuel Denney explained the transformation of British rugby into American football as the result of a lack of tradition. The 'hike' that puts the ball in play was one of their examples. In the absence of experienced older players who knew how to deal with ambiguities such as the 'heel-out' (which allowed a player to scoop up the ball and run with it), it was necessary for the ball to be 'hiked' into play from a stationary line of scrimmage.

Lack of tradition undoubtedly liberated Americans to experiment with the rules, but the *direction* of the experiments is what mattered most. Riesman and Denney noted, quite correctly, that the 'procedural rationalization' of American football 'fitted in with other aspects of … industrial folkways'.[14] Although 'instrumental rationality' is probably a better translation of Max Weber's *Zweckrationalität* than 'procedural rationalization', Riesman and Denney were right. The processes of rationalization reshaped the game of rugby until it became the unmistakably American form of football. By 1895, Caspar Whitney, the influential editor of *Outing* magazine, was able to dismiss rugby as 'an elementary game', clearly not on a level with gridiron football's 'scientifically developed play'.[15]

To a remarkable degree, the impetus behind the transformation came from a single man. Walter Camp played the game when he was a student at Yale. After his graduation, he found local employment as an engineer and remained in New Haven to coach the football team. And then, for 46 years, he was the dominant force on the Football Rules Committee that – step by step, year by year – transformed rugby into American football.

Camp, who worked for a clock manufacturer, approached the game from an 'essentially managerial and technocratic perspective'.[16] He was the man responsible for the introduction of the line of scrimmage in 1880. It was his idea, that same year, to reduce the squad from 15 men to 11. After the 1882 Yale-Princeton game had ended in a scoreless tie, each team having kept possession of the ball for half the game, Camp introduced a rule that had momentous consequences. Continued possession of the ball was made contingent upon the team's moving the ball forward five yards in three attempts (known as 'downs' because the ball was placed on the ground). Chalked lines enabled the players (and subsequently the officials) to judge whether or not the ball had indeed been carried the requisite five yards beyond the line of scrimmage. These chalked lines formed a grid, which gave the field of play its distinctive appearance.

The lines were a visible statement of the game's increased rationalization. They also gave the game a new name: gridiron football.

Camp understood the importance of specialization, another characteristic of modern sports.[17] 'Division of labor', he wrote, 'has been so thoroughly and successfully carried out on the football field that a player nowadays must train for a particular position'.[18] Thanks largely to Camp's obsessive commitment to instrumental rationality, Yale's football team trained harder and more scientifically than its rivals. Yale's squad became an engine of destruction that steamrollered other Ivy League teams. From 1885 through 1899, Yale won 46 straight games, trampling its hapless opponents by a combined score of 2,018 to 29.[19] Athletic success brought economic benefits. In 1914, Yale inaugurated a 75,000-seat stadium, an architectural materialization of the income earned by ticket sales and a source of even greater income.[20]

Students at southern colleges were eager to get into the game, but college presidents and boards of trustees frequently restrained them. Wake Forest College, in Winston-Salem, North Carolina, fielded its first football team in 1882, but there was tension between the churches and the colleges, most of which – like Wake Forest – were church-supported schools administered by clergymen. At a time when Ivy League football games were considered the quintessence of collegiate experience, the *Wesleyan Christian Advocate* complained that the game's violence unleashed 'the lower impulses of the physical man' and encouraged young males to 'find their pleasure in mere sensual energy'.[21] The journal's opposition to collegiate football was so fierce that Trinity College (now Duke University) abandoned the game in 1894 and did not resume play until 1920.

Christian faith was not the only impediment. President Andrew D. White of Cornell University, an adamant proponent of secular education, was unimpressed by the nation's enthusiasm for football. He rejected out of hand the team's request for an 'away' game: 'I will not permit thirty men to travel four hundred miles merely to agitate a bag of wind.'[22] President William Rainey Harper of the University of Chicago was shrewder. Recognizing the game's contribution to 'school spirit' and its enormous public-relations value, he hired Amos Alonzo Stagg to coach the football team, gave him professorial status, and told him to put the newly founded university on the academic map, which Stagg did. President Charles William Eliot of Harvard set aside his doubts about the educational value of football and did likewise. He hired William Reid to coach the team and paid him $7,000 a year, 30 per cent more than Harvard's highest paid professor.[23] Hundreds of students may have come to class to hear William James lecture on pragmatism, but 38,000 packed Harvard's grand new stadium to revel in the sight of Reid's football squad in action.[24]

Football had a long career as the chosen sport of Ivy League athletes eager to prove that they were real men and not the 'mollycoddles' ridiculed by Theodore Roosevelt and other upper-class exponents of the 'strenuous life'. Within the tight confines of instrumental rationality, football allowed for bravado and demonstrations of rugged masculinity. Caspar Whitney – one of Walter Camp's collaborators – explained in *Outing*, which he edited, that the 'instrumentality of sport [introduced] a certain amount of modern discipline' into a boy's life. Boston Brahmin, W. Cameron Forbes, articulated a widespread upper-class racist and Social Darwinist conception of the game when he told the readers of *Outing*, in 1900, that 'Football is the expression of the strength of the Anglo-Saxon ... It is the dominant spirit of a dominant race, and to this it owes its popularity and its hope of permanence'.[25] Blunter words and plainer pictures appeared in the *Police Gazette*, which found its way into saloons rather than salons. That journal highlighted football's anachronistic brutality and sexual allure.[26] The theme of masculinity was underlined and intensified when cheerleaders were inserted into the 'text' of a football game. Their 'bare and vulnerable bodies' elevated 'the armored male bodies... to mythical status'.[27]

The day of the Harvard-Yale game was, for years, a major event in the nation's sporting calendar. For the players and their coaches, it was a combination of Mardi Gras and Armageddon. 'You are now going out to play football against Harvard', intoned Yale's coach, 'never again in your whole life will you do anything so important'.[28] The more important the game, the greater the determination to win. And with the determination to win came the accelerated professionalization of intercollegiate football.

The students began the process when they, not the college's administration, hired coaches and voluntarily submitted to the coaches' rules and regulations. Driven by a desire to achieve victory no matter what the cost, students also secured the temporary services of robust farmboys and steelworkers whose only connection with the college was their hard work on Saturday afternoons. In 1894, for example, seven of Michigan's eleven starting players 'neither enrolled in school nor attended any classes'.[29] Shenanigans of this sort moved indignant faculties to take control of the game and to remind the students of their academic obligations. When the professors – perennially jealous of time diverted from research – proved unable to prevent repeated violations of the rules, collegiate administrations turned to men like Chicago's Stagg and Harvard's Reid.

The most serious problem faced by Stagg, Reid and their peers was the game's violence. By the turn of the century, changes in the rules had made football more 'scientific', but they had also allowed for increased levels of violence. Control of the ball at the line of scrimmage, for instance, allowed the offensive team to place the ball carrier within a human wedge that charged at full speed into the stationary line of defensive players. Princeton pioneered this tactic in 1889. 'There was nothing subtle about it', comments a recent historian of Ivy League football, 'just weight and brawn concentrated on breaking through a single point in the defense. It was effective but it was dangerous because once the V got its momentum going [the players] rolled over everything in their path.'[30] Harvard used this deadly tactic in its 1892 games against Yale and the University of Pennsylvania. The practice spread and football fields were littered with injured players. In 1894, Walter Camp stepped in and the rules were revised to limit the number of men in motion before the ball was 'hiked' into play. The wedge was banned, but brutal play continued to be the norm. A dozen players were killed in 1902. In 1905, 18 players were killed and 159 were seriously injured.[31]

In the 'civilizing process' that transformed Europe's emotional dynamics, the power and authority of the nation-state played a crucial role. It was, accordingly, fitting that the call for reform and restraint in American football came from the President of the United States. From the White House, Theodore Roosevelt, a great believer in football as a school of masculinity, intervened, not to abolish football but to save it from abolition. He delivered an ultimatum to Reid and his colleagues at Yale and Princeton: reform the game before the 'mollycoddles' banned it.[32] When the Ivy League colleges failed to respond to the presidential appeal, New York University Chancellor Henry McCracken took the lead. Several conferences at New York's Murray Hill Hotel climaxed in January 1906 with the birth of the 38-school Intercollegiate Athletic Association. Renamed the National Collegiate Athletic Association (in 1910), the organization eventually claimed – and very nearly attained – monopolistic control over intercollegiate sports.[33]

The promise of reform was insufficient for many schools. Stanford and the University of California dropped football in 1906 and did not return to the game until 1919. (In the interim, they played rugby.)[34] Columbia and the University of Chicago also abandoned the game.[35] The NCAA did make an effort to keep the promise of reform. The organization used its power to rewrite the rules of football. In 1906, the game was shortened from 70 minutes to 60. (Players who were less fatigued were, of course, less likely to be injured.) A gain of ten yards was required for a 'first down' (instead of five) and four downs were allowed (instead of three). This meant that the ball was kicked less frequently and that the danger of injury was somewhat reduced. (Players who caught or retrieved the kicked ball were especially vulnerable to tacklers who charged downfield at full speed.) These changes diminished the level of violence, but the diminution was minimal. In fact, while it is probable that the percentage of players fatally injured dropped after the rule changes of 1906, the absolute number *increased*, in 1909, to 30.

In 1910, the Rules Committee outlawed the 'flying tackle', a tactic that tended to injure the tackler more often than the ball-carrier. An even more important rule change that year eliminated the 15-yard penalty for an incomplete forward pass. This move greatly encouraged throwing the ball rather than running with it. A subsequent rule protected pass-receivers from injuries sustained when they were most vulnerable, that is, at the moment just before they caught the ball. Although it took some time for coaches and players to realize the importance of the forward pass, throwing the ball eventually became as important as running with it. Biomass ceased to be decisive. Deadly violence became much less frequent.

III

In the last quarter of the twentieth century, the level of physical violence increased. Serious injuries became much more frequent when players began to 'spear' opponents with their helmets. (Recall 'Woody' Hayes' enthusiastic advice to his players.) The

Table 1 NFL Television Rights (figures in $bn)

ABC	Monday night games plus three Super Bowls	4.4
ESPN	Saturday and Thursday night games	4.8
Fox	National Football Conference plus three Super Bowls	4.4
CBS	American Football Conference plus two Super Bowls	4.0

NCAA acted to ban the practice. And then a graver problem emerged. The quotation with which this essay began came from an era when a 200-pound player was considered large. Today, thanks to hours in the weight room and the marvels of the pharmaceutical industry, football players are much bigger and much stronger and much more likely to injure one another. The problem is intransigent because it cannot be solved by changes in the rules of play – unless the NCAA and the NFL were to ban all players weighing more than 200 hundred pounds, which is apparently an unthinkable restriction.

The alternative is for the authorities to attempt to regulate the athletes' behaviour off the field. Coaches in the past attempted, with mixed success, to ban the use of alcohol and tobacco. The NCAA and the NFL can attempt a similar ban. They can do much more than they have done to ban the use of anabolic steroids and human growth hormone (and – while they are at it – the use of amphetamines and the analgesic agents routinely used to send injured players back into the game).

Reluctance to enforce strict bans on drugs may be motivated by more than a human regard for the civil liberties of the players. It may also be that the men in control of American football and the fans who pay to watch the game *like* the fact that the game is now played by armoured behemoths who project the awesome power of creatures from another planet. When truck drivers spend the equivalent of a week's wages to sit in the endzone, when corporate executives invest tens of thousands of dollars to rent 'luxury boxes' overlooking the field of play, they expect to identify with 'real men' (even when the 'real men' are medically constructed cyborgs).

Material factors play a role, as they always do. The level of violence in intercollegiate and openly professional football increased more or less simultaneously with an increase in the number of spectators and in the amount of money that television networks were ready to pay for the right to broadcast football games. In the 1980s, the NCAA sold rights to intercollegiate play to ABC and CBS for $263.5 million. Notre Dame University, negotiating on its own rather than as a member of the NCAA cartel, received $38 million from NBC for the rights to four years of play.[36] The NFL was more profitable still. For the 1994–97 rights, ABC, ESPN, Fox TV, NBC and Turner Network Television paid a grand – indeed, a very grand – total of $4.38 billion. The figures for 1998–2005 – in billions of dollars – defy credulity (see Table 1). The total comes to $17.6 billion or $73 million per team per year.[37] Who wants to upset an apple cart that delivers fruit like this?

Whatever the reason, meaningful reform of on-the-field violence seems unlikely. In all probability, American football will continue to be characterized by the present level of violence. In the eyes of the fans, the violence is indeed, as George Stade remarked, the game's 'special glory'.

Notes

[1] Stade, 'Game Theory', 173.
[2] To tackle, in American football, means to seize and hurl to the ground.
[3] Quoted in A.J. Mandell, *The Nightmare Season*, 19.
[4] Quoted in Sharnik and Creamer, 'A Rough Day for the Bear', 16.
[5] Quoted in Dowling, *Coach*, 46.
[6] Dunning and Sheard, Barbarians, *Gentlemen and Players*.
[7] Gardner, *The Simplest Game*, 164
[8] Fischer, *Albion's Seed*, 149.
[9] Davis, *Football*, 35–37.
[10] Cady, *The Big Game*, 75; see also Oriard's brilliant *Reading Football*.
[11] Davis, *Football*, 45–50, 62–6.
[12] Ibid., 69; Dunning and Sheard, *Barbarians, Gentlemen and Players*, 111.
[13] Riesman and Denney, 'Football in America'.
[14] Ibid., 250.
[15] Whitney, *A Sporting Pilgrimage*, 192.
[16] Oriard, *Reading Football*, 37.
[17] On the characteristics of modern sports, see Dunning, 'The Structural-Functional Characteristics of Folk Games and Modern Sports'. Guttmann, *From Ritual to Record*, 15–55.
[18] Quoted in Gems, *For Pride, Profit, and Patriarchy*, 17.
[19] A. Sach, 'American Business Values and Involvement in Sport'. Rader, *American Sports*, 84–5.
[20] Sack and Staurowsky, *College Athletes for Hire*, 31.
[21] Doyle, 'Foolish and Useless Sport', 319–20.
[22] Quoted in Smith, *Sport and Freedom*, 74.
[23] Ibid., 160.
[24] Lucas and Smith, *Saga of American Sports*, 246–7.
[25] Forbes, 'The Football Coach's Relation to the Players', 339.
[26] Oriard, *Reading Football*, 168 (for Whitney) and 146 (for *Police Gazette*).
[27] Messner, 'Sports and Male Domination', 202.
[28] Quoted in Gems, *For Pride, Profit, and Patriarchy*, 55.
[29] Watterson, *College Football*, 46.
[30] Bernstein, *Football: The Ivy League Origins of an American Obsession*, 31.
[31] Moore, 'Football's Ugly Decades, 1893–1913'. McQuilkin and Smith, 'The Rise and Fall of the Flying Wedge'.
[32] Lawrence, *Unsportsmanlike Conduct*, 8.
[33] Moore, 'Football's Ugly Decades'. Smith, 'Harvard and Columbia'. McQuilkin, 'Brutality in Football'.
[34] Park, 'From Football to Rugby – and Back, 1906–1919'.
[35] Watterson, 'The Gridiron Crisis of 1905'.
[36] Smith, *Play-by-Play*, 143–76.
[37] Bellamy, 'The Evolving Television Sports Marketplace'. Leifer, *Making the Majors*, 133–34; Quirk and Fort, *Hard Ball*, 39; Cook and Mravic, 'Scorecard', 40.

References

Bellamy, R. V. "The Evolving Television Sports Marketplace." In *MediaSport*, edited by L. A. Wenner. London: Routledge, 1997: 73–87.

Bernstein, M. F. *Football: The Ivy League Origins of an American Obsession*. Philadelphia: University of Pennsylvania Press, 2001.

Cady, E. *The Big Game*. Knoxville: University of Tennessee Press, 1978.

Cook, K. and M. Mravic. "Scorecard: March to Madness." *Sports Illustrated* 91 (29 Nov. 1999): 40.

Davis, P. H. *Football: The American Intercollegiate Game*. New York: Scribner's, 1911.

Dowling, T. *Coach*. New York: Norton, 1970.

Doyle, A. "Foolish and Useless Sport." *Journal of Sport History* 24, no. 3 (Fall 1997): 319–20.

Dunning, Eric. "The Structural-Functional Characteristics of Folk Games and Modern Sports." *Sportwissenschaft* 3, no. 3 (1973): 215–32.

Dunning, E. and K. Sheard. *Barbarians, Gentlemen and Players: A Study of the Development of Rugby Football*. 2nd edn. London: Routledge, 2005.

Fischer, D. H. *Albion's Seed: Four British Folkways in America*. New York: Oxford University Press, 1989.

Forbes, W. C. "The Football Coach's Relation to the Players." *Outing* 37 (Dec. 1900).

Gardner, P. *The Simplest Game*. Boston: Little Brown, 1976.

Gems, G. R. *For Pride, Profit, and Patriarchy*. Lanham: Scarecrow Press, 2000.

Guttmann, Allen. *From Ritual to Record*. New York: Columbia University Press, 1978.

Lawrence, P. R. *Unsportsmanlike Conduct*. New York: Praeger, 1987.

Leifer, E. M. *Making the Majors*. Cambridge: Harvard University Press, 1995.

Lucas, J. A. and R. A. Smith. *Saga of American Sports*. Philadelphia: Lea & Febiger, 1978.

Mandell, A. J. *The Nightmare Season*. New York: Random House, 1976.

McQuilkin, S. A. "Brutality in Football and the Creation of the NCAA." *Sport History Review* 33, no. 1 (May 2002): 1–34.

McQuilkin, S. A. and R. A. Smith. "The Rise and Fall of the Flying Wedge." *Journal of Sport History* 20, no. 1 (Spring 1993): 57–64.

Messner, M. "Sports and Male Domination." *Sociology of Sport Journal* 5, no. 3 (Sept. 1988): 197–211.

Moore, J. H. "Football's Ugly Decades, 1893–1913." *Smithsonian Journal of History* 2 (Fall 1967): 49–68.

Oriard, M. *Reading Football*. Chapel Hill: University of North Carolina Press, 1993.

Park, R. J. "From Football to Rugby—and Back, 1906–1919." *Journal of Sport History* 11, no. 3 (Winter 1984): 5–40.

Quirk, H. and R. D. Fort. *Hard Ball*. Princeton University Press: Princeton, 1999.

Rader, B. G. *American Sports*. Prentice-Hall: Englewood Cliffs, NJ, 1983.

Riesman, D. and R. Denney. "Football in America: A Study in Culture Diffusion." In *Individualism Reconsidered and other Essays* by D. Riesman. Glencoe, IL: Free Press, 1954.

Sach, A. "American Business Values and Involvement in Sport." In *Women and Sport*, edited by D. V. Harris. University Park: Pennsylvania State University, 1972: 277–91.

Sack, A. L. and E. J. Staurowsky. *College Athletes for Hire*. Westport, CT: Greenwood, 1998.

Sharnik, M. and R. Creamer. "A Rough Day for the Bear." *Sports Illustrated* 17 (26 Nov. 1962): 16.

Smith, R. A. "Harvard and Columbia and a Reconsideration of the 1905–06 Football Crisis." *Journal of Sport History* 8, no. 3 (Winter 1981): 5–19.

Smith, R. A. *Sport and Freedom*. New York: Oxford University Press, 1988.

Smith, R. A. *Play-by-Play*. Baltimore: Johns Hopkins University Press, 2001.

Stade, G. "Game Theory." *Columbia Forum*, Fall 1966

Watterson, J. S. *College Football*. Baltimore: Johns Hopkins University Press, 2000.

Watterson, J. S. "The Gridiron Crisis of 1905." *Journal of Sport History* 27, no. 2 (Summer 2000): 291–98.

Whitney, C. W. *A Sporting Pilgrimage*. New York: Harper & Brothers, 1895.

Boxing Blind: Unplanned Processes in the Development of Modern Boxing

Patrick Murphy & Ken Sheard

Introduction

Elias's figurational sociology has been characterized by some people as being overly concerned with civilizing processes, violence and violence control. However, as the contributions to this volume make clear, and as has been abundantly demonstrated elsewhere,[1] such a characterization does not adequately convey the richness of the figurational approach, nor the contribution that Eric Dunning has made to the sociology of sport. This having been said, it is nevertheless true that figurational sociologists have had much to say about civilizing and de-civilizing processes and violence control. One of Dunning's early books, written in conjunction with Sheard, concerned the ways in which rugby football became, in the Eliasian sense, more civilized.[2] In the conclusion to that book ideas were raised which came to form the basis of Dunning's work on football violence and, in particular, the research he conducted into fan violence with other members of the 'Leicester School'.[3] Dunning was also the supervisor of Sheard's doctoral dissertation which concerned the development of the modern sport of boxing out of the relatively less restrained prizefighting of the eighteenth and nineteenth centuries.[4] It should be clear, then, that the interest of both the present authors in the development of modern sport owes much to their collaboration with, and the encouragement of, Eric Dunning.

The present contribution will focus on the development of boxing and will be particularly concerned to provide a demonstration of the centrality of the unplanned, unintended, dimensions of human activity, upon which Elias placed so much weight.[5] Elias himself displayed an interest in the development of modern boxing which he saw as very different from the combat 'sports' of the Ancient Greeks and Romans.[6] The development of boxing as a sport, he believed, had to be firmly located within the context of the twin processes of parliamentarization and sportization emerging in eighteenth-century England. As Elias put it, during this period:

> military skills gave way to the verbal skills of debate... rhetoric and persuasion... which required greater restraint all round and identified this change... clearly as a civilizing spurt. It was this change, the greater sensitivity with regard to the use of violence which, reflected in the social habitus of individuals, also found expression in the development of their pastimes. The 'parliamentarization' of the landed classes of England had its counterpart in the 'sportization' of their pastimes.[7]

Elias held that the civilizing spurt involved in the leisure side of this process could be demonstrated *inter alia* by the development of boxing:

> Like many other bodily contests, fighting with bare knuckles assumed the characteristics of a sport in England where it was first subjected to a tighter set of rules... the growth of sensitivity showed itself in the introduction of gloves and, as time went on, in the padding of gloves and the introduction of various classes of boxers which ensured greater equality of chances. In fact, it was only in connection with the development of a more differentiated and... tighter set of rules and the greater protection of the contestants from serious injury which followed... that a popular form of fighting assumed the characteristics of a 'sport'.[8]

While we will not diverge from this broad analysis, we shall change its emphasis and question whether *all* of the rule changes which accompanied and were part of the civilizing of boxing, and which led to its greater regulation, made it unambiguously safer and less seriously injurious. We shall begin our analysis by offering a truncated account of the development of boxing since the eighteenth century with a view to using it as a basis for highlighting the unplanned dimensions of this process.

The Emergence of Boxing as a Sport

Nowadays many people regard boxing as a brutal and degrading activity scarcely deserving of the name 'sport'. But what of earlier forms of boxing? Were they more or less brutal, more or less violent? Tracing the development of prizefighting in its entirety to the present day is an impossible task. Much of the required evidence is simply not available. Nevertheless, while acknowledging these difficulties, this essay will seek to shed some light on the above processes.

In most historical accounts of the development of boxing an eighteenth-century Oxfordshire man called James Figg is singled out as the person who 'invented' the sport. However, given that fist fighting was part of a British folk tradition this seems to be an unwarranted accolade. At the same time, Figg, himself a prizefighter, does seem to have been the first person to commercialize boxing and to develop it as a 'business'. In the eighteenth century the British state was becoming more effective at curbing the violence of the warrior nobility and cultivating less lethal ways of settling disputes than by sword and pistol. Figg tapped into this emerging market, drawing most of his clients from the younger members of the aristocracy and gentry.

Another prominent figure in this period was Jack Broughton, an ex-prizefighter, 'entrepreneur' and boxing tutor. He is held to have been the originator of the first written rules governing boxing. He is also attributed with introducing gloves, or mufflers as they were known, in 1747. They were advertised as helping his gentlemen pupils to avoid 'the inconveniencing of black eyes, broken jaws and bloody noses'.[9] Notwithstanding this innovation, or perhaps because of its inadequacies, gentlemen and aristocrats began to seek more vicarious excitement – in what was becoming an increasingly routinized society – by betting on the result of prizefights or by 'running' a fighter themselves, just as they ran stables of horses for racing. Over time, these involvements began to displace their own direct participation in fighting. Hence, a more civilized sport-like activity in which gentlemen indirectly participated, developed alongside the more traditional, brutal forms of prizefighting which had been the preserve of the lower classes.

There is no doubt that by present standards boxing was an extremely violent and bloody activity in this period. For example, it was possible to use what we would now call 'wrestling' holds. One such technique was the 'cross-buttock' throw in which the opponent could be thrown over one's hip to the ground. The fallen adversary could then be leapt upon and have knees smashed into his exposed rib cage. Moreover, eyes could be gouged, hair pulled, and the testicles attacked. Prizefights were 'supervised' by the respective fighters' 'seconds', perhaps assisted by the 'stake-holder', the person delegated to guard the money wagered on the fight. The winner was the fighter left standing at the end. Up until the 1860s a round ended with a fall. In Britain, the largest number of rounds fought under this system was the 276 fought between Jack Jones and Patsy Tunney in 1825. The English essayist, William Hazlitt, provides a description of the *bloody* nature of prizefighting in his account of the battle between Tom Hickman and William Neate in 1821. He wrote:

> All traces of life, of natural expression, were gone from him. His face was like a human skull, a deaths head, spouting blood. The eyes were filled with blood, the nose streamed blood, the mouth gaped blood.[10]

The Move from Urban to Rural Settings

In the eighteenth century urban boxing theatres started to develop where people could gather to watch and bet on contests. By the end of the eighteenth century people like Daniel Mendoza were making a good income by travelling the country on the theatre circuit and engaging in exhibition bouts.[11] These arrangements had their attractions, for both boxers and entrepreneurs, in that fighters tended not to get so badly hurt, and charging for admission was not difficult when prizefighting or exhibitions took place in a hall or theatre. Indeed, it is possible that these venues could have provided the context for the development of a more restrained form of prizefighting were it not for the increasing opposition of the commercial middle classes and religious groups. These groups took exception to activities which did not accord with their own standards of propriety and they brought pressure to bear on magistrates and later, the police, to exercise more control over these events. Had boxing been allowed to continue to flourish in these settings it might have formed a 'safer' foundation for the development of the sport. On the other hand, had exhibition boxing become more established, it might have moved in a direction more akin to modern professional wrestling, that is in the direction of becoming more of an entertainment than a sport.[12] That having been said, it is also the case that the increasing predictability of boxing in this form was making it more difficult for the links with gambling to be sustained. The importance of gambling can hardly be overstated. In this regard, it should be noted that Broughton's rules of 1747 were aimed primarily at protecting gambling interests rather than the health of the contestants. In the event, to avoid the constraints of the urban environment, prizefighting migrated to rural areas where it came under the control and protection of the less 'respectable' members of the aristocracy and gentry.[13] While collecting money from the huge crowds attracted to big fights in the rural areas was much more of a problem, the unpredictability of these contests enabled prizefighting to continue to develop primarily as a vehicle for gambling. The paradox is that this movement to a rural setting, with the attendant gambling, probably helped to advance the possibility that in the longer run prizefighting would develop into a 'genuine' sport.

The Accelerated Movement Towards Growing Regulation

During the nineteenth century the availability of increasingly effective means of social control – such as the establishment of Sir Robert Peel's police force in 1829 – meant that boxing was driven even further 'behind the scenes'. Under these conditions, boxing became more regulated and controlled in the context of private clubs such as the National Sporting Club (formed in 1891). Here it came under the influence of upper and middle-class groups who formalized it further and fought some of the more important battles over its 'respectability' when ring fatalities threatened to lead to its demise.

In Britain in the eighteenth and for most of the nineteenth centuries there were no nationally centralized rule-making and rule-enforcing bodies of any note or effectiveness. The Amateur Boxing Association was not formed until 1880 and it was 1929 before a body to administer British professional boxing at the national level – the British Boxing Board of Control – was established. This process of institutionalization was associated with greater control and more stringent formal rules. The Marquis of Queensberry Rules, introduced in 1865, were a landmark in this process. These rules were originally for amateur boxing. They were not deemed suitable for professionals – for prizefights – so they had to be adapted, and professionals for many years operated under the 'revised' Queensberry rules or what came to be known as the 'Queensberry Rules of Endurance'.[14] The Queensberry Rules of Endurance were a contraction of the London Prize Ring Rules, combined with the more humane aspects of the Queensberry amateur rules.[15] While it is not clear how this compromise was arrived at, what is clear is that over the century which followed the Queensberry Rules formed the basis of a series of increasingly constraining regulations.

The use of gloves for professional contests was adopted, albeit to defuse the abolitionist movement and to help establish the 'legality' of boxing. Even so, by this time gloves were not intended to protect the person being hit, but rather the hands of the hitter. The last heavyweight fight with bare knuckles for the British championship took place in 1885. The last official bare-knuckle fight in America took place in 1889. Other rules proscribed and defined the sorts of violence which were permitted in the ring. The type of blow allowed and the areas of the body which could be attacked were carefully circumscribed. Boxers could also be penalized for infringing these rules. For example, points could be deducted for hitting 'below the belt', using the head illegally, or holding and hitting. Weight divisions were introduced in an attempt to equalize conditions for all boxers, both in Britain and the United States. In earlier days men (and sometimes women) fought each other irrespective of weight. This introduction of weight divisions allowed boxing skill to have a greater impact on a contest and offset the advantages of extra poundage or longer reach. Later still, regulations were introduced aimed at protecting boxers from aspects of both the permitted and accidental violence they could inflict upon each other. These included, for example, the provision of equipment such as padded gloves, gum shields, head-guards and groin-protectors. Officials have the responsibility of ensuring that contests are properly managed and the rules observed. Restrictions were also placed upon the length of contests and the length of 'rounds'. Professional championship contests are now fought over 12 rounds. Until relatively recently, the stipulated 'distance' was 15 rounds and before this, the usual distance was 20 rounds of 3 minutes each. However, it was well into the twentieth century before there was any effective medical control in boxing. Nowadays, proponents of boxing claim that professional boxers, in particular, are subject to exacting medical tests and controls. All the officials in British boxing would claim to put the safety of boxers first, and that fights are stopped at the first sign that a boxer is no longer in a position to defend him/herself.

Intended and Unintended Dimensions of these Regulatory Processes

Over this extended period it is certainly the case that both insiders and outsiders have made attempts at controlling the level of violence involved in boxing and the amount of damage that can be inflicted on boxers, and they have done so with varying degrees of success and failure. Some reforms have been largely cosmetic in the sense that the intention of insiders, when introducing them, was simply to appear to be doing something about dimensions of boxing that were held to be unacceptable by certain outsider groups. It is also the case that other reforms were presented as safety measures when they were actually motivated by other, extraneous, concerns. Yet other reforms have involved a genuine attempt to make boxing safer but, in the event, to varying degrees, have proved to be misguided. It is hoped that the following examples will serve to illustrate the complexity of these processes.

When Intentions and Outcomes Diverge

The opposition of the rising commercial classes and religious groups to the development of urban boxing theatres in the eighteenth century was primarily aimed at prohibiting or controlling an activity which they perceived to be both threatening and offensive. They were certainly not trying to foster it and facilitate its development. In the event, the constraints they brought to bear forced boxing promoters into the countryside where they were subject to less oppressive control. In retrospect this move seems to have cut short any tendency for boxing to develop along the lines of professional wrestling and become a form of entertainment rather than a sport. The shift to rural settings also bolstered the competitive element that was so crucial if boxing was to maintain its links with gambling. Moreover, the rekindling of the competitive element reinforced and prolonged its bloody traditions. Retention of this competitive core was also an essential prerequisite for its later transformation into a genuine sport. As such, this outcome is an example of how groups opposed to an activity can inadvertently help to create conditions which ensure its longer-term survival.

Weight Divisions: A Sword with a Hidden Edge

As pointed out earlier, weight divisions in boxing were introduced in order to make contests more equal and, thereby, reduce the obvious dangers involved in two fighters of distinctly different physical stature fighting one another.[16] Understandably, this was a measure over which there was substantial agreement. Some of the supporters of this move may have been more concerned with making contests more open in the interests of gambling, while others may have been more concerned with fairness *per se*. Whatever the initial balance of opinion, it is certain that none of the parties involved, including the anti-boxing lobby, foresaw the dangers inherent in this move. How could they? The consequences would only become apparent on the basis of considerable advances in medical knowledge. It is, however, now firmly established that this reform did have unforeseen consequences, one of which has been detrimental to the long-term health of boxers. Weight divisions mean that boxers fight within a relatively narrow weight band. This in turn has meant that many of them have encountered difficulties in making the requisite weight. In their efforts to do so, it is not uncommon for them to 'crash diet' just prior to fights. For example, the boxing reporter John Rawling reported that Ricky Hatton, the World Boxing Union light-welterweight champion, lost 'around two and a half stone in little more than five weeks to make the 10-stone light-welterweight limit', this weight loss amounting to 20 per cent of his body weight.[17] Such a process is dehydrating and any boxer who enters the ring in a dehydrated state is more prone to brain damage. Thus, a reform over which there was general unanimity on its positive implications for the safety of boxers has had insidious consequences which remained hidden for an extended period of time.

An Iron Fist in a Leather Glove

It is possible to argue that certain innovations, while introduced under the guise of making boxing safer, have actually made it more dangerous. As with the introduction of weight categories, the development of boxing gloves has had hidden damaging consequences for the wellbeing of boxers. Boxing gloves were first introduced in the belief that they would protect the features of gentlemen. It is now more widely appreciated that gloves in some significant respects increase the damage that boxers can inflict upon one another. Since the hands are protected, more, and harder, punches can be thrown with relative impunity. While it is still possible for a boxer to sustain a hand injury, it is certainly not a regular occurrence in the modern ring. Rarely are fights stopped for this reason. The former heavyweight champion of Britain, Henry Cooper, was of the view that:

> The boxer whose hands are covered by only the minimum of protection would think twice before throwing a punch unnecessarily – as they did in the bare-knuckle days. There is a tendency now to regard that era of boxing as barbaric. That is a matter of opinion, but what is a matter of fact is that because of the risk of a boxer hurting himself, fewer punches were thrown. The big one didn't go in until the deliverer of the blow was virtually assured of hitting the target.[18]

It is likely that the empirical basis for the original belief that gloves were less damaging lay in the fact that they led to fewer cuts and therefore less bloody contests. However, by the time gloves became mandatory in the late nineteenth century, they were seen as a means of protecting the hands of the boxers. Nevertheless, because they cut down on the blood and gore, they were also seen as a means of placating the growing anti-boxing lobby. Yet the reality is that while the outwards signs of damage are reduced by gloves, the actual damage to the brain is increased. The journalist, Nick Pitt, puts the argument in the following way:

> Little did the magistrates, who permitted glove-fighting contests... or the public, whose conscience was spared by the comparative lack of blood, realise the trade-off

they had condoned. Gone were the gore, the broken bones and bunged-up eyes...
but in their place was a more brutal and insidious legacy that even today is difficult
to measure or predict: brain-damage.

He continues:

It is ironic, then, that the introduction of gloves helped to save competitive boxing
from the threat of extinction at the very time that the law, the public and many
influential patrons were turning against it. Prize fighting with bare-knuckles was so
obviously bloody and barbaric that it was increasingly difficult to defend.

Of the gloves themselves he writes:

Their luxurious padding appears to be designed to soften a blow, to protect the
recipient. But really they protect the striker's hands, making the hitting of an
opponent as painless as pulling a trigger. With the protection of the glove, it is
possible to hit a person as hard and as often as you like (and the modern, trained,
well-fed boxer hits very hard and very often) with impunity. Indeed, gloves add
weight to a boxer's blows. They are in effect, weapons.[19]

Thus, the introduction of gloves not only resulted in more brain damage, it led to new
techniques of fighting. In bare-knuckle fighting, punches tended to be straight and
cutting. Without gloves, aiming hooks or slogging shots to the side or back of the head
involved the risk of breaking one's fingers. Indeed, because of the ever-present danger
of damage to one's hands, fighters were much more inclined to throw fewer punches.
The introduction of gloves also led to more excitement in that there were more
knockouts, the knockout being a euphemism for brain damage. Thus, the history of
gloves involves a complex combination of conscious strategies and unforeseen
consequences.

Pursuing Commercial Interests under the Guise of a Welfare Measure

In the mid-1980s the World Boxing Council, World Boxing Association and
International Federation changed their rules on the length of championship contests,
reducing the number of three-minute rounds from 15 to 12. This move was presented
as a safety measure. However, Ellis Cashmore has argued that this reform was
primarily geared to the interests of television companies and, therefore, their own
commercial interests. He writes:

Fifteen three-minute rounds, as well as fourteen one-minute intervals, preamble and
post-fight interviews amounted to an awkward seventy to seventy-five minutes.
Twelve rounds yielded forty-seven minutes, as well as, say, thirteen for padding,
which fitted perfectly into a one-hour time slot.[20]

Cashmore's argument certainly seems to have a degree of plausibility. The primary
interests being advanced when championship fights were reduced in length to 12
rounds could well have been commercial ones.[21] The appeal of this move might also
have been further enhanced by the opportunity to present it as an enlightened reform
aimed at protecting the welfare of the boxers. Yet even if this was a fundamentally
cynical move on the part of the boxing establishments and the media, it still serves

to demonstrate the way in which their powers are limited and mediated by other groups. In common with many other sports, the length of contests is inherently unpredictable. Regardless of the desire of boxing promoters to accommodate the requirements of television schedules, a 12-round contest can still end abruptly in the first round due to knock-out, an injury caused by a blow or a clash of heads or disqualification. It is also the case that the reduction in the length of championship contests occurred before the satellite and digital revolution, when television programmers worked under tighter restrictions. If this reform was motivated predominantly by commercial concerns, it may be that its proponents now regret it. It would, however, be very difficult for them to reverse this decision. Even powerful groups have a limited ability to predict the future and have to live with the, perhaps now unwelcome, consequences of their own actions.

The Chowdhry Scoring System: A Case Study of the Complexity of Human Figurations

As the foregoing analysis has shown, the struggle between the pro- and anti-boxing lobbies is a long-standing one. Of the two forms of boxing – professional and amateur – it is the latter which, in many respects, is presently under greater threat. This greater vulnerability stems from the relational network in which the International Amateur Boxing Association (IABA) is located. While the IABA runs its own world championships, the fact that it is an amateur sport means that its broader standing in the world of sport is very much dependent on its Olympic status.

In recent years the Olympic status of amateur boxing has been threatened on three fronts. Firstly, there are those who are implacably opposed to it on the grounds that it is too brutal and degrading to be an Olympic sport. It is held to offend 'Olympic ideals'. Secondly, there are those who are disturbed by amateur boxing's connections with professional boxing and the latter's alleged links with organized crime. The third source of pressure comes from those who are concerned by its history of controversial decisions made by competition judges. While some of these judgements have undoubtedly been due to incompetence, others have been perceived as being linked to organized crime or tainted by political corruption. Nevertheless, it is also probably the case that some members of the anti-boxing lobby are using the controversy surrounding such decisions as a convenient stick with which to beat the sport. We say this because other sports are not immune from questionable decisions by judges and yet these do not seem to threaten their Olympic status. There are, therefore, good grounds for the amateur boxing authorities to be apprehensive about the future of their sport and, as such, it is not surprising that they 'have been sensitive to the demands of abolitionists, fearful that boxing's status as an Olympic sport is under threat, and (consequently) are more prepared to accede to safety demands'.[22]

The example of Olympic boxing may be used as a short case study to demonstrate how actions aimed at resolving one perceived problem in boxing can inadvertently exacerbate another dimension of the sport which is also deemed by some to be a source of concern. The initial problem in question related to the reliability of judges.

This issue surfaced in the 1984 and 1988 Olympics, coming to a head in Seoul when the American boxer, Roy Jones, was widely held to have been deprived of a gold medal when the verdict went in favour of his apparently outclassed South Korean opponent.[23] The issue resurfaced at the World Championships in Houston, Texas, in 1999 and triggered a walk out by the powerful Cuban team, amidst accusations that their boxers had been the victims of a series of unjust decisions. John Rawling has commented that, 'it was the suspicion of corruption, bribery and even Mafia influences which provoked the Cuban actions'. He adds that, 'it is common knowledge that boxers from the former Soviet Union are coveted by underworld figures seeking to capitalize on their successes' and, in light of these connections, 'few businesses have been more damningly tainted with corruption than professional boxing. And sometimes its amateur relation appears determined not to be outdone.' Rawling is of the view that the 'outrage', following the Jones decision, 'almost killed boxing as an Olympic sport'.[24]

Understandably, particularly given the wider challenge to boxing's Olympic credentials, the IABA executive felt compelled to take remedial action. Their response was the introduction of a new scoring system aimed at resolving the problem of unreliable judges. It was the brainchild of Professor Anwar Chowdhry, the President of the AIBA. Another journalist, Michael Hughes, describes the principles of the system as follows: it 'awards a boxer a point when three of the judges press a button, to signify seeing a punch landed, within a second of each other'.[25] This information is relayed to a computer and the final result is calculated automatically.[26]

While Chowdhry was confident that this technological innovation had solved the problem, seasoned observers of the boxing scene were more sceptical. Rawling referred to the system as 'controversial and baffling'. He wrote: 'the system was meant to be foolproof but soon proved otherwise. What if a judge was not scoring fairly? What if he was looking at punches thrown only by one fighter?'[27] Michael Hughes was of a similar view. The system 'works fine when boxers are throwing big punches but means that often a combination of punches can be missed because of the angles – one judge can see a punch but two others may see nothing. And in the speed of the action it is possible for judges to score different punches.'[28] The Cuban walk out in Houston in 1999 forced Chowdhry to acknowledge the shortcomings in his system and his response was to move further down the technology road. At the world championships in Belfast in June 2001, video surveillance cameras were introduced to monitor the actions of the officials and an adjudication committee was appointed to handle any appeals. This practice was continued at the Sydney Olympics. Chowdhry's faith in technological solutions is captured in the following statement: 'if a judge has pressed a (scoring) button, you can see what the position of the two boxers was . . . How did he press the button? They (the boxers) were maybe not within scoring distance. So we will know exactly whether the judge has done it correctly or not . . . so we will have the proof.'[29] It is difficult to determine whether Chowdhry genuinely believed that the system bearing his name could achieve the stated objectives; perhaps it was a case of his commitment to finding a solution blinding him to its rather obvious shortcomings.

These actions and reactions are, of course, expressions of the complex power struggles which are a fundamental characteristic of these regulatory processes. While the Chowdhry system was explicitly intended to resolve the problem of incompetent or corrupt judges, it has had other ramifications. The nature of the system has encouraged boxers to concentrate their punches on their opponent's head because, when compared with body blows, head punches are more likely to be seen from outside the ring and, specifically, from the designated vantage points taken up by the judges. While body blows can be launched from long range, they are usually much more effectively delivered at close quarters, when infighting is taking place. Such blows might be seen by one, perhaps two judges, but they are far less likely to be seen by three. Consequently, targeting the head has become a more central part of the strategy of amateur boxers and their coaches. Body punching plays a greater part in the armoury of some professional boxers. This is because attacking the body has two primary aims. Firstly, effective body punches can lower the guard of an opponent and open up the head as a target. Secondly, heavy body punching is in itself an effective way of weakening an opponent and, on occasions, bringing about a stoppage. Moreover, some boxers are particularly susceptible to body punching. However, such punching usually takes a number of rounds to take its toll and, given the shorter length of amateur bouts, this time is only available in the professional ring. Nevertheless, even to the limited extent that body punching was a characteristic of the amateur sport, the Chowdhry system has greatly reduced the incentive to pursue this tactic. *Prima facie*, an increase in the number of punches taken on the head is likely to exacerbate the amount of brain damage sustained. Vivienne Nathanson of the British Medical Association is in no doubt about the brain damage caused. She distinguishes between treating the occasional blood clot, as was the case with Paul Ingle, and 'the chronic insidious brain damage that will blight so many boxers' lives' which is cumulative. 'In the extreme you get severe Parkinson's disease or punch-drunk syndrome.'[30]

Part of the IABA's strategy to counter this long-standing criticism was the introduction in 1984 of mandatory head-guards in amateur boxing. It was, and is still, widely believed that head-guards reduce the likelihood of brain damage. As Jim Smart, chairman of the British Amateur Boxing Association put it: 'the safety of boxers must be paramount, and I think head-guards prevent more trouble than they cause'. The hint of ambivalence in this statement may be traced to two related reservations. Firstly, his belief that 'head-guards diminish some of the sport's interest, as spectators struggle to identify with 'anonymous' figures' and, secondly, his feeling that 'head-guards have taken some of the character out of boxing'.[31] John Rawling decodes some of the concerns possibly underlying Smith's reflections when he writes: 'Fighters wearing head-guards may be less palatable for television companies as they cannot be easily distinguished'.[32]

The jury is very much out on the issue of whether or not head-guards make boxing safer. Their introduction was based on the belief that they cushion the effect of blows to the head. Traditionally, they have been used by professional boxers when sparring in preparation for a fight. In addition to the belief that they offer some protection from punches *per se*, they also make it less likely that a boxer will sustain a cut prior to a fight, which is a major consideration when a costly and lucrative promotion is in the offing. John Rawling puts the counter-argument in the following way:

> There is no real proof that guards reduce injuries and critics suggest they increase the target area, make it more difficult to avoid punches because of impaired vision and give fighters a false sense of safety. Some suggest impact may even be increased with the guard causing greater resonance and movement of the brain when punches connect.[33]

It is this whirling motion of the brain inside the skull which is held to be the principal cause of brain damage.

Thus, it seems we have at least two processes at work here. One has been driven by a combination of external and internal pressure to clean up the sport and ensure fairer competition. The other, in the first instance, has been driven by external groups who hold boxing to be too dangerous and by insider groups who have bowed to this pressure by introducing a series of 'safety measures', among them the head-guard, in the belief that such concessions will satisfy at least some of the critics. Of course, when making concessions of this kind, the boxing authorities are probably aware that they will cut little ice with committed members of the anti-boxing lobby. They can hardly not be cognisant of the fact that this section of public opinion is unreachable and not likely to be satisfied with anything other than a total ban. Therefore, by introducing such reforms they appear to be trying to win over or placate the less committed who might be open to persuasion.

There are strong grounds for believing that many of the ramifications of the above figuration were not anticipated by any of the groups involved. Indeed, it seems that some of these outcomes have still not been fully grasped by many insiders and outsiders, and/or by many members of the pro- and anti-boxing lobbies. Such outcomes are prone to be described as paradoxes, but to describe them as such tends only to mystify the processes still further. Once unravelled there is nothing mysterious about them. They are a consequence of the complex interweaving of human beings with different beliefs, associated misconceptions and divergent objectives. It is the sheer complexity of the interaction, as these groups seek to defend, maintain and advance their perceived interests, which generates outcomes which were unforeseen. Some of these ramifications become immediately apparent to at least some groups, while others will go unrecognized for extended periods of time. This being so, this case study constitutes but a microcosm of human history.

The Commingling of Civilizing and De-civilizing Processes: The Case of Unlicensed Boxing

If we retain a firm grip on the premise that human history is best understood in terms of the dynamics of differential power relationships, we are well placed to appreciate the way in which these human figurations express themselves in the shifting balance between civilizing and de-civilizing processes. To hold that, in Western Europe, civilizing processes have been in the ascendancy for the last 500 years or so, is not to deny the fact that throughout this period they have co-existed uneasily with de-civilizing processes. Indeed, it could be argued that they are actually different sides of the same coin. Throughout history more powerful groups have endeavoured to contain and restrain actions of less powerful groups which threatened or were perceived to threaten or offend them. On some occasions these efforts to suppress certain forms of behaviour have been relatively successful. On other occasions they have met with resistance. The likelihood is that on all occasions the resultant interactions can be conceived of as a complex combination of the intended actions of the groups involved and, as we have set out to demonstrate above, the unforeseen consequences of these same dynamic figurations. Civilizing and de-civilizing processes are both elements in, and expressions of, these processes.

The growing pacification of boxing is hardly in doubt. There can be no argument about the fact that by present-day standards traditional prize-fighting was a bloody and brutal affair. Nevertheless, the development of boxing still exemplifies the hostile co-existence of civilizing and de-civilizing processes. These processes have been expressions of bitter and acrimonious power struggles stretching back over the centuries. They have been characterized by insiders who have resisted reform; insiders who have pragmatically accepted reform, albeit reluctantly; insiders who have embraced the 'need' for reform; outsiders who have been indifferent to the struggle and the debate over boxing; outsiders who have been vaguely hostile to boxing; and members of the trenchant anti-boxing lobby who have looked forward to the day when boxing ceases to exist. Some of the reforms have been cosmetic, some have been driven by extraneous concerns, some have been genuine and made boxing safer and some were believed by all concerned parties to constitute an advance in safety standards but, in the event, proved to be otherwise.

Within the limitations of this essay we have tried to demonstrate the complexity of these processes. However, there is another figurational dimension of these processes that has not so far received sufficient attention, namely, de-civilizing processes. There have always been those groups within the 'world' of boxing who have been unwilling to accept reforms and who have seen specific reforms as 'a step too far', as a de-masculinizing imposition. Some of these groups have taken their opposition to the point of breaking away and running unlicensed, 'no holds barred', promotions outside the jurisdiction of the boxing establishment and, sometimes, outside the law. While it is entirely possible under certain conditions for such de-civilizing processes to become dominant, in the case of unlicensed boxing we seem to be witnessing a sideshow, with a limited appeal. But, then again, perhaps it is too early to make such a judgement.

Conclusion

The twin themes of this essay have been, firstly, the extent to which the development of boxing has been increasingly hedged in by controls and regulation and, secondly, the centrality of the unplanned dimensions of these processes. We have endeavoured to demonstrate a range of ways in which unintended outcomes can emerge and ramify. The focus throughout has been unerringly on the composite unit, the human figuration. Many critics of the theory of civilizing processes misunderstand the argument. It is not held that civilizing processes are somehow the 'prime mover' in human history, an equivalent of the role that, say, Marxists assign to 'economic forces'. Civilizing processes are as much an outcome of other processes of social development as they are a cause of subsequent change. Civilizing processes have intertwined with an array of other processes, among them nation-state formation and economic development. In describing them as processes we strive to avoid the temptation to slip into a mode of thought which conceives of them as having a reified existence of their own, somehow independent of human beings. It is, in our view, crucial never to lose sight of the fact that social processes are human beings in action, nothing more and nothing less. As the term human figurations is intended to convey, the focus for sociologists needs to be on dynamic networks of differentially interdependent human beings. Such a perspective does not neglect people as individuals, but recognizes that individuals can only be more adequately understood in terms of the networks of which they are a part.[34] These figurations consist of human beings pursuing their individual and/or their group interests. The figurations in which they are located, and of which they are a part, both constrain and enable action. However, the very complexity of the interactions leads to many outcomes that were unintended and unforeseen. In some instances these unanticipated outcomes become apparent to all concerned almost immediately. On other occasions they only become apparent to specific individuals and groups. And on yet other occasions, the unforeseen consequences can remain hidden elements in human figurations for extended periods of time. The important thing to recognize is that these unplanned outcomes are not the work of the mysterious reified forces to which so many sociologists have recourse; they are the outcomes of the interactions of dynamic, differentially interdependent human beings. These differential inter-dependencies can with equal validity be conceived of as differential power relationships and as such human history can appropriately be conceived of as on-going power struggles.

While conspiracy theories of history are often transparently simplistic, this does not prevent us from recognizing the fact that human beings do often conspire, plot and withhold information and knowledge from other groups in the process of trying to achieve their ends. At the same time, even the most powerful groups are constrained by the nature and complexity of the human figurations in which they are located and their aspirations and their strategies are more or less continuously mediated and even thwarted by less powerful groups. Of course, if and when unanticipated outcomes become apparent, more powerful groups are likely to be better placed to respond, but whatever actions they take will only be part of another 'cycle' in the human figuration.

Overall, the failure of people to achieve their objectives may be traced to three principal and interrelated sources: (i) their objectives may be impracticable, unrealizable, (ii) even when they are realizable, their attempts to achieve them may be undermined by their limited perspective and knowledge and an important aspect of this restricted vision stems from the prevailing tendency to view the world through eyes which are preoccupied with ideological concerns, (iii) perhaps, above all, their pursuit of their goals is undermined or at least mediated by the sheer complexity of the relational network that, ideally, their strategies should have taken into account. But in truth, the depth of this complexity is such that even the most sophisticated of thinkers can only aspire to develop strategies which prove, in the event, to have a degree of adequacy. Given these social and psychological obstacles, it is hardly surprising that history is fundamentally characterized by the unplanned, unforeseen consequences of human actions geared to other ends.

Notes

 [1] Murphy, Sheard and Waddington, 'Figurational Sociology and its Application to Sport'.
 [2] Dunning and Sheard, *Barbarians, Gentlemen and Players*.
 [3] Williams, Dunning and Murphy, *Hooligans Abroad*; Dunning, Murphy and Williams, *The Roots of Football Hooliganism*; Murphy, Williams and Dunning, *Football on Trial*; Dunning *et al.*, *Fighting Fans*.
 [4] Sheard, *Boxing in the Civilizing Process*.
 [5] Elias, *Involvement and Detachment*.
 [6] Elias, 'The Genesis of Sport as a Sociological Problem'.
 [7] Elias, 'An Essay on Sport and Violence'; Dunning, *Sport Matters*, 56.
 [8] Elias, 'The Genesis of Sport', 21.
 [9] Atyeo, *Blood and Guts*, 142.
[10] Hazlitt, 'The Fight', 8.
[11] Wignall, *The Story of Boxing*, 55–8; Sheard, 'Aspects of Boxing in the Western "Civilizing Process"', 41–2.
[12] Stone, 'Wrestling; The Great American Passion Play'.
[13] Sheard, 'Aspects of Boxing', 41.
[14] Sheard, *Boxing in the Civilizing Process*, 218–24.
[15] Ibid., 264.
[16] Sheard, 'Aspects of Boxing'.
[17] Rawling,. 'Hatton gets World Title Shot'.
[18] Cooper, *Henry Cooper's Book of Boxing*, 31.
[19] Pitt, 'Bare Fists and the Thinking Fighter', 27.
[20] Cashmore, *Making Sense of Sport*, 146–7.
[21] Sheard, 'Aspects of Boxing', 49.
[22] Rawling, 'Gloves off in the Safety Debate', 1.
[23] Rawling, 'Boxing Hoping for end to Amateur Dramatics'.
[24] Ibid., 1.
[25] Hughes, 'Ringside Judges are put on Probation after Wigging', 2.
[26] International Amateur Boxing Association, *Rules for International Competition or Tournaments*, Rule XVII, Directives 4a, 1 and 2. http://www.aiba.net/AIBA%20Rules.pdf.

[27]   Rawling, 'Boxing Hoping for an end to Amateur Dramatics', 2.
[28]   Hughes, 'Ringside judges are put on Probation after Wigging', 2.
[29]   'Boxing Judges Warned of Spy Camera', *Dawn*, the Internet Edition, 10 Sept. 2000.
[30]   BBC Sport, 'Minister Rejects Boxing Ban'.
[31]   BBC Sport, 'Amateur Boxing Hits on Safety'.
[32]   Rawling, 'Gloves off in the Safety Debate', 1.
[33]   Ibid., 1.
[34]   Elias, *What is Sociology?*, 104–57; Elias, *The Society of Individuals*.

References

Atyeo, D. *Blood and Guts: Violence in Sports*. New York: Paddington Press, 1979.

BBC Sport. "Amateur Boxing Hits on Safety." http://news.bbc.co.uk/sport1/hi/other_sports/1109763.stm, accessed 10 Jan. 2001.

BBC Sport. "Minister Rejects Boxing Ban." http://news.bbc.co.uk/sport1/hi/other_sports/1074209.stm, accessed 18 Dec. 2000.

Cashmore, E. *Making Sense of Sport*. London: Routledge & Kegan Paul, 1990.

Cooper, H. *Henry Cooper's Book of Boxing*. London: Arthur Barker Ltd, 1982.

Dawn, the Internet Edition. "Boxing Judges Warned of Spy Camera." 10 Sept. 2000.

Dunning, E. *Sport Matters: Sociological Studies of Sport, Violence and Civilization*. London: Routledge, 1999.

Dunning, E. and K. Sheard. *Barbarians, Gentlemen and Players: A Study of the Development of Rugby Football*. Oxford: Martin Robertson, 1979, Second edition with a new introduction, London: Frank Cass, 2004. .

Dunning, E., P. Murphy, and J. Williams. *The Roots of Football Hooliganism: An Historical and Sociological Study*. London: Routledge and Kegan Paul, 1988.

Dunning, E., P. Murphy, I. Waddington, and A. Astrinakis. *Fighting Fans: Football Hooliganism as a World Phenomenon*. Dublin: University College Dublin Press, 2002.

Elias, N. "The Genesis of Sport as a Sociological Problem." In *The Sociology of Sport: Selected Readings*, edited by E. Dunning. London: Frank Cass, 1971: 88–115.

Elias, N. *What is Sociology?* London: Hutchinson, 1978.

Elias, N. "An Essay on Sport and Violence." In *Quest for Excitement: Sport and Leisure in the Civilizing Process*, edited by N. Elias and E. Dunning. Oxford: Basil Blackwell, 1986: 150–74.

Elias, N. *Involvement and Detachment*. Oxford: Basil Blackwell, 1987.

Elias, N. *The Society of Individuals*. Oxford: Basil Blackwell, 1991.

Hazlitt, W. "The Fight." *New Monthly Magazine*, 1822

Hughes, M. "Ringside Judges are put on Probation after Wigging." *The Guardian*, 2 Aug. 2002

International Amateur Boxing Association. *Rules for International Competition or Tournaments*, Rule XVII, Directives 4a, 1 and 2. http://www.aiba.net/AIBA%20Rules.pdf.

Murphy, P., J. Williams, and E. Dunning. *Football on Trial*. London: Routledge, 1990.

Murphy, P., K. Sheard, and I. Waddington. "Figurational Sociology and its Application to Sport." In *Handbook of Sports Studies*, edited by J. Coakley and E. Dunning. London: Sage, 2000, 92–105.

Pitt, N. "Bare Fists and the Thinking Fighter." *Sunday Times*, 3 June 1984.

Rawling, J. "Gloves off in the Safety Debate." *Guardian Unlimited*, 19 Dec. 2000.

Rawling, J. "Boxing Hoping for end to Amateur Dramatics." *The Guardian*, 4 April 2001.

Rawling, J. "Hatton gets World Title Shot." *The Guardian*, 14 July 2004.

Sheard, K. "Boxing in the Civilizing Process." Ph.D. diss., Anglia Polytechnic University (1992).

Sheard, K. "Aspects of Boxing in the Western "Civilizing Process"." *International Review for the Sociology of Sport* 32, no. 1 (1997): 41–2.

Stone, G. P. "Wrestling; The Great American Passion Play." In *The Sociology of Sport: Selected Readings*, edited by E. Dunning. London: Frank Cass, 1971: 301–35.

Wignall, T. C. *The Story of Boxing*. London: Hutchinson, 1923.

Williams, J., E. Dunning, and P. Murphy. *Hooligans Abroad*. London: Routledge and Kegan Paul, 1984, 2nd edn, 1989.

'Amateurism' as a Sociological Problem: Some Reflections Inspired by Eric Dunning

Richard Gruneau

Introduction

Eric Dunning helped me to clarify how amateurism in sport could be seen as a distinctively sociological problem. Here is how it happened. As a graduate student in the early 1970s I conducted a survey of the socioeconomic backgrounds of Canadian amateur athletes and was struck by the extent to which so many athletes in the sample came from families where both parents were highly educated and where fathers were employed in professional or managerial occupations.[1] A few years earlier an influential Canadian government report on sports participation had concluded that Canadian amateur sport in the late nineteenth century had been overly exclusive, reflecting a lingering 'aristocratic conception'. But, the report went on to suggest that the 'aristocratic conception of sport has democratized; a whole new world of human activity has been born in which millions take part'.[2] Based on my data, I argued that the report was overly optimistic about the level of democratization in Canadian amateur sport, reflecting a broader ideological conception that Canada had 'evolved' over the twentieth century into an essentially meritocratic and fully democratic society.[3] While upper middle-class (a more accurate description than 'aristocratic') conceptions of sport may have been a thing of the past, systemic socioeconomic differences were still clearly evident in Canadian amateur sport. However, I increasingly began to feel that proper consideration of such issues demanded a much different kind of study to the one I had undertaken. The questions that were beginning to interest me were historical questions. Finding answers would require a detailed historical analysis of the institutional development of sport in Canada, with specific reference to the changing relationships between various ways of organizing sport (for example, amateur sport versus professional sport) and social class.

At the time, there were few models available to suggest how such a study might look. My first impulse was to design a study comparing and contrasting the backgrounds of people who had the greatest influence in the organization of sport at key points in Canadian history. With this in mind, I did some preliminary historical research in the mid 1970s on the backgrounds of 'organizational elites' in Canadian sport. Along the way, I discovered two essays that helped me to conceptualize my work in new and broader ways.[4] The first of these essays was Eric Dunning's brilliantly suggestive discussion of 'Industrialization and the Incipient Modernization of Football'.[5] The second was Dunning's fascinating essay, with Kenneth Sheard, on 'The Bifurcation of Rugby Union and Rugby League'.[6] These two essays were later reworked and published in Dunning and Sheard's path-breaking book *Barbarians, Gentlemen and Players*.[7]

I was particularly struck by Dunning's, and Dunning and Sheard's, discussions of nineteenth-century amateurism. In their view, amateurism could be understood as a distinctly modern *ideological* 'ethos' that emerged to articulate and to promote the world view of nineteenth-century 'public school elites'.[8] The emergence of organizations and rules designed to give institutional support to this ethos – and the development of organizations and rules opposed to it – involved a complex play of social class struggles and regional cultural dynamics in late nineteenth-century Britain. This view of amateurism as *both* an ideological discourse and as a set of class practices was a revelation. The key point for me was the way that Dunning, and Dunning and Sheard, analyzed amateurism in distinctly historical and sociological terms rather than treating it simply as an abstract moral or philosophical category.

As a young graduate student in sociology, I had already begun to piece together my own kind of social analysis of the origins and meaning of amateurism as a form of class-based 'ideology'. Indeed, in the early 1970s I promoted this view vigorously in a number of on-campus debates about the continuing efficacy of the ideal of 'amateurism' as a guiding principle in the face of the growing professionalization of high-level Canadian sport in the twentieth century. However, my understanding of the issues involved was still confused by a tendency to view amateurism as a transcendent moral principle – something to contrast to the allegedly 'corrupting' influences in sport of financial or bureaucratic rationality. In this view, I was influenced by Huizinga's analysis of the problems of excessive 'seriousness' in sport, assuming that 'amateur sport' was somehow closer to the spirit of fair play and simple enjoyment than more 'professionalized' sporting activities. Separated from its initial class exclusiveness, the philosophy of amateurism even seemed at times like a viable standpoint for social criticism. Viewed, as an abstract moral and philosophical principle, amateurism seemed to keep alive the romantic notion of free human expression in sport. With some stretching, and in the context of the 'counter cultural' movements of the late 1960s and early 1970s, this conceptual linkage between free expression and the romantic *ideal* of amateur sport did not seem inconsistent with the student left's equally romantic rejection of the rationalizing forces of technology and capitalist markets.

The force of Dunning's, and Dunning and Sheard's, sociological analysis of amateurism proved immensely useful in helping me to clarify my thinking on these issues. Whatever value the dream of amateurism may hold as an ethos stressing fairness and simple enjoyment in sport, their work demonstrated the theoretical utility of understanding the dream as a distinctively modern, socially-produced conception – a discourse – that was grounded in material interests and social struggles. This discourse took its institutional and cultural form through clearly observable social practices of rule making, exclusion and inclusion. Thinking about these ideas against the background of broader reading in radical political economy and social theory led me to a conclusion that seemed inescapable: the basic constituting structures of sport – and, indeed, the social definition and meaning of sport – are constantly in play in human history. The key task of sociological analysis is to understand the shifting conditions within which – and the practices through which – the 'making' and 'remaking' of sport occurs.

Pierre Bourdieu outlined a similar view with arresting clarity in an essay published in 1978:

> sport, like any other practice is an object of struggles between the fractions of the dominant class and also between social classes ... *the social definition of sport* is an object of struggles ... in which what is at stake *inter alia* is the monopolistic capacity to impose the legitimate definition of sporting practice and the legitimate functioning of sporting activity.[9]

This passage virtually jumped off the page at me when I first read it. However, I also had the feeling that many of the key ideas promoted by Bourdieu in 1978 were implicit in Dunning's, and in Dunning and Sheard's essays, two years earlier. Bourdieu, Dunning and Sheard all shared the view that it is never adequate to analyze sport reductively – as a passive reflection of abstract social forces, a mirror of society. Neither is it adequate to view sport simply as an expression of some inherent human essence for play, nor as some socially-constituted 'corruption' of that essence. The more useful view is to see sport as something constituted by a shifting set of social practices and socially-produced discourses.

In various ways this latter assumption has guided my work in the sociology of sport for nearly 30 years. I never heeded Dunning's calls to fully embrace the 'figurational' sociology of Norbert Elias, and I was never fully persuaded by the theoretical conclusions that

Dunning and Sheard arrived at in *Barbarians, Gentlemen and Players*. Still, empirically and analytically my work has been greatly influenced by many of the ideas that Eric Dunning has consistently championed throughout his career: notably, a belief in the virtue of pursuing resolutely sociological approaches to analysis; commitment to a dynamic historical and 'developmental' sociology; strong emphasis on the importance of social context; and a focus on both the enabling and constraining features of social structures. So, whether he cares for the idea or not, Eric Dunning has to bear at least some of the responsibility for the style and focus of my work in the sociology of sport.

In this essay, I want to honour this intellectual debt by revisiting 'amateurism' as a sociological problem, broadening and extending the analysis of amateurism in new ways.[10] My discussion will begin with a general overview of the social and cultural conditions which led to the emergence of amateurism in western sport as an ethos or social philosophy, a set of social, organizational and cultural practices, and even as a broad social movement. Following this I explore a range of significant contradictions within amateurism both as an ideal and as a more concrete organizing principle in sport and I examine the international export of amateurism, especially via amateurism's incorporation into the Olympic 'movement' in the early twentieth century. I conclude by discussing how the early ideal of amateurism became unsustainable not only within the Olympic movement, but within western sport more broadly. The IOC removed the word 'amateur' from the Olympic Charter in 1974; however a number of key ideas associated with the amateur ideal continue to stay alive within the Olympic movement, only now their primary function seems more to demarcate the saleable features of the Olympic brand than to provide guidelines for the social and cultural meaning of sport.

The Emergence of Amateurism in Western Sport

Modern organized sport in western societies has its roots in the eighteenth and early nineteenth centuries, in a wide range of older local folk games, masculine physical contests of different types, including various para-military arts (for example, fencing, shooting, boxing), and a diverse array of contests and gaming activities practiced at fairs, picnics, taverns, social clubs and community outings. Initially, these activities tended to be periodic, and were minimally-organized, and many activities were more socially-oriented than competitive. However, in other instances competition could be extremely intense, involving significant amounts of both emotional energy and money.

In the United States especially, a great many of these activities were imbued with an aura of casual commercialism in their earliest forms. Steven Pope has noted, for example, how commercial harness-racing drew huge crowds of well-heeled patrons in Long Island early in the nineteenth century.[11] Boat racing, often for prizes that ranged as high as 20,000 dollars was also popular in the US at this time, along with early circuit professionalism in sports such as pedestrianism and boxing.[12] More notable was the development of a vibrant regional saloon culture in the larger cities and towns. This saloon culture catered primarily to male working-class patrons and it provided a haven for prizefighting along with other small-scale commercial sporting spectacles such as ratting, dog fights and cockfights.[13] Even US College sports had commercial connections in the middle of the nineteenth century. During the 1860s Harvard crews competed for cash prizes as high as $500 in Boston Regattas, college track and field athletes often engaged in prize-hunting, pitting their prowess against local favourites, and Harvard baseball teams often played games against teams of professional players.[14] Baseball was one of the earliest US sports to emerge with ongoing professional leagues.

A number of historians have commented on the pluralistic – some even use the word 'democratic' – features of this informal and casually commercial approach to sport.[15] Throughout much of the nineteenth century, saloon keepers, small-time promoters and sports facility owners were behind many of the events that grabbed headlines in the sporting magazines that were becoming increasingly popular throughout North America. In some instances, in the first half of the century, these events were even sponsored by members of upper-class sporting clubs that had formed at the time. In this sporting environment, it was not unusual for athletes from privileged family backgrounds to compete in the same competitions with manual labourers and tradesmen.

Somewhat similar patterns of cross-class competition and sponsorship were not uncommon in other western societies as well, although arguably not to the same extent as in the United States. Britain also had a vibrant tavern culture which promoted various physical contests among rural people and the working classes. This partial openness could also be found in some sporting clubs. Indeed, Dunning and Sheard note how 'there was initially little middle- and upper-class opposition to the participation of working men in soccer and Rugby'.[16] Furthermore they note how social relations in the industrial North of England encouraged lower degrees of status-exclusiveness than in Southern England and this played a role in the development of 'open' and 'working class' clubs in the North and of 'open', often commercial, competitions in the mid-to late nineteenth century.[17] A few trend-setting sporting clubs sponsored open competitions as early as the 1850s where 'gentlemen' would compete against working men.[18] In another example of mid nineteenth-century cross-class sporting contact, Dr W.P. Brookes, a tireless promoter of sport at the time, was instrumental in organizing 'Olympic Games' in his community that featured cash prizes and were open to all competitors. Brookes commented that 'such meetings as these bring out free minds, free opinions, free enterprises, free competition for every man in every grade of life. The Olympic Games bring together different classes and make them social and neighbourly.'[19]

Research on the history of Canadian sports reveals parallel tendencies. Throughout much of the nineteenth century a diverse array of sporting activities were sponsored by tavern owners, facility operators and local promoters, sometimes bringing men from the privileged classes and the working class into similar venues, and, on occasion, into similar competitions. At the same time, following the lead of developments in the US, organized baseball in Canada grew quickly in rural areas between the 1830s and 1860s, often featuring payment for player's services, prizes and gate receipts. Organized lacrosse revealed similar commercial tendencies, with skilled aboriginal players and teams frequently setting a high standard of play. Meanwhile, in the cities, a handful of upper-class recreational sporting clubs occasionally sponsored open competitive sporting contests that brought athletes together from a diversity of social backgrounds: whites and aboriginals, professionals and manual workers, French and English, British colonials and native-born Canadians.[20] Anticipating the initiative of W.P. Brookes in England – by nearly a decade – a Montreal Olympic Athletic Club was formed in 1842 by 241 leading citizens of the city. This club staged a local 'Olympic Games' in Montreal in 1844 that featured open competitions. Archival records note that races were won by 'Sergeant McGillvary of the garrison; Tarisonkwan, an Indian; E. Burroughs, a lawyer; and "Evergreen" Hughes'.[21]

The presence of such open competitions in the United States, Britain and Canada in the first half of the nineteenth century undoubtedly gives substance to the claim that sporting cultures at this time were pluralistic. But, it is a gross overstatement to call them 'democratic'. In all three countries the cultural meanings of sporting events throughout the nineteenth century were tightly framed by the class, gender and racial prejudices of the time. Even the most 'open' sporting competitions were widely understood to be virtually synonymous with demonstrations of masculine vitality and prowess and therefore excluded females without a thought.[22] By the same token, although 'Indians' might occasionally compete against 'lawyers', as in the Montreal 'Olympics' of 1844, racial and class prejudices were ingrained in the competitions in significant ways – notably through the common practice of awarding medals and trophies to 'gentlemen' and cash prizes to everyone else. From the 1850s through the remainder of the century these class and racial prejudices in sport began to crystallize into a set of more formal rules of exclusion. The concept of amateurism emerged as a key element in this process.

But, where exactly did the idea of amateurism come from? One commonly-voiced argument is that the roots of amateurism can be found to lie far back in classical antiquity, notably in Greek sport. The ancient Greeks, the argument runs, initiated competitive athletics 'out of a deep, genuine love of sport for sport's sake, and as an appropriate activity for praising their gods'.[23] Baron Pierre de Coubertin's creation of the so-called 'modern' Olympics in 1896 is the event that has played the greatest role in perpetuating this link between amateurism and antiquity. Many of the early leaders in de Coubertin's Olympic movement promoted this argument passionately – the late Avery Brundage, a former IOC president, is an especially notable example.[24]

However, more recently, historians have substantially challenged the idea that the roots of amateurism lie in western antiquity.[25] We now know with certainty that the ancient Greeks really had no conception of amateur sports. Indeed, in Greek games, gambling, cheating, violence, regional chauvinism, profit-taking, and prejudice were 'the norm for most athletic competitions of public note'.[26] A more compelling argument is to see amateurism as an 'invented tradition', *a distinctly modern creation* that grew out of a unique and highly complex set of circumstances in western life during the nineteenth century.[27] Amateurism emerged in the nineteenth century as a unique pastiche of both reactionary and – for the time – progressive ideas. These ideas were connected to two seemingly contradictory impulses: the class-conscious, and often racist, desire to exclude from sport people who might be defined as social inferiors; and the belief that sport could be an important arena in which to school young men and, later, young women, in a set of rational and positive cultural values. Dunning and Sheard correctly associate this latter impulse with the middle-class evangelical project of late nineteenth-century 'muscular Christianity'. However, I believe the impulse has even deeper roots in the broader 'project' of modernity that began to take form amongst western European intellectuals in the late eighteenth century.

Liberalism, Industrial Society and the Philosophy of Amateurism

This last point requires clarification. Both of the impulses noted above are connected to the ways that social and economic organization, politics and cultures in western nations began to change during the late eighteenth and early nineteenth centuries. An increased confidence in science and human reason, along with the expansion of markets in Europe during the eighteenth century, fuelled a widespread reaction to older ideas about the naturalness of social hierarchies and to the legitimacy of established religious doctrine. Against the feudal idea of every person having their place, more and more people began to argue that human beings had the capacity to rise or fall in social life on the basis of their abilities. Even more notable were the modern liberal ideas that citizens had inalienable civil and political rights; that individual citizens should be treated equally and fairly; and that 'the people' in any society had the capacity to govern themselves.

These tendencies were felt acutely in turn-of-the-century Britain, where the close proximity of Jacobinism, post-enlightenment republicanism and democratic thinking in France seemed to pose a very real challenge both to older conceptions of aristocratic rule, and to the place of the aristocracy as leaders in the definition and maintenance of the national culture. To Britain's conservative Tory establishment, the twin spectres of the storming of the Bastille and the terror of the guillotine elevated fears about the dangerous irrationality and power of the masses.[28] Over the next half-century, the advent of new industrial technologies, the enclosures of feudal estates, and the migration of thousands of workers to new industrial cities created additional insecurities for Britain's ruling class. In addition, as the nineteenth century progressed, burgeoning industrial capitalism promised new opportunities for people wanting to raise their social station, and contributed to a strengthening middle class. Urban poverty and the popularity of seemingly irrational and rough leisure activities among the new urban masses – such as drinking, gambling and blood sports – stimulated middle-class movements for social and moral reform. At the same time, the oppressive conditions of early industrial work spawned an actively democratic opposition from an increasingly organized working class. All of these developments contributed to a growing sense of crisis throughout the nineteenth century, fuelled both by upper-class insecurity and growing middle-class fears of social unrest, social decay and moral decline.

In this increasingly volatile environment in Britain over the course of the nineteenth century it shouldn't be surprising that upper-class patrons of games and sports became less inclined to sponsor sporting competitions likely to include large crowds of people who they viewed as their social inferiors, and who they began to fear. Upper-class sportsmen were also less likely to want to compete against such people. Dunning and Sheard were the first writers I know of to make this important, albeit speculative, argument. In a social environment where the privileged felt secure in their positions, a 'well-born' person might well test his prowess in open sporting competition. But, an upper-class person's sense of identity and self-worth was not greatly at risk in such sporting competitions, and there was little need to be concerned about the symbolic consequences of losing a contest to a person of lower station. This meant that the emotional stakes for the privileged in such games were likely to be fairly low. A certain amount of casual commercialism could be readily tolerated in the promotion of public amusement and public displays of masculine prowess. Moreover, occasional instances of cross-class sporting competition offered little threat to the established order.[29]

Things were simply not the same in an increasingly industrial society, with its undercurrents of liberal democratic political ideas, unfettered individualism, social mobility through the market, and accompanying class competition and class tension. The most patrician of the sporting clubs that formed in Britain, Canada and the United States early in the nineteenth century – especially the aristocratically-inclined hunt clubs and yacht clubs – began to act in a more defensive and isolationist manner in the face of these changes. Formed initially as upper-class social and recreational clubs, these patrician enclaves rarely demonstrated great enthusiasm for open sporting competitions. Still, whatever limited interest such clubs may have had in open competitive sport seems to effectively disappear by the 1850s. In the latter half of the nineteenth century, the most exclusive sports clubs in Britain, Canada and the United States simply concentrated their energies on providing isolated social and recreational opportunities for the well-born and the rich.

Elsewhere, though, older sporting cultures were adapting in innovative ways to the broader changes that were affecting life in western societies during the nineteenth century. The team sports that were starting to develop in early nineteenth-century British public schools provide one of the most important examples. As Britain became a more entrepreneurial and industrial society the public schools emerged as a site where the sons of aristocrats, wealthy merchants and new industrialists began to intermingle. The culture of 'gentlemanly' athleticism that emerged within these schools drew on older notions of aristocratic pedigree, privilege and duty, but mixed them with newer bourgeois ideas about the importance of self-help and self-improvement.

The playing field became a vital element in the creation and promotion of this new cultural formation. On the playing field young men were taught that in order to proceed fairly games had to be set apart from the broader rules of social privilege. The goal was to create a new community of peers who recognized and agreed to be bound by higher rules of regulative authority.[30] It was obvious in football, for example, that there could be no fair demonstration of prowess if the son of a bottle merchant was prevented by his lower rank in social life from tackling the son of a Lord. At the same time, the old idea that sporting contests were valuable training grounds for virility and courage was subtly integrated with new ideas about self-development and the educative and moral value of games. British schoolboy games dramatized the need to balance the push for self-advancement, and the demonstration of individual masculine prowess, with a responsibility to duty and a commitment to one's peers – precisely the kinds of values that would help to forge and to solidify a powerful new bloc of aristocratic and high bourgeois class alliances in British society.[31] Unlike the comparatively open commercial culture of the tavern, the new public school sports culture offered a far more restricted approach to the idea of 'equality' in sporting competition. While the culture of the early British public school was evangelistic in its promotion of the virtues of sport, the public school promotion of sports participation was also closely aligned with the idea that 'gentlemen' were distinct from – and morally superior to – everyone else. Nonetheless, British schoolboy sport was an important vehicle for fostering a self-consciously competitive and achievement-oriented approach to sport within the Victorian upper and middle classes.

This growing emphasis on achievement and prowess in British public school sport merely extended the trend already established by earlier open competitions, and it was fully consistent with the rapid spread of popular sport imbued with an air of casual commercialism. The ethos of achievement – on sport as a kind of meritocracy – also resonated powerfully with broader struggles for more open, more equal societies in the west. However, it was an ethos that was at odds with lingering – yet still powerful – paternalistic sentiments about the naturalness of social distinction based on class, racial, ethnic and gender lines. The view of sport as an open competitive enterprise also raised new questions about exactly *who* in society should take responsibility for organizing sport, and about the kind of morality that should accompany sport.

In Canada – the case I know best – a new generation of upward-striving, native-born, professional and business men took control in the 1870s of the most prominent sports clubs.[32] The directors of these clubs began to see sport as something more than simple upper-class recreation or as periodic displays of masculine physical prowess. Instead they came to view sport in a way that reflected key aspects of a British public school sensibility. Sport was important not only because it promoted masculine strength and vigour but also because it presumably helped to teach good 'character'. These new directors of sports clubs were themselves often temperance-minded men, Methodist by inclination, with strong conservative values. But their conservatism had little connection to older upper-class sensibilities. Their world view grew out of the broader culture of business and professional life in Canada at the time – a culture that had come to place great emphasis on organization, regulation, competition, vitality, energy and the values of self-improvement. Prominent businessmen and professionals struggled to apply these values to create new forms of sporting organization in the image of their own cultural ambitions. With that in mind, the most prominent clubs set out to finance and build new sports facilities, and to create standardized rules for competition that would allow athletes and teams from across the country to compete with one another. It wasn't long before a number of these clubs in the largest cities had spun off self-designated 'national' organizations designed to promote their sport across Canada by seeking affiliate clubs, publishing national rule books, adjudicating disputes, and organizing sanctioned 'national' championships.

Sport historians in the United States have pointed to a similar development of prominent sporting clubs in the latter half of the nineteenth century, along with the proliferation of a great many other clubs who sought to organize sporting activities in small and medium-sized towns. In a fast changing industrial world many local business groups, churches, unions and occupational and ethnic associations throughout both Canada and the United States had began to use sport as way of promoting a sense of membership and identity with the sponsoring community. This lent itself to often intense local rivalries, for example, between civic boosters in adjacent industrial communities, working-class and middle-class club teams, or teams from differing ethnic and religious communities. When a baseball club from a small industrial community played a club from New York or Boston, or, in Montreal, when an Irish working-class lacrosse team challenged a team of clerks and professionals of English origin, the results *mattered* to the communities in question. In other words, by the 1870s, athletes were already beginning to act as the symbolic representatives of rival communities in North America and this added new incentive to find ways to win. That sometimes meant actively recruiting players from outside the community and paying them, playing a little tougher than the rules allowed, or finding a set of backers to finance a team of community professionals. The successes of sports teams began to be seen as a significant indicator of a community's character and prosperity.[33]

All of this fuelled a myriad of disputes: for example, about what was fair and what was not fair in sporting competition; how to control cheating and violence; how gate or prize money should be allocated between competing teams; and the kinds of limits, if any, that should be placed on any one team's efforts to recruit good players. Compounding these issues, by the latter third of the nineteenth century, the casual commercialism of earlier years was becoming much more systematic. By the 1870s there was an increasingly clear delineation between work and leisure in western nations, creating a situation where large groups of people became available for the consumption of commercial entertainment at regular and predictable times. The consolidation of an industrial system based on wage labour and machine production – matched with organized labour's push for 9-hour work days and holidays on Saturdays – created the conditions necessary for the development of mass audiences. These audiences became new markets to be exploited through the ongoing professionalization of sporting activities. At the same time, the growing demand for sporting equipment in North America was creating an increasingly prominent sporting goods industry. Industry leaders, such as the Spalding corporation, got into the business of publishing rule books, sponsoring leagues and seeking alliances with 'the leading sports clubs' in various regions.[34]

The Contradictions of Amateurism

The rapid emergence of organized sport into a prominent feature of North American cultural and economic life in the late nineteenth century was not something that everyone viewed as a positive development. For many religious leaders and educated professionals, sport still appeared to be little more than a valueless diversionary spectacle closely connected to idleness, gambling, drink and violence.[35] Earlier in the century, movements to prevent cruelty to animals, along with those promoting temperance and moral reform in growing industrial cities, had decried the seemingly destructive and irrational features of such popular male working-class recreations as cockfighting, ratting, and prizefighting. With the rapid expansion of cities as specialized sites for commerce and industrial production this moral concern about seemingly irrational and socially-destructive uses of leisure became closely linked with economic and political expediency. The drinking, merrymaking, and sometimes disorderly recreations popular among working-class men were viewed as activities that disrupted the daily routines of business by encouraging absenteeism, debt and insubordination. As a result, throughout the nineteenth century, governments in North America made play in the streets illegal, heavily regulated tavern locations and hours, and controlled alcohol consumption at public events. They also often banned sports that they saw as encouraging gambling, cruelty or irrational violence, and they promoted more seemingly 'rational' forms of recreation in their stead.[36]

Still, the question remained whether sport of any kind should be promoted as a socially-desirable, rational and 'civilizing' activity. The most militant critics of sport in the late nineteenth and early twentieth centuries argued that sport could never be anything other than a socially worthless activity. Sports were not truly 'productive' activities, the argument ran. Even worse, not only do sports contribute nothing of value to society, they distract people from things that are of greater importance. By the early twentieth century this initial resistance to sport was often tacitly linked to a broader type of conservative cultural criticism. Conservative critics typically argued that the thirst revealed by the modern industrial masses for diversionary amusement – and especially through increasingly spectacular entertainments – revealed the spread of dangerously irrational tendencies in western cultural life. Sport seemingly stood out as a graphic demonstration of such tendencies. Like the Roman Circus in antiquity, the argument continued, the spread of modern sport should be understood as an indicator of growing social decay, even barbarism.[37]

Against these views, nineteenth and early twentieth-century physical educators, and middle-class proponents of sporting competition, took their leads from 'modern' educational theories that stressed the importance of training both the mind and the body. Most notable was Locke's widely-cited reference to 'a sound body and a sound mind' in his essay on 'Some Thoughts Concerning Education'. This dictum became a key motto in the 'muscular Christian' movement that grew in England throughout the nineteenth century.[38] Middle-class proponents of sport also championed the perceived virtues of English schoolboy athletics, arguing that rationally organized sport, pursued for its own sake, could indeed be a 'civilizing' endeavour. The older argument that sport could develop health and virility among young men – very important for the expansion and defence of empire – was made routinely. But, the new nineteenth-century upper and middle-class evangelists for sport typically emphasized other socially-desirable values as well: self-reliance, modesty, an appreciation of the importance of fairness, control of one's emotions and respect for one's adversary. The challenge was to ensure that schools, sporting clubs and sporting organizations all supported and promoted this rational civilizing agenda in sport and physical education.

Still, many critics remained unconvinced that this civilizing agenda was either possible or desirable if pursued on a broad scale. Certain people in society, the argument ran, were simply not capable of living up to this imagined civilizing agenda. Physical training and gymnastics in schools for military purposes may be appropriate, but the working classes, or the so-called 'primitive races', arguably lacked the refinement to appreciate the higher virtues of sports. The masses seemed too tied to rough and irrational recreations and, more importantly, they seemed to invest the outcomes of sporting competitions with too much significance.

A far better strategy, the argument continued, was to limit the teaching of civilizing sport to young 'gentlemen' amateurs – people most likely to approach sport with a strong moral foundation, and with a necessary sense of proportion. Here, the view of amateurism drew inspiration from the Renaissance image of the leisured gentlemen who excelled effortlessly at a variety of tasks, merging it with aspects of an older aristocratic valorization of physical vitality, and the more recent English schoolboy obsession with fair play and sportsmanship. In addition, proponents of this socially-exclusive view of competitive sport began to extend the argument to suggest that there were classes of people in society who had definite physical advantages in certain games because of the nature of the work they performed. A mechanic or labourer, for example, could logically be expected to be stronger than a white collar clerk. Competition between the two was therefore unlikely to create the conditions for fairness necessary to stage socially-desirable recreations.

These sentiments circulated and took root in the student-sport culture of Oxford and Cambridge in the 1850s and soon found their way into the official declarations of a growing number of amateur clubs and amateur associations, beginning with a few key clubs in England who restricted their membership to 'gentlemen amateurs' and who barred members of the 'working classes' from club-sponsored competitions.[39] The first sporting association in England with the word 'amateur' in the title was formed in the mid 1860s, and the popularity of social restrictions on sporting competition quickly spread.[40] These restrictions received their most famous formulation in the Henley Regatta's exclusion of mechanics, artisans and labourers, and, eventually, anyone 'engaged in any menial duty'.[41] Elsewhere, other forms of social exclusion by statute were also added to the definition of amateurism. For example, in Canada in 1873, the Montreal Pedestrian Club defined an amateur as 'one who has never competed in any open competition, or for public money, or for admission money, or with professionals for a prize, public money or admission money, nor has ever at any period of his life taught or assisted in the pursuit of athletic exercise as means of livelihood or is a labourer or Indian'.[42]

In this definition, the class and racially-based prejudices are obvious. The problem of losing to imagined social inferiors, or of opening the door to unwelcome cultural values, is solved through a conscious and aggressive strategy of social exclusion. However, a great many athletes and sports organizers rejected such an exclusive definition of socially-valuable 'amateur' sport. If sport did have important educative potential, the argument ran, it surely made sense to try to promote it as broadly as possible. With this in mind, many sports organizers from the 1870s through to the early twentieth century began to act as self-conscious moral entrepreneurs, aggressively selling their particular vision of positive social values as an imagined universal standard for evaluating sport's social worth. The most committed moral entrepreneurs believed that there was no reason why anyone should be formally excluded from participation in amateur sports on the basis of their social origins, as long as they demonstrated complete devotion to the idea of sport as a fair and morally-grounded area of cultural life. Indeed, the men who became amateurism's most committed moral entrepreneurs in the early twentieth century were themselves often from humble social origins – including the American Athletic Union's early leader, John Sullivan, born of Irish-immigrant parents, and Avery Brundage, International Olympic Committee president and the son of a stone mason.[43]

In his path-breaking history of the Olympic Games in the nineteenth century, David Young demonstrates clearly how tensions between the socially exclusive view of amateur sports participation, and the more evangelical view of amateur sport as a broad 'civilizing' force in western life, were clearly evident in Britain as early as the 1850s and 1860s. W.P. Brookes was a notable early champion of the universalist moral entrepreneurial view. 'As Christians', Brookes announced, 'we should, on moral grounds, endeavor to direct the amusement of the working class'. This put Brookes at odds with the advocates of class-exclusive amateurism, creating 'constant and furious conflict' that eventually killed the fledgling British Olympic movement.[44]

Even those people who were inspired by Brookes' view – including Pierre de Coubertin, years later – were unsure exactly how it would be possible to ensure that a moral agenda could be maintained in universally-open sporting competition. The only way to ensure this seemed to be to accept the idea that sports participation should be accompanied by a distinctive world view – a state of mind. From this perspective, amateurism should not be limited to a particular social class; rather, it should be something to which *anyone* might aspire.

But, the incorporation of this abstract goal into any precise organizational definition proved to be virtually impossible. The most popular solution was to define the philosophy of amateurism in negative terms; that is, to define it in terms of what it is not. The seemingly obvious conclusion was to point the finger at the allegedly corrupting powers of money. Like money in the biblical temple, the existence of material rewards seemed to pose the greatest threat to the inherited public school ideal of playing the game for its own sake. It was argued that money raised the stakes of games to a point where games lost their intrinsic value and were pursued simply as a means to a financial pay-off. Money promotes greed and cheating, the argument ran, and it sustains professionalism. Professionalism, in turn, can be associated with gross ambition, gambling and moral laxity. Therefore, it seemed that the best way to define amateurism in sport was to juxtapose it to professionalism.

Unfortunately, there was no magic formula to determine what this exactly meant, and there were a myriad of possible interpretations. For example, amateur purists typically believed that anyone who had ever made any money in sport, say, as a teenage lifeguard, was a professional and therefore ineligible to compete in sanctioned amateur competitions. Even to have been found to have competed in a competition against someone who had ever earned money for teaching or playing sport was enough to risk excommunication from the amateur church. Others wanted the rule only to apply to money earned directly from sporting exhibitions. Still others believed in the heretical conception that limited forms of compensation were acceptable, as long as a person was not making their sole livelihood form the activity.

From the 1870s through to the First World War amateur sports organizers in western nations spent an enormous amount of time and energy debating these issues and staking out competing positions on them. The stakes were high. At issue was the degree of control that certain individuals, and certain sports organizations, would exercise over the developing worlds of national and international sport. In these struggles, the major differences between competing individuals and organizations were often little more than where each person or group stood on the amateur question.

The Olympics and the International Export of Amateurism

Viewed from the broadest perspective – and distanced from its most aggressively exclusive tendencies – the emergence of amateurism as a guiding principle in sport was simply an expression of the more widespread attempt by the educated western middle classes to regulate and to reform the uses and meanings of leisure time among 'the people'. For example, by the early years of the twentieth century in Britain and North America a clear distinction between the rational use of leisure time and seemingly irrational amusement had become fully institutionalized. Rational recreation was promoted in amateur sports organizations, schools, municipal parks and libraries. Irrational leisure – typically associated with the older saloon culture, gambling and 'rough' sport was patrolled by the police.[45] Professional sports still carried the stigma of an earlier attachment to rough leisure, but they increasingly began to occupy a cultural position that seemed to move fluidly between the two poles of rational and irrational recreation. Despite their exclusion from amateur organizations, promoters of professional sport in the early twentieth century didn't hesitate to adopt some of the moral entrepreneurs' rhetoric about sport as a character builder. Moreover, in the fast-growing commercial popular culture of the time, most commentators in the commercial media tended not to differentiate between amateur and professional sport stars. Simply stated, commercialism of various types in sport remained a widely accepted part of the cultural landscape among legions of sports fans, and professional sports continued to grow in popularity.

To add to the confusion, even some of the most ardent promoters of amateurism clearly admired the skills of the best athletes in their sport, professional or not. More notably, many of the clubs, teams and schools that were formally affiliated with the new national organizations that developed to promote and to police amateur sport – such as the Amateur Athletic Union (AAU) or the National Collegiate Amateur Athletic Association (NCAAA) in the United States – were by no means as ideologically committed to amateurism as the bureaucrats were who ran these organizations. In this environment, many sports clubs simply proclaimed a public commitment to amateurism while quietly accepting professionalism of varying degrees.[46] In addition, as late as the turn of the twentieth century, even the most powerful amateur organizations in North America had yet to consolidate full control over the diverse regions of the United States and Canada.

This was the context in which Pierre de Coubertin – taking up some of the agenda championed earlier by W.P. Brookes – explored the idea of creating an international modern Olympic Games.[47] And, like elsewhere, while there was a great deal of talk about the philosophy of amateurism in the early years of de Coubertin's Olympics, the reality of the fledgling movement was often quite different. Initially, in order to stage the games at all, significant compromises with commerce and professionalism were made. For example, the 1900 and 1904 Olympic games in Paris and St Louis were held in conjunction with international expositions and the athletic events were literally surrounded by celebrations of commerce. Furthermore, at the insistence of some IOC members, professional fencers were allowed to compete in 1896 and 1900. The Olympic champion cyclists from the United States in 1904 were also paid performers.[48]

Such compromises led to increased pressure from amateur purists to define the Olympic mandate more clearly. As a result, the IOC formed committee after committee to study the meaning of amateurism and to try to define it in practical terms. A parallel series of debates about the precise meaning of amateurism occurred within the major amateur sport organizations in the United States and Canada, with the amateur purists and moral entrepreneurs eventually taking control.[49] The successes of the moral entrepreneurs at the national level – especially in the US – added momentum to the lobby for a very tough anti-commercial position within the IOC. In 1912, the IOC agreed to adopt a definition of amateurism that officially precluded participation by anyone who had ever received any monetary gain at any time for teaching or participating in any kind of sport. This puritanical conception was modified slightly just over a decade later to allow for greater latitude in interpretation, but moral sentiment continued to be paramount: 'An amateur is one who devotes himself to sport for sport's sake without deriving from it, directly or indirectly, the means of existence. A professional is one who derives the means of existence entirely or partly from sport.'[50] IOC Presidents from the 1920s through to the 1960s – Avery Brundage in particular – became fierce defenders of this 'anti-professional' definition of amateurism as a standard for participation in the Olympics.

The growth of the Olympics as an international 'movement' with self-professed moral overtones gave new life to the amateur code. Ironically, considering the internationalist aspirations of the Olympic movement, 'amateur sport' became closely linked to the burgeoning nationalism of western industrial societies.[51] This in turn strengthened the influence of National Olympic Committees in their home countries, along with the most prominent amateur associations. But, the very successes of the Olympics put new pressures on amateurism, because now the symbolic representational power of modern sport was moved beyond the local realm of small town rivalries, cross-class or inter-ethnic and inter-racial conflicts, and into the international arena. Winning was something that came to matter more and more to sports fans in the countries that competed in the Games, and this put mounting pressures on National Olympic Committees to field the best possible teams, even if that meant bending the rules of amateurism to the limit.

So, even when the victory of purified amateurism as a standard in international sport seemed virtually complete, the amateur ideal continued to be compromised by a set of deeply-rooted contradictions. Amateurism was supposedly connected to a self-consciously educative and civilizing *project* – the promotion of an imagined culturally superior 'state of mind' – but it often simply seemed to operate as an inflexible bureaucratic reflex. Amateurism was supposedly a hymn to fairness and equality, but it preached these virtues through a policy that implicitly favoured the wealthy, and early on had discriminated in more obvious ways against non-Caucasians and women.[52] Amateur sport, through its association with the Olympics, became closely associated with the goals of internationalism and global fraternity, but it also contributed to the contradictory project of building an imagined national vitality within different nations, and to the creation of national programmes designed to demonstrate national prowess through sport. At the same time, the concept of amateurism had to accommodate a philosophical commitment to *both* versatility and specialization. Amateur sport was something to be done as an avocation, but in the Olympics it was also guided by a commitment to the motto 'Citius, Altius, Fortius'. To take this motto to its logical conclusions implied specialization and professionalization. Finally, amateurism committed itself, ironically, to a non-commercial cultural ideal in a world that was in the process of becoming more and more self-consciously commercial – a world of international capitalism, where popular cultural goods, such as music, films and sports, were in the process of becoming some of the most important and prized commodities of all. Then too, there was the obvious fact that amateurism was meant to reference a universal code of fairness, but amateur sports organizations around the world – and the IOC especially – often seemed to be in the business of negotiating compromises in interpretation in the interests of political expediency.

Amateurism, Commercialism and the 'Aestheticization' of Modern Sport

Given these deep contradictions it is small wonder that the national and international sports governing bodies who took responsibility for promoting and regulating the ideal of amateurism were mired in controversy throughout much of the twentieth century. These controversies were played out most prominently in the IOC. Problems with 'commercialism', and debates around acceptable definitions of 'amateurism', or about the legitimacy of the entire concept, plagued the IOC from its inception all the way into the early 1980s.[53] Contemporary histories of the 'modern' Olympics are filled with stories about the IOC's ongoing struggles with such things as industry endorsements to national sports federations, sponsorship money and broken time payments to athletes. Among these struggles, historians often point to the significance of Avery Brundage's infamous suspension of Austrian ski racer, Karl Schranz, from the 1968 Olympics as a pivotal transitional moment in the IOC's eventual retreat from the principles of 'amateurism' in the 1970s.[54] The Schranz episode was significant because it powerfully dramatized the immense gulf that had developed between puritanical amateur ideals and actual practices in international sport by the 1960s. But, the broader retreat from amateurism as a guiding principle in national and international sport had begun much earlier, with many so-called 'amateur' organizations in Europe and North America all but abandoning their moral entrepreneurial mission as early as the 1930s. Now, in the age of NBA (National Basketball Association), NHL (National Hockey League) and FIFA (Federation Internationale de Football Association) 'dream teams' in the Olympics, along with prominent professional players in sports such as tennis, the concept of amateurism seems little more than a distant memory.

I want to argue that the most relevant question in the history of amateurism is not to ask 'why did amateurism ultimately collapse as a guiding principle in sport?' Given amateurism's many contradictions, obvious class exclusiveness, and existence in a world where sport was a widely accepted part of commercial popular culture, the more relevant question is 'why was the principle of amateurism able to become so influential, and to last as long as it did?' I don't have the space here to discuss this latter question in depth; rather, I merely want to highlight a few speculative points and arguments.[55]

The most obvious explanation for the fleeting 'successes' of amateurism lies in the extent to which the growing popularity of the Olympics in the twentieth century had the effect of elevating the promoters of amateur sport to an international monopoly position. Anyone who wanted to participate in the Olympics was simply forced to follow the amateur line, or at least claim to be following it. The link that developed between Olympic sport and nationalism pushed international sport in a more competitive and commercial direction, much to the chagrin of the defenders of 'pure' amateurism. But, at the same time, nationalism briefly strengthened the hand of the moral entrepreneurs by providing increased international interest in the Olympics. After the Second World War, when the contradictions of amateurism appeared to be sharpening to an untenable state, the entry of socialist countries – with their deep aversion to commercialism – into the Olympics gave amateurism another temporary reprieve.

Still, these historical and structural circumstances only tell part of the story. The philosophy of amateurism was *deeply appealing* to many people because it suggested that sport could serve a higher cultural purpose beyond mere amusement or crass commerce. Promoting this higher cultural purpose became the ideological core of what we might call the distinctively modern 'project of amateurism'. This project was itself influenced by a much broader set of social and cultural movements in western nations from the late eighteenth through to the mid twentieth century. Particularly relevant was the emergent cultural modernism in the eighteenth century that celebrated human creativity and scientific discovery – along with the more general pursuit of individual excellence – in the name of human progress.[56] In this view, the ultimate goal was for human societies to 'progress' by developing 'objective science, universal morality and law, and autonomous art according to their inner logic'.[57] Under the ambit of amateurism, sport could make a claim to being a rationally-organized and legitimate part of the historical march in the west toward progress through human self-improvement. Seen as a state of mind, rather than a narrow set of rules, amateurism sought to transform lowbrow 'uncontrolled' sport into a more regulated and socially worthwhile form of creative physical expression.

But the real evocative power of amateurism – and especially Olympian amateurism – did not lie in these modernist elements alone. Rather, it lay in the unique way in which traces of cultural modernism were blended with ideas from late Victorian romanticism. Particularly relevant here was the widespread interest that grew in late nineteenth-century Europe and North America for all things 'classical'. De Coubertin tapped into this interest when he surrounded his imagined festival of international amateur sport with symbols from a so-called pre-modern 'western' world. His contemporary Olympic Games suggested an imagined continuity between the apparent emergence of western civilization in classical antiquity and the great heights reached by western civilization at the turn of the twentieth century. At the same time, the modernist emphasis on reason and universalism in human affairs was both reaffirmed and softened by his attempt to build strong links between sport, art and poetry.

Once more, there is an intriguing irony about all this: in the push to celebrate sport as a form of rational civilizing culture, the proponents of amateurism – particularly in the Olympic movement – chose to reference a host of non-rational images and visceral collective rituals. We might say that de Coubertin and his colleagues were fascinated by the fact that the ancient Greeks set out consciously to 'aestheticize' sport in addition to simply participating in it. Odes to athletes, paintings, frescos and sculptures all spoke to a view of sport as something that went beyond a merely agonistic enterprise. In this sense, the promoters of modern amateurism sought to link their moral entrepreneurial vision to a renewed aesthetic and ideological project. In roughly the same way that fascist philosophy sought to 'aestheticize' politics, the evangelists for amateurism sought to aestheticize sport as part of a self-consciously modern promotional enterprise.[58] Linked to the modern Olympics, these aesthetics – of classically-sculpted male bodies; mythical flames and torches; flags, ritual ceremonies and mass displays; paintings, sculptures, hymns and poetry; and public incantations of honour and duty – briefly gave amateur sport a cultural status that no form of sport in western life ever had in the past.

More importantly, this unique combination of modern rationalist principles, and anti-modern romanticism, made for a powerful and intoxicating cultural brew. In its new aestheticized form, early twentieth-century amateurism had a remarkable capacity to appeal to *both* political progressives and reactionaries. For progressives, international amateur sport, spearheaded by the Olympics, clearly seemed to be a positive cultural innovation. International amateur sport embodied the dream of a new kind of rational internationalism, steeped in universally-agreed upon rules for international cultural exchange and within a moral system that emphasized sportsmanship and fairness. As part of this dream, amateur sport was promoted as an activity that the working classes, and people in poor or developing countries, might use to improve themselves. For reactionaries, the romanticism associated with international amateur sport provided a new way to glorify a number of older non-rational cultural themes and values: strength, duty, authenticity and masculine vitality. The Olympic Games in particular not only provided a framework for the celebration of individual will and prowess, they also dramatized the strength derived from the subordination of will and prowess to higher forms of national or racial purpose.

Against the background of this intriguing combination of cultural influences, the social philosophy of amateurism developed to become a kind of pseudo-religion for its most ardent followers.[59] The Olympic 'movement' in the early twentieth century provided a vast socializing mechanism for the ongoing rehearsal of this pseudo religion. This self-conscious aestheticization of sport did not emerge 'naturally' in any way; rather, it was developed by interested intellectuals who took it upon themselves to define and to debate the amateur philosophy, to write its history, and, in many instances, to simply spread the gospel. Within the circles of international sports governing bodies, and among physical educators and sports people around the world, these intellectuals worked hard to establish the philosophy of amateurism as a new kind of common sense. But, in the end, the cultural battle simply could not be sustained in a world where commerce was becoming increasingly ubiquitous as the social form most responsible for the mediation of human life. So amateurism gradually 'disappeared', slipping quietly into the sepia-tinted imagery of sporting history.

Does amateurism have any significant residual effect at all in sport today? Amateurism may be *passe* at the Olympics, but in community sports and in schools around the world the idea that sport has a higher social or moral purpose is far from dead. It is also interesting to note, despite the absence of the word 'amateurism' in the Olympic charter, that the IOC continues to insist that the Olympic Games are committed to higher purposes than mere commercial spectacle. The IOC's new version of 'common sense' is that it is still possible to promote 'Olympism' as a 'philosophy of life' while opening up sport fully to commercial interests. However, once again, it simply isn't clear exactly what this philosophy of life actually entails, and how the Olympic spectacle serves higher social and cultural interests. Indeed, there is great difficulty in defining and agreeing upon such 'higher interests' in any case, and we have seen how the evolution of the apparent universal civilizing mission of amateur sport emerged out of a very clear set of western, masculine, and class-based moral conceptions. In this respect, there was never anything inherently universal about them.

More than 25 years ago Eric Dunning and Ken Sheard reminded students of sport to avoid a view of history as a set of seemingly abstract and impersonal social processes. Rather, students of sport should always stay attuned to 'clashes of group interest and ideology'. When you adopt this perspective in studying the historical emergence, evolution and apparent demise of the concept of amateurism in modern sport you cannot help but be struck by the manner in which aesthetics and moral philosophy became so closely intertwined with a powerful ideological project. In their attempt to aestheticize sport, and to regulate it in the interests of a self-professed moral universalism, the promoters of amateurism in the nineteenth and twentieth centuries spun a web of historical illusions. Today, despite the fact that amateurism is officially gone, these illusions soldier on as a vital part of Olympic marketing. The whole idea that the Olympic Games are a social and cultural 'movement', and therefore different from other forms of international sporting spectacle, such as the World Cup, is a centrally defining feature of the Olympics as a commercial 'brand'. In the end, the kind of sociological analysis of amateurism first begun by Eric Dunning in the early 1970s, and extended into the present day, leads you inescapably to consider an immense historical irony. The faint residues, rhetoric and imagery of a self-consciously anti-commercial ideology, forged in the nineteenth century, now arguably play the major role in sustaining the value of the Olympic Games as a global commercial spectacle.

Notes

[1] Data from this study are discussed in Gruneau, 'Class or Mass?'
[2] *Report of the Task Force on Sport for Canadians*, cited in Gruneau, 'Class or Mass?', 112.
[3] It also struck me forcefully that this 'ideological conception' was buttressed rather conveniently by a variety of arguments in contemporary social science that variously celebrated post-war affluence and the emergence of a modern society based on 'achievement values' more than older standards of social ascription. More detail on this point can be found in Gruneau, 'Class or Mass?', 108–14.
[4] Some of this preliminary work was published in conference proceedings in the late 1970s and one of these working papers was reprinted a few years later. See Gruneau, 'Elites, Class and Corporate Power in Canadian Sport'.
[5] Dunning, 'Industrialization and the Incipient Modernization of Football'.
[6] Dunning and Sheard, 'The Bifurcation of Rugby Union and Rugby League'.
[7] Dunning and Sheard, *Barbarians, Gentlemen and Players*.
[8] Dunning and Sheard, *Barbarians, Gentlemen and Players*
[9] Bourdieu, 'Sport and Social Class', 826.
[10] Much of the material on amateurism discussed in this chapter is derived from a public lecture that I presented at the University of Utah in 2001, in a pre-Olympic lecture series hosted by the Tanner Center for the Humanities. An edited version of that lecture was published under the title 'When Amateurism Mattered'.
[11] Pope, *Patriotic Games*, 20.
[12] Pope, *Patriotic Games*, 20
[13] Pope, *Patriotic Games*, 20 20–1. For a more developed discussion of sport and early saloon culture in the United States see Gorn and Goldstein, *A Brief History of American Sports*, 3–46. For a discussion of similar issues and events in Canada, see Gruneau and Whitson, *Hockey*

Night in Canada, 56–67. A highly-detailed case study of this 'saloon culture' in Montreal, Canada, can be found in DeLottinville, 'Joe Beef of Montreal'. Additional materials on sport and saloon culture in Canada can be found in Metcalfe, *Canada Learns to Play*.

[14] Pope, *Patriotic Games*, 20–1.

[15] In Canada, for example, several early sport historians linked the development of sport to the supposedly democratic 'frontier spirit' of the late eighteenth and early nineteenth centuries. See Howell and Howell, *Sports and Games in Canadian Life*, 54–6; and Roxborough, *One Hundred – Not Out*. I offer a critique of this position in Gruneau, *Class, Sports and Social Development*, 93–108.

[16] Dunning and Sheard, *Barbarians, Gentlemen and Players*, 139.

[17] Dunning and Sheard, *Barbarians, Gentlemen and Players* 141.

[18] See Dunning and Sheard, 'The Bifurcation of Rugby Union and Rugby League'.

[19] Young, *The Modern Olympics: A Struggle For Revival*, 25.

[20] Metcalfe, *Canada Learns to Play*, 22–6. Also see our discussion in Gruneau and Whitson, *Hockey Night in Canada*, 39–43.

[21] Metcalfe, *Canada Learns to Play*, 23.

[22] The importance of masculinity was highlighted by Sheard and Dunning, 'The Rugby Football Club as a Type of Male Preserve'.

[23] Pope, *Patriotic Games*, 18.

[24] See Guttmann, *The Games Must Go On*, 116.

[25] See Young, *The Olympic Myth of Greek Amateur Athletics*.

[26] Pope, *Patriotic Games*, 19.

[27] This idea is discussed in Pope, *Patriotic Games*, 37–40 and noted earlier by Kidd, 'The Myth of the Ancient Games'. A more detailed discussion of relationships between amateurism and 'modernity' can be found in Gruneau, 'The Critique of Sport in Modernity', 85–93.

[28] Thompson, *The Making of the English Working Class*, 441–3.

[29] For more developed discussions of these ideas see Gruneau, *Class, Sports and Social Development*, 98–103; and Gruneau and Whitson, *Hockey Night in Canada*, 46–77.

[30] Dunning, 'Industrialization and the Incipient Modernization of Football'.

[31] The classic statement on the role of the British public school is Wilkinson, *Gentlemanly Power*. Also see Arnstein, 'The Survival of the Victorian Aristocracy'. A more recent and comprehensive treatment can be found in Mangan, *Athleticism in the Victorian and Edwardian Public School*.

[32] For an early statement of this point see Wise, 'Sport and Class Values in Old Ontario and Quebec'. More recent discussions include: Gruneau, *Class, Sports and Social Development*; Metcalfe, *Canada Learns to Play*; and Gruneau and Whitson, *Hockey Night in Canada*.

[33] A more developed discussion of the 'representational' importance of sport in the late nineteenth century can be found in Gruneau and Whitson, *Hockey Night in Canada*, 67–77.

[34] Hardy, '"Adopted by all the Leading Clubs"'.

[35] David Young argues that an 'anti-athletic' stance among the Christian clergy in the west goes back to St Paul. In addition, he argues, that there was a deep-rooted intellectual precedent in Aristotle's *Politics* for not 'mixing the physical and the mental', thereby strengthening the western intellectual's antipathy to sport; *The Modern Olympics*, 188–9, n.18. However, it is important to distinguish here the differences between Catholicism and Protestantism on matters pertaining to the relationships between body and mind. Protestant movements, for example, were generally more accommodating to the uses of gymnastic exercise in schools. This kind of accommodation was given additional impetus by secular movements in educational philosophy after the Renaissance which claimed to recover classical Greek ideals of balance and harmony. See my discussion in Gruneau, 'The Politics and Ideology of Active Living in Historical Perspective', 201–10.

[36] There is now a very substantial literature that describes movements for the regulation and reform of leisure and 'popular' culture – and popular reactions to these movements – in western societies in the nineteenth century. Some influential early statements include: Bailey, *Leisure and Class in Victorian England*; Cunningham, *Leisure in the Industrial Revolution*; Hall, 'Notes on Deconstructing "the Popular"'; Rozensweig, *Eight Hours for What We Will*; Yeo and Yeo, *Popular Culture and Class Conflict: 1590–1914*.

[37] My discussion here is indebted to Brantlinger, *Bread and Circuses*. Also see Gruneau and Whitson, *Hockey Night in Canada*, 11–30.

[38] See my discussion in Gruneau, 'The Politics and Ideology of Active Living in Historical Perspective', 208– + 10.

[39] Young, *The Modern Olympics*, 30–4.

[40] Young, *The Modern Olympics* 32–5.

[41] Young, *The Modern Olympics* 193, n.65.

[42] Kidd, *The Struggle for Canadian Sport*, 27–8.

[43] I am indebted to Steve Hardy for alerting me (in personal correspondence) to this point.

[44] Young, *The Modern Olympics*, 31.

[45] My discussion here draws broadly on ideas found in Bailey, *Leisure and Class in Victorian England*; Hall, 'Notes on Deconstructing "the Popular"'; Cunningham, *Leisure in the Industrial Revolution*; and Bennett, 'The Politics of "the Popular" and Popular Culture'.

[46] See the discussion of amateurism and Canadian hockey in Gruneau and Whitson, *Hockey Night in Canada*, 56–92.

[47] On de Coubertin see MacAloon, *This Great Symbol*. MacAloon's work is usefully read in conjunction with the somewhat different interpretation offered by Young, *The Modern Olympics*.

[48] Guttmann, *The Games Must Go On*, 21.

[49] On the amateur/professional debate in the United States see Pope, *Patriotic Games*, 23–45. The Canadian case is well covered in Metcalfe, *Canada Learns to Play*, 99–132.

[50] Guttmann, *The Games Must Go On*, 55.

[51] On relations between nationalism and amateurism see Pope, *Patriotic Games*, 40–9.

[52] Hoberman makes a compelling case for the argument that the adoption of amateurism, merged with a strong appreciation of masculine vitalism, in the early stages of de Coubertin's Olympic 'movement' was never very far from a reactionary – indeed racist – vision of 'social harmony'. See Hoberman, *The Olympic Crisis*.

[53] See for example, Guttmann's catalogue of numerous issues around 'amateurism' in *The Games Must Go On*. Also see the discussion of tensions created by Olympic commercialism in Barney, Wenn and Martyn, *Selling the Five Rings*.

[54] On the Schranz case see Senn, *Power, Politics and the Olympic Games*, 146–7 and Guttmann, *The Games Must Go On*, 119–20.

[55] Very useful material for this kind of analysis can be found in Hoberman, *The Olympic Crisis*, Chapters 1 and 2.

[56] My discussion of cultural modernism is indebted to Harvey, *The Condition of Postmodernity*, especially Chapters 1 and 2. For a complementary, but rather different perspective, see Berman, *All That's Solid Melts Into Air*.

[57] Habermas, cited in Harvey, *The Condition of Postmodernity*, 12.

[58] Benjamin, 'Art in the Age of Mechanical Reproduction'.

[59] See Hoberman, *The Olympic Crisis*, 30–1 and Guttmann, *The Games Must Go On*, 116.

References

Arnstein, W. "The Survival of the Victorian Aristocracy." In *The Rich, the Well-born and the Powerful*, edited by F. C. Jaher. Urbana, IL: University of Illinois Press, 1973.

Bailey, P. *Leisure and Class in Victorian England*. London: Routledge, 1978.

Barney, R., S. Wenn, and S. Martyn. *Selling the Five Rings: The IOC and the Rise of Olympic Commercialism*. Salt Lake: University of Utah Press, 2002.

Benjamin, W. "Art in the Age of Mechanical Reproduction." In *Illuminations*, translated by H. Zohn edited by W. Benjamin. London: Fontana, 1970.

Bennett, T. "The Politics of "the Popular" and Popular Culture." In *Popular Culture and Social Relations*, edited by T. Bennett, C. Mercer, and J. Woolacott. Milton Keynes: Open University Press, 1986.

Berman, M. *All That's Solid Melts Into Air: The Experience of Modernity*. London: Verso, 1983.

Bourdieu, Pierre. "Sport and Social Class." *Social Science Information* 17 (1978): 819–40.

Brantlinger, Patrick. *Bread and Circuses: Theories of Mass Culture as Social Decay*. Ithaca, NY: Cornell University Press, 1983.

Cunningham, H. *Leisure in the Industrial Revolution*. New York: St Martin's Press, 1980.

DeLottinville, P. "Joe Beef of Montreal: Working Class Culture and the Tavern, 1869–1889." *Labour/Le Travailleur* 8 (1981/82): 9–40.

Dunning, E. "Industrialization and the Incipient Modernization of Football." *Stadion* 1, no. 1 (1975): 103–39.

Dunning, E. and K. Sheard. "The Bifurcation of Rugby Union and Rugby League: A Case Study of Organizational Conflict and Change." *International Review of Sport Sociology* 11, no. 2 (1976): 31–68.

Dunning, E. and K.Sheard. *Barbarians, Gentlemen and Players: A Study of the Development of Rugby Football*. 1st edn. Oxford: Martin Robertson, 1979.

Gorn, E. and W. Goldstein. *A Brief History of American Sports*. New York: Hill and Wang, 1993.

Gruneau, R. "Class or Mass? Notes on the Democratization of Canadian Amateur Sport." In *Canadian Sport: Sociological Perspectives*, edited by R. Gruneau and J. Albinson. Don Mills: Addison Wesley Canada, 1976.

Gruneau, R. "Elites, Class and Corporate Power in Canadian Sport." In *Sport, Culture and Society: A Reader on the Sociology of Sport*, edited by J. Loy, G. S. Kenyon, and B. D. McPherson. Philadelphia: Lea and Febiger, 1981.

Gruneau, R. *Class, Sports and Social Development*. Amherst: University of Massachusetts Press, 1983.

Gruneau, R. "The Critique of Sport in Modernity: Theorizing Power, Culture and the Politics of the Body." In *The Sports Process: a Comparative and Developmental Approach*, edited by E. Dunning, J. Maguire, and R. Pearton. Champaign, IL: Human Kinetics, 1993.

Gruneau, R. "The Politics and Ideology of Active Living in Historical Perspective." In *Physical Activity in Human Experience*, edited by J. Curtis and S. Russell. Urbana, IL: Human Kinetics Press, 1997.

Gruneau, R. "When Amateurism Mattered: Class, Moral Entrepreneurship, and the Winter Olympics." In *The Winter Olympics: From Chamonix to Salt Lake City*, edited by L. Gerlach. Salt Lake City: University of Utah Press, 2004.

Gruneau, R. and D. Whitson. *Hockey Night in Canada: Sport Identities and Cultural Politics*. Toronto: Garamond Press, 1993.

Guttmann, A. *The Games Must Go On: Avery Brundage and the Olympic Movement*. New York: Columbia University Press, 1984.

Hall, S. "Notes on Deconstructing "the Popular"." In *People's History and Socialist Theory*, edited by R. Samuel. London: Routledge, 1981.

Hardy, S. ""Adopted by all the Leading Clubs": Sporting Good and the Shaping of Leisure, 1800–1900." In *For Fun and Profit: The Transformation of Leisure into Consumption*, edited by R. Butsch. Philadelphia: Temple University Press, 1990.

Harvey, D. *The Condition of Postmodernity: An Enquiry Into the Origins of Cultural Change*. Oxford: Blackwell, 1989.

Hoberman, J. *The Olympic Crisis*. New Rochelle, NY: Aristide D. Caratzas, 1986.

Howell, M. and N. Howell. *Sports and Games in Canadian Life*. Toronto: Macmillan, 1969.

Kidd, B. "The Myth of the Ancient Games." In *Five Ring Circus: Money, Power, Politics and the Olympic Games*, edited by A. Tomlinson and G. Whannel. London: Pluto Press, 1984.

Kidd, B. *The Struggle for Canadian Sport*. Toronto: University of Toronto Press, 1996.

MacAloon, J. *This Great Symbol: Pierre de Coubertin and the Origins of the Modern Olympic Games*. Chicago: University of Chicago Press, 1981.

Mangan, J. A. *Athleticism in the Victorian and Edwardian Public School*. Cambridge: Cambridge University Press, 1981.

Metcalfe, A. *Canada Learns to Play: The Emergence of Organized Sport 1807–1904*. Toronto: McClelland and Stewart, 1987.

Pope, S. W. *Patriotic Games: Sporting Traditions in the American Imagination, 1876–1976*. New York: Oxford University Press, 1997.

Report of the Task Force on Sport for Canadians. Ottawa, Queen's Printer, 1969.

Roxborough, H. *One Hundred – Not Out: the Story of Nineteenth Century Canadian Sport*. Toronto: Ryerson Press, 1966.

Rozensweig, R. *Eight Hours for What We Will: Workers and Leisure in an Industrial City*. London: Cambridge University Press, 1983.

Senn, A. *Power, Politics and the Olympic Games*. Urbana, IL: Human Kinetics Press, 1999.

Sheard, K. and E. Dunning. "The Rugby Football Club as a Type of Male Preserve." *International Review for the Sociology of Sport* 5, no. 1 (1973): 5–24.

Thompson, E. P. *The Making of the English Working Class*. Harmondsworth: Pelican Books, 1968.

Wilkinson, R. *Gentlemanly Power: British Leadership and Public School Tradition*. New York: Oxford University Press, 1964.

Wise, S. F. "Sport and Class Values in Old Ontario and Quebec." In *His Own Man: Essays in Honour of A.R.M. Lower*, edited by W. H. Heick and R. Graham. Montreal: McGill-Queen's University Press, 1974.

Yeo, E. and S. Yeo. *Popular Culture and Class Conflict: 1590–1914: Explorations in the History of Labour and Leisure*. Sussex: Harvester Press, 1981.

Young, D. C. *The Olympic Myth of Greek Amateur Athletics*. Chicago: Ares Publishers, 1984.

Young, D. C. *The Modern Olympics: A Struggle For Revival*. Baltimore: Johns Hopkins University Press, 1996.

The Leicester School and the Study of Football Hooliganism

Alan Bairner

Introduction

The overall contribution that Eric Dunning and his University of Leicester colleagues, past and present, have made to the sociology of sport is an established fact. In the early 1960s, as Dunning himself recalls, he and Norbert Elias began their 'preliminary examination of sport'.[1] Thanks in no small measure to the initial efforts of Dunning and a handful of other pioneering scholars, the sociological neglect of sport has been increasingly addressed in the intervening years. It should also be added that, as a consequence of these developments, sociology has acquired a hegemonic status in the overall social scientific study of sport with historians, political scientists and anthropologists all engaging with, and benefiting in no small measure from, the work carried out by their counterparts in sociology.

Dunning describes the sociology of sport as 'one of the liveliest areas in the subject'.[2] For Dunning, 'a central part of this liveliness consists in the fact that the subdiscipline has become a terrain contested by protagonists of all the main sociological paradigms'. [3] He counsels, however, that 'it is a situation full of potential for further development but also fraught with danger, particularly the danger that representatives of the different paradigms will misconstrue the positions of their rivals, in that way contributing less to fruitful debate than to sterility and perhaps destructive conflict'. [4] According to Dunning the figurational approach that was introduced by Norbert Elias and subsequently adopted by the Leicester School 'has been frequently misconstrued'. [5] Interestingly, however, Dunning also concedes that 'figurational sociologists have undoubtedly misconstrued the work of others'. [6] The fact that Dunning has referred to this problem in one of his more recent works is interesting. Within sociology in general and specifically within the sociology of sport, the figurational approach that is so closely associated with Dunning and the Leicester School has attracted admirers and critics in almost equal measure. This is reflected in virtually all of the major debates in which sociologists of sport have engaged. Nowhere, however, has it been more apparent than in relation to the contribution that has been made by Dunning and his colleagues to the study of football hooliganism.

This essay documents the Leicester School's work on football hooliganism. It examines the attacks that others have made on this corpus and attempts to distinguish between gratuitous invective and constructive criticism. The general aim of the essay is to give credit where it is due. The validity of some of the critical comment is acknowledged. Overall, however, it is argued that no group of scholars has made such influential interventions in the debate on football hooliganism and that much of the criticism that has been levelled at Dunning and his fellow researchers is misplaced and ultimately unhelpful.

Understanding Football Hooliganism

According to Anthony King, 'it may be the case that legitimate concerns about hooliganism have unreasonably biased research into football, so that issues such as the administration of the game and its political economy have been wrongly relegated to a secondary position'. [7] There is some truth in this argument. On the other hand, as events during the 2002–03 English season and Euro 2004 illustrated, football hooliganism and football-related violence remain a major problem not only for the game itself (and, by implication, its governance and its finances) but also for society as a whole. As Dunning and his colleagues have consistently argued, it is not a new phenomenon, it is not uniquely British (or English), and association football is not the only sport that is accompanied by violence perpetrated by people who describe themselves as fans. The fact remains, however, that despite the introduction during the 1990s of countless measures aimed at eradicating the problem, football in Britain is still haunted by the spectre of hooliganism. Whilst not the first to actually write about this specific problem, the Leicester School members have undeniably established themselves as the most influential analysts of the social roots of football hooliganism.

Popular explanations of the phenomenon have focussed on excessive drinking and incidents on the field of play (including violent conduct and over-exuberance on the part of the players or questionable decisions by referees and their assistants). There has also been a tendency to blame this particular form of deviant behaviour, along with all other anti-social activities, on the so-called permissive society. Inevitably such responses have pointed in the direction of punitive solutions.

Academic analyses of various types have been rather more sensitive inasmuch as they have sought genuinely to explain why hooligan behaviour occurs, instead of simply seeking excuses to demonize the perpetrators. Psychologists have sought answers in the dynamics of group behaviour and in forms of ritualized aggression. Marxists have explained hooliganism primarily with reference to economic deprivation and social exclusion. In that way, the hooligans could be presented as engaging in a form of social resistance. At no stage has the Leicester School sought to dismiss either of these approaches in their entirety. Instead, Dunning and his colleagues, like Elias before them, have always been willing to engage with other academic disciplines and alternative theoretical perspectives in an attempt to construct a body of knowledge that it is capable of doing justice to the social phenomena to be studied.

As Hughson comments, 'as the dominant "school" of theory in the field, the work of Dunning and his associates is unavoidably addressed in subsequent scholarship on football hooliganism'. [8] Astrinakis goes further and remarks on the 'hegemonic' position of the Leicester research group. [9] As we shall see, not everyone who feels compelled to address the Leicester School's contribution is impressed by the group's position of authority on this or other matters. Nevertheless, it is hard to imagine any academic researcher in this area simply ignoring what Dunning and his colleagues have written over the course of the past 20 plus years. Indeed it is worth noting that even some of the hooligans themselves have come to recognize the Leicester School as a voice of some considerable authority. For example, in their book on Cardiff City's 'Soul Crew', David Jones and Tony Rivers note approvingly that Dunning and his colleagues described the Cardiff City-Manchester United game played in September 1974 as 'a watershed in the reporting of football hooliganism'.[10] Other hooligans (and former hooligans), as we shall see, have of course been less generous about academic commentators on their activities.

In 1988, having already written a study of the behaviour and control of English football fans in continental Europe, Eric Dunning, together with Patrick Murphy and John Williams, published a major work on the roots of football hooliganism.[11] The second text begins with the claim that the phenomenon is deeply rooted in two main ways – firstly, because 'contrary to popular belief, forms of it have been a frequent accompaniment of association football in this country [Britain] ever since the 1870s and 1880s, the period when the game emerged in a recognizably modern form'.[12] Football hooliganism is also deeply rooted because for those who engage in it most persistently 'it is part of a way of life and they cling to it despite all the preventative measures that the football authorities and the government have tried'.[13] As a consequence, they argued, 'this lays stress on the need to study long-term processes and recommends a synthesis of sociology and history'.[14] Such an approach, it should be added, would be consistent with Eliasian sociology from which the authors drew their inspiration. Indeed, they themselves acknowledged that they wished 'to relate the problem of football hooliganism to Elias's theory of "civilizing processes".[15] The Leicester researchers argued that 'the fact that football hooliganism is more deeply rooted than is often supposed suggests that the current understanding of its "causes" is deficient'.[16] Their own study, they claimed, was 'an attempt to probe these causes – the past and present roots of football hooliganism – more deeply than has been done so far'.[17] Theirs was to be an inquiry into 'the social circumstances inside and, more importantly, outside the game within which such behaviour is recurrently generated' and an examination of 'the reasons why its frequency and seriousness vary over time'.[18] This inquiry has continued into the 1990s and beyond and many of the same central arguments have remained at the heart of the Leicester School's analysis.

Certain 'discoveries' have been constantly revisited by Dunning and his fellow researchers. These include the fact that soccer hooliganism is not and never has been a solely English or British phenomenon. It is also repeatedly emphasized that hooligan behaviour attaches itself to sports other than association football, that football-related hooliganism is by no means a new phenomenon and that it is mainly an expression of patterned male aggression usually found, at least in the English case, in the rougher sections of the working class. This latter claim suggests a relatively deterministic approach not unlike that adopted by Marxist analysts of the hooligan phenomenon. In fact, however, the Leicester School's approach, in keeping with its overarching theoretical perspective, is considerably more multi-faceted.

Rather than espouse a mono-causal explanation of football hooliganism, the Leicester School has consistently referred to a multiplicity of factors that include social class and masculinity, as well as some of the more popular 'causes' such as alcohol. In addition, because they refuse to accept that football hooliganism is a new phenomenon, they have also adopted an eclectic approach that involves historical as well as sociological sources and results in 'a synthesis of sociological, historical and psychological approaches to the study of football hooliganism'.[19] According to Richard Giulianotti, 'the civilizing process is used by the Leicester School to explain football hooliganism in two main respects'.[20] Firstly, Dunning and his associates seek to explain how our broader social attitudes towards violence at football matches have changed over time. This includes a close examination of the role that the media have played not only by highlighting, but also by ignoring, hooligan activity at different stages of the game's development. As Dunning and his colleagues wrote as recently as 2002, 'the label "football hooliganism" is not so much a scientific sociological or social psychological concept as a construct of politicians and the media'.[21] Secondly, the Leicester School has attributed most fan violence to social groups that have been relatively unaffected by the civilizing process. Thus, young men from what is described as the 'rough' working class are put forward as the main perpetrators of this form of anti-social behaviour.

Dunning and his colleagues admit that there is a lack of 'hard' evidence about the social origins and current stratification rankings of English football hooligans.

They claim, however, that between 70 per cent and 80 per cent of football hooligans are working class with low levels of formal education, and are most commonly employed in manual occupations. Their lower-class male habitus is exhibited in a complex of learned traits that appear to derive principally from early socialization characterized by the ready resort to violence, and adolescent socialization on the streets where violence is used to acquire membership of, and status within, groups that are held together by the principle of 'ordered segmentation'. As a consequence, these young males 'learn to associate adrenaline arousal in fights and physical confrontations with warm, rewarding and thus pleasurable feelings, rather than the anxiety and guilt that tend to accompany the performance and witnessing of "real" (as opposed to "mimetic") violence in the broader context of societies in which a majority of people consider themselves to be "civilised"'.[22] For the hooligans themselves, 'football hooliganism is basically about masculinity, struggle to control territory, and excitement' and fighting 'is a central source of meaning, status or "reputation", and pleasurable emotional arousal'.[23]

According to Dunning and his co-researchers, 'the figurational approach to football hooliganism does not constitute some kind of "super theory" which purportedly explains everything'.[24] However, such is the group's hegemonic standing in this area of sociological inquiry that critics have tended to react to the Leicester School as if it has been engaged in a form of intellectual imperialism. Although this essay will focus on only a few of the criticisms that have been levelled at the figurational interpretation of football hooliganism, it is worth establishing at the outset the entire range of critical comment.

Steaming in

Giulianotti has sought to classify the criticisms that have been levelled at Dunning and his associates. Firstly, there is the general charge that Elias's sociology is a medley of 'untestable' and 'descriptive' generalizations and not a genuine theory. Secondly, it has been argued that the Leicester approach contains historical inaccuracies. Thirdly, Dunning and the rest fail to show sufficient understanding when they seek to consider other, that is, non-English, cultures. Fourthly, the approach suffers from methodological weaknesses, not least a failure, especially in more recent years, to engage directly with the hooligans. Finally, the Leicester School stands accused of ethnographical failings.[25] There are also concerns about the extent to which Dunning and his colleagues have been primarily interested in trying to substantiate the validity of the idea of 'the civilizing process', even when this has led to inaccurate analysis of football hooliganism. For example, the claim that the overwhelming majority of hooligans belong to a 'rough', unincorporated section of the working class complements Elias's thoughts on civilization, but does not necessarily offer an accurate portrayal of the people who engage in football hooliganism. In addition, Giulianotti claims that 'these published criticisms mask what is often a deeper, more bitter professional relationship between the figurationalists and their opponents, especially those in England'.[26] In his opinion, 'part of this reflects the tendency of Dunning and his colleagues to dismiss the work of other researchers, and to over-react (even by academic standards) to any criticisms of their work'.[27]

On the basis of the quotes that appear in the introduction to this essay, it is reasonable to assume that Dunning himself would be willing to accept that the debate on how best to interpret football hooliganism has been rather more acrimonious than it might have been, and that the Leicester researchers have not been entirely blameless in this regard. On the other hand, when people have invested so much time and effort in developing a theoretical approach in which they wholeheartedly believe, it is scarcely surprising, and by no means reprehensible, that they should wish to defend that approach with vigour. For this reason, it is not worth devoting too much time at this point in the discussion to considering the pernicious influence that Giulianotti claims the Leicester School has exerted on academic debate on football hooliganism. Criticisms of the substance of the figurational approach and of the Leicester School's research methods are, however, different matters altogether. Most significant in this respect are the group's characterization of the social background of the hooligans, its ethnographic credentials, the slavish adherence to figurational theory and the ability (or inability) of the Leicester School to understand the hooligan problem outside of the English context.

Class Matters

Dunning and his colleagues refer consistently to the 'rough' working class, thereby attracting criticism not only from those who fail to see the need to compartmentalize the working class for the purposes of understanding football hooliganism, but also from those who argue that the hooligans are representative of a wide range of social backgrounds. According to Giulianotti, 'for anyone who really meets with the hooligan groups themselves, what is most striking is the ordinariness of it all'.[28] Arguing for a more inclusive understanding of the social origins of the hooligans, Giulianotti writes, 'A first glance at their clothes, girlfriends, parents, homes, cars, jobs, wider environment and leisure interests, testifies comprehensively to the mundane, even banal lifestyles of those who are well incorporated into mainstream UK society (though perhaps not to the polite endogeny of academic conferences and dinner parties)'.[29] The concluding remark looks like a cheap shot aimed at undermining the ethnographic credentials of the Leicester School – a subject to which this essay will return in due course. The original point, however, is one that receives some support from observations made by the hooligans themselves. For example, Jones and Rivers claim that 'the majority of football boys are, believe it or not, decent lads with good jobs and families, out for a release from the day-to-day pressures of life'.[30] According to them, 'there are Cardiff lads who have run around with the Soul Crew while holding down jobs like solicitor and doctor and a couple are even linked to the club in some capacity'.[31] Even though this claim is virtually unverifiable, it is not impossible. That said, it is not inconceivable that these middle-class hooligans are nothing more than exceptions to the general rule formulated by Dunning and his co-researchers.

Despite their reference to doctors and solicitors, Jones and Rivers tend to support this latter inference throughout the rest of their account of the Soul Crew's activities. They comment on 'the working class supporters of Cardiff City', 'the rugged miners and dockers of South Wales' together with the industrial towns, the tough places, such as Ely and the Docks, and the massive council estates.[32] They also describe Barry, one of Cardiff City's strongholds, as 'a rough little dockside town, ten miles outside Cardiff, with many council estates and one of the worst crimes' rates in the country'.[33] This sounds uncannily like the habitus in which, according to Dunning and his associates, the roots of football hooliganism are most effectively nurtured. Another insider account of the hooligan phenomenon also makes constant reference to this type of social context. Writing about the hooligans who have attached themselves to Hull City over a number of years, Shaun Tordoff alludes throughout to the 'hardness' of Hull and its working-class estates in which 'fighting was a way of life'.[34] Tordoff also supports another Leicester School claim – that hooligan behaviour attaches itself to sports other than football – by describing the scale of hooliganism among the fans of the city's two rugby league clubs, Hull FC and Hull Kingston Rovers. He writes, 'any football lads who bumped into Rovers in services or train stations will bear testimony to the fact that, number for number, they were as good as any football lads'.[35]

It is undeniable of course that the character of the British working class has changed considerably even in the period that the Leicester School has been studying the hooligan phenomenon. As a result of increased home ownership, de-industrialization resulting in fewer opportunities to engage in manual labour and a decline in unemployment, far more working-class people possess the attributes of incorporation. As Dunning and his colleagues note, 'social class raises complex and contentious sociological issues of definition and measurement'.[36] Yet there is reason to believe that far from disappearing, the essential characteristics of the unincorporated working class have been appropriated by men who may now possess the material trappings of incorporation, but who have responded to a crisis of masculinity that has partially been created by that process of incorporation by adopting and exaggerating 'rough' working-class behavioural traits. This point is well brought out by John Sugden in his study of football's underground economy.[37]

As Sugden observes, 'the social and regional make-up of England's travelling support is complex'.[38] But it is predominantly male and white. According to Sugden, 'England football provides them with opportunities to celebrate and reinforce traditional masculine identities: ones based on physical prowess and an unquestioned working-class patriarchy generated in the labour-intensive, urban, industrial economies of the last century'.[39] Few people now occupy positions associated with such economies. But, as Sugden correctly argues, 'there remains, nevertheless, for a certain type of man, a need to hang on to this muscular, factory-floor, barroom image of manliness'.[40] Although Sugden is disinclined to offer a purely sociological explanation for the behaviour of

England's fighting fans, his attribution of shaven heads and bulging tattooed muscles to 'a distinctly English masculine identity crisis' helps us to understand the extent to which the Leicester School's approach is still plausible, even in an era when the 'rough' working class of which they initially wrote has been superficially transformed if not quite obliterated.[41] Garry Robson makes some similar observations in relation to Millwall hooligans. 'It is clear', he writes, 'that their experience cannot be contained within the increasingly creaking apparatus and categories of conventional class analysis'.[42] They appear to be working class but they are not. They may seem to have gone through a process of embourgeoisification; but they are not embourgeoisified. Of one fan, Robson comments, 'being Millwall helps him to negotiate, survive and prosper in new and challenging circumstances'.[43] As a consequence, 'he lives at a distance from the working-class traditions that shaped him, but is able and eager to reconnect with them'.[44] It is by way of such negotiation that the values and attitudes of the 'rough' working class survive in an altered material environment.

It is inevitable that researchers who enter the field on a regular basis will encounter exceptional cases. That was certainly the experience of this author when he accessed the world of the Black Army, the unofficial supporters' club of leading Swedish club AIK and the traditional base for many of the most feared football hooligans in Sweden.[45] Those who spoke most were undoubtedly better educated and relatively affluent, albeit in a society in which class difference is much harder to establish than in Britain. Given that they were more likely than some of their peers to speak fluent English, it is perhaps unsurprising that they took the initiative when it came to talking to a visiting researcher. At no stage, however, did the articulate explanations that these young men offered for their hooligan behaviour disguise the fact that the overwhelming majority of their fellow Black Army members belonged to that category of people who, according to the Leicester School, are most likely to be attracted to hooliganism. Researchers in this area need to be wary of drawing general conclusions from the experiences of their key informants. This is a point not lost on Sugden, who clearly strikes up a close relationship with 'Fat Tony', the gatekeeper who allows him access to the world of the football grafters and who is able to explain his behaviour in rational terms. But this does not lead Sugden to ignore the fact that the world that he has entered is 'rough' and uncivilized.[46] Critics might argue, however, that even if the Leicester School is correct about the social origins of the hooligans, it has arrived at that conclusion without having entered the field – at least for many years.

Entering the Field

The Leicester School has certainly been criticized for its increasing lack of ethnographic engagement with the objects of their analysis. Giulianotti notes the difficulties that can arise when conducting research with football fans but consistently implies that he and a few others have managed to overcome these. The Leicester School, however, stands condemned of viewing the hooligans from a safe distance. In fact, Dunning and his colleagues recognize all too well the problems involved in conducting ethnographic research into hooliganism. Indeed, they stated as early as 1984 that the fieldwork for their initial studies had been carried out by John Williams, and not by Dunning or Patrick Murphy, because 'he is young enough and sufficiently "street-wise" and interested in football to pass himself off as an "ordinary" English football fan'.[47] Meanwhile the others would be able to focus on theory. There seems little wrong with this kind of academic division of labour. Moreover the fact that one does not spend large amounts of time with the hooligans would not necessarily disqualify trained sociologists from commenting on what they see around them – at football grounds, in pubs, at railway stations and so on. Not being 'in the field' is not synonymous with being in 'the ivory tower'. Furthermore, there is often something slightly disturbing about sociologists involved in football studies who constantly seek to establish their intellectual credentials on the basis of street credibility.

Unsurprisingly, some of the hooligans themselves are fiercely critical of certain types of academic analysis. Martin King and Martin Knight praise the work of Gary Armstrong who 'really has done his research, unlike previous academic efforts'.[48] Many of the latter, they argue, subscribe to 'the theory regarding unemployment and poverty, which was always crap'.[49] Without resorting to such colourful language, of course, the Leicester School has also dismissed simple economistic explanations for football hooliganism. In addition, 'the quest for excitement', which lies at the heart of the figurational approach, is consistent with what most of the hooligans themselves have to say by way of critiquing academic analysis. Jones and Rivers, for example, observe that 'the buzz of kicking off at a match, seconds before conflict, cannot be beaten by recreational or hard drugs'.[50] 'The adrenaline rush is amazing', they claim, 'so strong, in fact, that the only way you can kick the habit is to stay away'.[51] According to Giulianotti, 'sociologists have tended to underestimate the psycho-social pleasures of football violence'.[52] This can scarcely apply to the Leicester School, which consistently endorses the view that for the hooligans, 'the "pleasurable battle-excitement" engendered in hooligan confrontations forms a central life interest'.[53] In sum, therefore, without spending as much time in the field as they once did or, indeed, spending sufficient time in the right part of the field, the Leicester School has arrived at conclusions which, in broad terms, are sensitive to and reflective of the experiences of the hooligans. It is doubtful if more time spent with the hooligans would have led to different results. On that point though, some critics might argue that the reason why the analysis would not change dramatically, regardless of the precise research methodology employed, is the fact that the entire contribution of the Leicester School to the football hooligan debate is aimed at consolidating Eliasian sociology as opposed to explaining the actual phenomenon.

Theorizing the Problem

Implied in the criticisms made by Giulianotti and others is the idea that Dunning and his associates seek to ensure that their exploration of football hooliganism fits in with the theoretical propositions of Elias, even at the expense of accurately describing and explaining the hooligan phenomenon. However, King argues that much of the work on football hooliganism, including that of the Leicester School, is exemplary precisely because it is informed by 'an awareness of sociological theory and procedure'.[54] He is considerably less sanguine about the condition of the sociology of football more generally. In some instances there is what he describes as a 'retreat from sociology' with rich data being left undertheorized.[55] This need not mean an absence of theoretical language. According to King, 'Giulianotti's recent contributions to the analysis of hooliganism constitute a very special case of this trend of uncritical, undertheorized writing because, on the surface, Giulianotti's sentences are replete with philosophical terminology, and they are obscurely constructed in a manner which suggests theoretical sophistication and erudition'.[56] In itself, this does not invalidate Giulianotti's view that the Leicester School is let down as a result of an attempt to make the evidence fit a theory that is not necessarily the most helpful for seeking to come to terms with football hooliganism. Indeed, even King suggests that 'Dunning's Eliasian approach tends, in its less self-critical moments, towards teleology'.[57] That said, King's attack on Giulianotti reminds us of how difficult it is to unify theory and practice. There are few social scientists, if any, who can claim never to have given primacy to their theoretical perspective. The resultant findings should still be taken on their own intrinsic merits.

Certainly Robson, whose methodology would almost certainly find greater favour with Giulianotti, recognizes the positive aspects of the figurational approach, which emerge directly out of Eliasian theory. He comments that 'the greatest virtue of this body of analysis is its detached historical focus and consequent stress upon the significance of continuities in relationships between class, masculinity and English football'.[58] He notes the criticisms of its theoretical coherence and of its empirical content and he himself remarks on the high level of generality, the apparent 'irrefutability' and a tendency towards over simplification. But 'despite these shortcomings this account of the development and construction of the hooligan phenomenon has its strengths'.[59] In particular, according to Robson, it has made a major contribution to 'a stable terrain of received knowledge about the development of the hooligan phenomenon'.[60] The Leicester School's approach may not be perfect either theoretically or empirically or in terms of the relationship between theory and empiricism. Nevertheless, it has made an important contribution at every one of these levels to the analysis of the English hooligan phenomenon. It remains to be seen, however, whether it has also been able to understand hooliganism in other settings.

Border Crossings

Armstrong disputes the validity of the concept of 'ordered segmentation' in the Sheffield case.[61] He argues that the hooligans do not have values that differ markedly from the rest of society and that there is little hard evidence that they come from the most deprived and 'roughest' working-class estates. Once more, however, the leading critic is Giulianotti, who argues that Dunning and his colleagues lack empathy when they seek to apply their general theory to non-English contexts. Specifically he claims that his own research into football hooliganism in Scotland reveals the presence of stable working-class as well as middle-class hooligans, thereby disproving the Leicester School's general proposition that the perpetrators of this type of violence belong only to the 'rougher' section of the working class.[62] It should be noted, however, that Giulianotti's early studies were of hooligans in Aberdeen, a city with a relatively homogeneous working class and, at least at that time, a degree of prosperity centred on the North Sea oil industry. It is more surprising though that he makes these general claims about Scotland given that some of his other research has taken him to Edinburgh, where a number of housing estates have acquired a reputation for precisely the kind of social bonding and associated violence that Dunning and his colleagues first identified in Leicester. It should in any case be noted that Dunning recognizes that 'it is unlikely that the phenomenon of soccer hooliganism will be found everywhere to derive from the same roots'.[63] Indeed, he and his co-authors observe that the phenomenon is not always or everywhere a consequence solely or mainly of social class. It is important to seek out the major fault lines in specific societies in order to uncover the roots of football violence. In both Scotland and Northern Ireland, for example, sectarianism is a crucial factor. Nevertheless, in attempting to establish a sociological understanding that is capable of transcending national boundaries, the Leicester School notes that in all cases the shared characteristic consists of social formations that involve intense 'we-group' bonds.[64]

Armstrong denies that this is necessarily a shared feature of hooliganism, even within the English context. Yet it is certainly an accurate description of the source of the problem in Northern Ireland where, despite the presence of an alternative fault line, much of the hooliganism that has occurred owes more to segmental bonding within lower working-class Protestant communities than to divisions between nationalist and unionist fans. In recent years, most football hooliganism in Northern Ireland has involved fans of Belfast's two most successful clubs – Glentoran and Linfield.[65] Both attract the bulk of their support (which is almost exclusively male) from the working-class loyalist housing estates of greater Belfast. Such estates are themselves characterized by the kind of bonding to which Dunning and his colleagues refer. This is notable in relation to loyalist paramilitarism within which internecine feuds are as likely to be linked to the defence of specific spaces – the Shankill, the Lower Newtownards Road, Sandy Row and Ballybeen – as to ideological differences of opinion. Inevitably, the fact that the majority of Glentoran's fans live in east Belfast whereas Linfield's support is arguably more diffuse, means that devotion to locality is further intensified in the attitudes and activities of the hooligans.[66] Young men seek excitement and status in the first instance by fighting for their respective estates and then for their team which, at least in the case of Glentoran fans, also means fighting for Protestant East Belfast.

Such an analysis does not work as well for other European countries, where the game itself as well as the social context may have followed very different trajectories. In Italy, for example, according to Roversi and Balestri, 'the social basis of the ultras does not consist predominantly of the lower and roughest strata of society'.[67]

It is worth noting, however, that this claim is made in a collection of essays edited by Dunning and some of his Leicester colleagues – evidence perhaps not only of a willingness to accept national differences in this respect, but also to promote open discussion within the sociology of sport, all of which runs counter to specific and general criticisms that have been levelled at them.[68] In fact, *Fighting Fans* represents a major attempt to bring together a variety of scholars and case studies written from a variety of perspectives. Far from setting themselves up as an omniscient elite, they have made every effort to encourage debate and to uncover difference even if that might potentially undermine the 'truth' of their figurational approach.

Grounds for Concern

To date, every effort has been made in this essay to defend the Leicester School from its critics. Constructive criticism, however, is always worth offering and in at least two respects Dunning and his colleagues have arguably brought some of the opprobrium upon themselves. It has been argued above that those who criticize the Leicester School for trying to arrange the 'facts' in such a way as to substantiate Norbert Elias's theories are themselves equally guilty of keeping an overly watchful eye on their theoretical credentials when writing about the hooligan phenomenon. However, the fact that others are guilty of the same error of judgement is scarcely sufficient to absolve Dunning and his associates from criticism.

The Leicester School has made an eminently sensible (some might think an almost commonsensical) contribution to the study of football hooliganism. Despite what the hooligans themselves might say about academic analyses of their activities, their own emphasis on the pleasure that such behaviour brings is catered for and, indeed, explained in some depth by Dunning and his colleagues. The latter's focus on masculinity is also insightful. The attempt to segment the working class is altogether more problematic, particularly in an era when the generic term itself is open to question. Nevertheless, the point made by Dunning and his fellow researchers makes basic rudimentary sense, even though it is always possible to uncover exceptions to the general rule that they have established. One is left to wonder, however, to what extent these convincing conclusions about football hooliganism actually need, or were at all times prompted by, the figurational approach. Of course, Dunning and the rest will argue that it is impossible to separate their findings from the theoretical perspective out of which they emerged. Yet one cannot help but think that their analysis owes more to their own powers as solid social scientific researchers than to any single theoretical approach. That they would deny this vehemently leads to another criticism, which was touched on quite briefly earlier but certainly needs to be addressed.

Without going nearly as far as Giulianotti, it is still possible to argue that the Leicester School has found itself in the middle of some fairly rancorous debates both within the group itself and between the group and other researchers. It is difficult sometimes for the outsider to understand why the wounds that these disputes have opened have continued to fester over an extended period of time. The people who are most involved are certainly not making such radically different claims about football hooliganism as to make this level of enmity inevitable. It would appear therefore that *amour propre* is heavily involved, with the various groups of researchers, the Leicester School included, fighting to defend their status. Indeed, without wishing to trivialize some of these academic rivalries, one can see similarities between their behaviour and that of the people whom they study. They are nearly all male. They are not exclusively English although England, and specifically Leicester, has been very much in the forefront of the activities involved. They are not of course working class, although one might hazard a guess that given their close affinity with association football many of them have working-class or lower middle-class origins. They have clearly bonded together in such a manner as to make 'them' and 'us' rivalry a distinct possibility. Perhaps the intra-academic rivalry provides an element of excitement in an otherwise drab world of teaching, assessment and administration. Finally, they are highly motivated to fight for a particular cause – in this instance not a football club or a specific neighbourhood, but rather a theoretical perspective. All of these factors have conspired to produce a struggle for supremacy – a battle to be 'top lads' in the academic study of a social phenomenon in which the status of being a 'top lad' is highly sought after. The Leicester School's devotion to Elias and their dogged commitment to espouse the figurational perspective is admirable, but one is left to ponder as to whether it is absolutely necessary and how far it has been responsible for alienating countless fellow researchers who would, in other circumstances, find much to agree with in the writings of Dunning and the rest.

Conclusion

The major contribution that Dunning and his colleagues have made to the study of sport's social significance is incontrovertible. More specifically, in relation to the analysis of football hooliganism as a world phenomenon, their work has been more substantial and more influential than that which has been produced by any other individuals or research groups. It would be difficult to question any of the 'discoveries' that they have made, although arguably they protest too much when arguing that hooliganism is a problem for sports other than football. Hooliganism certainly occurs in the course of other sporting events. It is doubtful, however, if it is endemic in other sports in the way that it appears to be within the context of football.

Using an eclectic research methodology, the Leicester School arrived at an explanation of football hooliganism. Their main findings are insightful and difficult to refute. Although there is scope for debate on the questions of what constitutes the 'rough' working class and to what extent it is the habitus of the overwhelming majority of football hooligans, there are no grounds for denying that the phenomenon involves young working-class men who, for a variety of reasons, either are, or else seek to be, marginal to mainstream society. Nor should we ignore the Leicester School's recognition that far from being helpless victims, these young men actively seek pleasure from their hooligan activities.

Those who do not subscribe wholly to the figurational approach will be tempted to argue that everything that Dunning and his colleagues have impressively revealed about the hooligan phenomenon could have been said without an almost slavish adherence to figurational sociology. But only the most jaundiced could use that as a reason for dismissing or underestimating the importance of the Leicester School's findings. In any case, it would be the height of arrogance to refute without reservation the epistemological trajectory that Dunning and his colleagues believe links their theoretical upbringing and their sociological interventions.

Notes

[1] Dunning, *Sport Matters*, 2.
[2] Ibid., 13.
[3] Ibid.
[4] Ibid.
[5] Ibid.
[6] Ibid.
[7] King, *The End of the Terraces*, 3.
[8] Hughson, 'Australian Soccer's "Ethnic" Tribes', 41.
[9] Astrinakis, 'Subcultures of Hard-core Fans in West Attica', 91.
[10] Jones and Rivers, *Soul Crew*, 3.
[11] Dunning, Murphy and Williams, *The Roots of Football Hooliganism*. A year later the triumvirate's first book was republished: Williams, Dunning and Murphy, *Hooligans Abroad*.
[12] Dunning, Murphy and Williams, *The Roots of Football Hooliganism*, 1.
[13] Ibid.
[14] Ibid., 1–2.
[15] Ibid., 2.
[16] Ibid., 5.
[17] Ibid.
[18] Ibid.
[19] Ibid., 217.
[20] Giulianotti, *Football*, 45.
[21] Dunning, Murphy and Waddington, 'Towards a Sociological Understanding of Football Hooliganism as a World Phenomenon', 1.
[22] Ibid., 21.
[23] Ibid., 16.
[24] Ibid., 15.
[25] Giulianotti, *Football*, 46.
[26] Ibid., 47.
[27] Ibid.
[28] Ibid., 49.
[29] Ibid.
[30] Jones and Rivers, *Soul Crew*, 90.
[31] Ibid.
[32] Ibid., *passim*.
[33] Ibid., 59.
[34] Tordoff, *City Psychos*, 128.

[35] Ibid., 125.
[36] Dunning, Murphy and Waddington, 'Towards a Sociological Understanding of Football Hooliganism as a World Phenomenon', 17.
[37] Sugden, *Scum Airways*.
[38] Ibid., 159.
[39] Ibid., 159–60.
[40] Ibid., 160.
[41] Ibid.
[42] Robson, '*No One Likes Us*', 150.
[43] Ibid., 151.
[44] Ibid.
[45] Bairner, 'Sweden and the World Cup'. Bairner and Shirlow, 'Territory, Politics and Soccer Fandom in Northern Ireland and Sweden', 5–26.
[46] Sugden, *Scum Airways*.
[47] Williams, Dunning and Murphy, *Hooligans Abroad*, xiii.
[48] King and Knight, *Hoolifan*, 217.
[49] Ibid.
[50] Jones and Rivers, *Soul Crew*, 90.
[51] Ibid.
[52] Giulianotti, *Football*, 52.
[53] Dunning, *Sport Matters*, 148.
[54] King, *The End of the Terraces*, 4.
[55] Ibid.
[56] Ibid., 7.
[57] Ibid., 4.
[58] Ibid.
[59] Robson, '*No One Likes Us*', 26.
[60] Ibid., 29.
[61] Armstrong, *Football Hooligans*.
[62] Giulianotti, *Football*. According to Giulianotti, 'many of the modern Scottish hooligans, the "casuals", come from fairly stable upper working-class and middle-class areas, especially in cities like Aberdeen and Edinburgh' (46). Citing evidence from other research, Dunning disputes this claim (*Sport Matters*, 157).
[63] Dunning, *Sport Matters*, 158.
[64] Dunning, Murphy and Waddington, 'Towards a Sociological Understanding of Football Hooliganism as a World Phenomenon', 22.
[65] Bairner, 'The Dog That Didn't Bark'.
[66] See also Bairner, '"Up to their Knees?"' A. Bairner, 'Soccer, Masculinity and Violence in Northern Ireland'. Bairner and Shirlow, 'Loyalism, Linfield and the Territorial Politics of Soccer Fandom in Northern Ireland'. Bairner and Shirlow, 'Real and Imagined: Reflections on Football Rivalry in Northern Ireland.
[67] Roversi and Balestri, 'Italian Ultras Today', 142.
[68] See Dunning *et al.*, *Fighting Fans*, for a review of these criticisms.

References

Armstrong, Gary. *Football Hooligans. Knowing the Score*. Oxford: Berg, 1998.
Astrinakis, Antonios. "Subcultures of Hard-core Fans in West Attica: An Analysis of some Central Research Findings." In *Fighting Fans. Football Hooliganism as a World Phenomenon*, edited by E. Dunning, P. Murphy, I. Waddington, and A. E. Astrinakis. Dublin: UCD Press, 2002.

Bairner, A. "Sweden and the World Cup: Soccer and Swedishness." In *Hosts and Champions. Soccer Cultures, National Identities and the USA World Cup*, edited by J. Sugden and A. Tomlinson. Aldershot: Arena, 1994.

Bairner, A. "Up to their Knees"? Football, Sectarianism, Masculinity and Protestant Working-Class Identity." In *Who Are 'The People'? Unionism, Protestantism and Loyalism in Northern Ireland*, edited by P. Shirlow and M. McGovern. London: Pluto Press, 1997.

Bairner, A. "Soccer, Masculinity and Violence in Northern Ireland – between Hooliganism and Terrorism." *Men and Masculinities* 1, no. 3 (1999): 284–301.

Bairner, A. "The Dog That Didn't Bark." In *Fighting Fans. Football Hooliganism as a World Phenomenon*, edited by E. Dunning, P. Murphy, I. Waddington, and A. E. Astrinakis. Dublin: UCD Press, 2002.

Bairner, A. and P. Shirlow. "Loyalism, Linfield and the Territorial Politics of Soccer Fandom in Northern Ireland." *Space and Polity* 2, no. 2 (1998): 163–77.

Bairner, A. and P. Shirlow. "Territory, Politics and Soccer Fandom in Northern Ireland and Sweden." *Football Studies* 3, no. 1 (2000): 5–26.

Bairner, A. and P. Shirlow. "Real and Imagined: Reflections on Football Rivalry in Northern Ireland." In *Fear and Loathing in World Football*, edited by G. Armstrong and R. Giulianotti. Oxford: Berg, 2001.

Dunning, Eric. *Sport Matters: Sociological Studies of Sport, Violence and Civilization*. London: Routledge, 1999.

Dunning, E., P. Murphy, and I. Waddington. "Towards a Sociological Understanding of Football Hooliganism as a World Phenomenon." In *Fighting Fans. Football Hooliganism as a World Phenomenon*, edited by E. Dunning, P. Murphy, I. Waddington, and A. E. Astrinakis. Dublin: UCD Press, 2002.

Dunning, E., Murphy, P., Waddington, I., and Astrinakis, A. E., (eds). *Fighting Fans. Football Hooliganism as a World Phenomenon*. Dublin: UCD Press, 2002.

Dunning, E., P. Murphy, and J. Williams. *The Roots of Football Hooliganism. An Historical and Sociological Study*. London: Routledge and Kegan Paul, 1988.

Giulianotti, Richard. *Football. A Sociology of the Global Game*. Cambridge: Polity Press, 1999.

Hughson, John. "Australian Soccer's "Ethnic" Tribes: A New Case for the Carnivalesque." In *Fighting Fans. Football Hooliganism as a World Phenomenon*, edited by E. Dunning, P. Murphy, I. Waddington, and A. E. Astrinakis. Dublin: UCD Press, 2002.

Jones, D. and T. Rivers. *Soul Crew. The Inside Story of Britain's Most Notorious Hooligan Gang*. Bury: Milo Books, 2002.

King, Anthony. *The End of the Terraces. The Transformation of English Football in the 1990s*. Revised edn. London: Leicester University Press, 2002.

King, M. and M. Knight. *Hoolifan. Thirty Years of Hurt*. Edinburgh: Mainstream, 1999.

Robson, Gary. *'No One Likes Us, We Don't Care'. The Myth and Reality of Millwall Fandom*. Oxford: Berg, 2000.

Roversi, Antonio and C. Balestri. "Italian Ultras Today: Change or Decline." In *Fighting Fans. Football Hooliganism as a World Phenomenon*, edited by E. Dunning, P. Murphy, I. Waddington, and A. E. Astrinakis. Dublin: UCD Press, 2002.

Sugden, John. *Scum Airways. Inside Football's Underground Economy*. Edinburgh: Mainstream, 2002.

Tordoff, Shaun. *City Psychos. From the Monte Carlo Mob to the Silver Cod Squad: Four Decades of Terrace Terror*. Bury: Milo Books, 2002.

Williams, J., E. Dunning, and P. Murphy. *Hooligans Abroad. The Behaviour and Control of English Fans in Continental Europe*. London: Routledge and Kegan Paul, 1984, 2nd edn. London, Routledge, 1989.

Millwall and the Making of Football's Folk Devils: Revisiting the Leicester Period

Joseph Maguire

Football hooliganism is deeply rooted in British society. Pioneering work in this area, led by Eric Dunning, was done at the University of Leicester during the late 1970s and early 1980s. I was fortunate to have been both part of the broader project as a doctoral student, and to have been supervised by him. Given that this is a contribution to a *Festschrift* for Eric, it seems appropriate to reflect on my time at Leicester (1979–85) and to base the substantive part of this essay on the work conducted then. Yet, revisiting the past brings with it several opportunities and challenges. In particular, this is an opportunity to focus on work that I have not looked at for quite some time. In so doing, I want to highlight one specific case study conducted at the time, but which was never published by me or incorporated into the work of the others involved in the 'historical' research (Eric Dunning and Patrick Murphy) or the project as a whole (Dunning, Murphy and John Williams). This case study provides an opportunity to reflect on Eric's guidance and supervision, and the challenge of examining to what extent the analysis has stood the test of time.

Arriving at the Sociology Department at the University of Leicester proved more daunting than a young doctoral student might have expected. Within the space of what, from memory, seems days, Ilya Neustadt, then Head of Department, had invited me to his office for what I assumed was a welcome address. I was ambushed with the killer question regarding my potential doctoral work: 'What is your sociological problem?' With hindsight, there may have been a double or many layered meaning to this question. However, at the time I took him to mean that *I* had to sort out the nature and focus of *my* doctoral work. This was not to prove easy. My Ph.D. – which may have been the first one completed on football hooliganism – was funded by a linked Social Science Research Council (SSRC) studentship, one of the last given in the pre-Thatcher period. It was linked to a project, directed by Dunning and Murphy, which already had a clear direction. Within a year SSRC had been replaced by the Economic and Social Research Council (ESRC) – seemingly I could no longer study society 'scientifically' – and, by the end of my doctorate, Mrs Thatcher had famously declared that society did not exist! These were difficult times for the discipline. My area of the project would focus on the 'socio-historical' or what Eric more correctly (as I was to discover) referred to as the 'developmental' aspects of football hooliganism.

At this stage, we did not know, but would soon discover, that spectator misconduct and moral panics[1] had been a persistent feature of the game since the foundation of the Football League in the 1880s. Initially, Eric directed me to the valuable work of Wray Vamplew[2] and others and, of course, to his own work and that of Norbert Elias. However, at that point much of Elias's work had yet to be translated into English; in this respect, my work over the last 20 years – as Elias's work has become increasingly available in English – has been an extension of my doctoral study of a sociological framework that has helped me make sense of sport, culture and society. This reading was combined with a wider search of the literature on violence,[3] Marxist social history,[4] and general accounts of deviance.[5] Eric seemed content with this literature trawl and, although I did not realize it, he was allowing me the intellectual space in which to carve out a distinctive position relative to the project as a whole. However ill-formulated it was in the early stages, I began to understand that more adequate explanations of the genesis of football hooliganism had to examine both the social roots of the violence but also how fans and their behaviour were subjectively defined. That is, in order to understand the 'limits of decent partisanship', attention had to be paid to both the objective conditions and the subjective definitions of the social problem.[6]

I worked initially at the Birmingham Public Library and the national newspaper library at Colindale. From there I went to the Football Association headquarters (then at Lancaster Gate), before moving on to Leicester Public Library where I worked closely with Patrick Murphy. A picture of the general trends regarding football hooliganism since the 1880s began to emerge. When I returned to Leicester, Eric would remind me that it was as important to 'find nothing' as it was to find evidence of a specific incident – for 'nothing' meant 'something'. The episodic nature of the condition, and of its reporting, became clearer. The linkages between youth culture, fear of working-class leisure, under-reporting, moral panics, football and 'spectator misconduct' could be established. The data, which covered the 1880s through to the early 1980s, were always a subject of debate between Eric, Patrick and me. Eric's mantra, 'think until it hurts', still echoes out from the past and I still use it when supervising my own students! Eric's attributes as an advisor, then and now, remind me of the argument that I have presented recently regarding the role of theory, that is, that theory provides us with 'resources of hope' and acts as a guide and compass, a friend and colleague.[7] Eric certainly did this and more. Perhaps even more importantly, Eric passed on to me the Weberian notion of 'sociology as a vocation' – the study of sport and society involves a serious, life-long commitment.

Much, but not all of the 'historical' work surfaced in the book by Dunning, Murphy and Williams.[8] Here, I want to consider another case study from my doctorate which examined the specific history of Millwall and its fans. In particular, I will focus on the emergence of their violent reputation as the *enfants terribles* of English soccer during the twentieth century. Though groups of Millwall supporters have been involved in serious disorder, it is the *perception* of these supporters by powerful outsiders that has proved to be more crucial in establishing their violent reputation and fuelling successive moral panics. By returning to this case study, I hope to show that the insights of the project as a whole still have resonance today and that, in certain respects, the paradigmatic war that engulfed the study of football hooliganism in the 1990s need not have happened. The project was 'ahead of its time' and this was in no small measure due to Eric Dunning.

Millwall FC and the Making of Football's Folk Devils

In 1885, workers at Morton's factory in South East London formed a soccer team that would become the present day professional club, Millwall. Little is known of these early beginnings (though now, with the work of Robson,[9] we are seeing renewed interest in the study of the club and its fans). Uncertainty exists concerning the motivation for the club's foundation and the social origins of those who were involved in its control and organization. By 1893, however, it had turned professional. In the following year, its development was such that the club was formed into a limited company. At this stage, Millwall were members of the Southern League. During the late Victorian and Edwardian periods, the club consecutively occupied several grounds, most notably at East Ferry Road, North Greenwich and 'The Den'. The common factor was that all the grounds were situated in South-East London. With regard to the move to the Den, which remained, until early 1994, Millwall's home ground, the motivation appears to have been financial. According to a near-contemporary report:

> It is perfectly true that the Directors have been looking around for a suitable ground in the midst of a populous district. Several likely spots have been carefully considered, and eventually a ground situated in the neighbourhood of the Old Kent Road was thought to be about the best.[10]

The crucial distinguishing feature was that the district was dominated by dockland. People who lived in the area would have been drawn mainly from the less respectable elements of the working class who, if employed, would have been connected with the semi-skilled or unskilled occupations associated with the East End of London. The occupational structure of dockland tends to confirm the types of relationships which traditionally existed in working-class communities. New workers were usually recruited from the sons of dockers.[11] Having gained entry into this hard manual job, sons would be taught their trade by their fathers and dockers were either organized in family 'gangs' or belonged to different 'gangs' but helped their relatives when they could. Perhaps as a result of the close-knit nature of such patterns of employment, when disputes arose between groups of dockers, a resort to violence was a frequent outcome.

Disorder during the late Victorian and Edwardian Periods: 'Free-fights' and the 'Coster-Sans' Class

By the turn of the century, with the club competing in the Southern League, the press reported what is the first case of disorder involving Millwall supporters that I uncovered. An article in the *Daily Chronicle*, in September 1901, claimed that during a match W. Smith, a Portsmouth player, 'was a victim of a cowardly assault, being struck by a stone. It behoves the Millwall directors to take greater precautions to prevent miscreants causing the closing of the ground.'[12] The incident was reported by the referee to the FA, who ordered the club to 'Publish notices in the district of the offence which had been committed, and warning spectators that any recurrence of misconduct on the ground might seriously prejudice the club'.[13] In addition, the club was obliged to give 'full publicity' to the warning via the local press.

Occasionally, reports of disturbances inside the grounds of other local clubs surfaced in match reports. Take the following report of the West Ham and Millwall match in September 1906:

> The 'Rivals' at Upton Park. Unseemly Scenes.

> From the very first kick of the ball it was seen that there was likely to be some trouble, but the storm burst when Dean and Jarvis came into collision, the former pressing the latter, so that seizing Dean by the waist, Jarvis threw him with great force against the railings. This aroused considerable excitement among the spectators... The crowd on the banks having caught the fever, free fights were plentiful.[14]

The importance of this example is two-fold. Firstly, it documents various forms of disorder. Secondly, the more serious free fighting took place, significantly, on the 'banks' or terracing (where working-class fans gathered) while other reports indicated that barracking originated from the grandstand. It should also be noted that the fighting between rival supporters took place at a 'derby' game – that is a game involving near neighbours. The violent masculine style, which Dunning *et al.* argued characterizes the dominant males in such lower working-class communities,[15] and the concomitant clashes between neighbourhood 'gangs', have long been a feature of English society and were certainly not uncommon in the streets within the vicinity of the Den.

In September 1901 the *Kentish Mercury* commented on the widespread disorder in the district in which the ground was located:

> Rowdyism in New Cross Road is no new thing. Our columns have for years borne witness to its existence . . . the condition of affairs in that important thorough-fare is as bad as ever, more particularly on Sunday nights, when noisy gangs of youths

of both sexes perambulate the road. The majority of them are respectably dressed, in many cases the lads are apparently office boys or shop assistants, each with the cheap and poisonous cigarette in mouth, but there is a considerable proportion too, of the Coster-Sans collar class, with neckerchief tightly knotted round the throat. These young hooligans are specially offensive just about the time that more respectable folk are making their way home from church.[16]

This article highlights the clash between the 'roughs' and 'respectables' who lived in and around the district. It also uses terms such as 'rowdyism'. It is clear that the writer identified two main elements to the disorder – a more 'respectable' section and what he called the 'coster-sans collar class'. The latter seemingly were perceived as the more offensive of the two. It is difficult to imagine that, if such groups were involved in disorder on the streets in this area and if they were attracted to local football matches, similar behaviour would not also have occurred in and around the ground at East Ferry Road.

From early on, those involved in spectator misconduct were not averse to travelling to support Millwall at away fixtures. Such trips were marked by confrontations with groups of supporters probably drawn from similar communities of the rival team.[17] As the report of the match between West Ham and Millwall in 1906 illustrated, 'free fights' in the context of such games were not unknown. Such venues provided a stark demonstration of, firstly, the loyalty to, and identification with, one's own district and, secondly, the antagonism towards rival supporters, who were equally defiant in defending the 'honour' of their district. Misconduct of this kind has been a persistent feature of spectating at the Den throughout the twentieth century.

What did this free fighting tradition entail and which social groups were involved? A clue to the latter – and indeed to the generating conditions of such a tradition – can be found in the work of Jerry White.[18] In his analysis of Campbell Bunk, a North London working-class community, White makes passing reference to the fact that a member of this community would 'On Saturday afternoons... often travel to the Lion's Den at Millwall and pick up a pile of coppers by singing to the football crowd'.[19] But what type of community was it? White refers to the conflicts and tensions which permeated all relationships:

> Violence was Campbell Bunk's dominant characteristic. It was never far beneath the surface. There was violence within families, between neighbours, even between streets; for good reasons and for no reason; leaving grudges and cementing friendships... The fist, boot, pudding basin, chair leg, flat iron, were often the first resort in arguments between neighbours, and even within families. Little of this violence was confined discreetly behind the closed doors. Generally it took place in the street.[20]

Violence permeated all social relations. Rivalries emerged and grudges were maintained – the vendettas to which Dunning *et al.* refer. Such communities were not confined to North London. Arthur Harding, known as the 'Terror of Brick Lane', has reminisced about his life in the East End of London. Once more, a picture emerges of violence as a dominant characteristic of everyday social relations. Unfortunately, as in White's account, no connection is made to sporting experiences; however, the violent encounters are vividly described. Those involved in the more serious forms of spectator misconduct may well have been drawn predominantly from such communities in which violence was a part of everyday life.

Disorder in the Inter-War Years: The Development of a Fighting Reputation

In 1920 Millwall became a member club in the then recently formed Division Three of the Football League. Following the First World War, Millwall were attracting attendances in excess of 20,000 for home games. The *Lewisham Borough News* reported an incident in one home game in 1920:

> In the second half Cooper, the Newport goalkeeper had an argument with the crowd, and actually climbed the railings to enforce his point of view, and a spectator at the other end, incensed at the manner in which the game was being mishandled, entered the field to give the referee the benefit of his wisdom. Just as the 20,000 spectators had been worked up to fever heat, Keen, the Millwall centre-forward scored a goal, and this acted as a safety-valve.[21]

At this stage in its emergence as a social problem, misconduct was still reported as involving 'over-excitement' due to partisanship, and hence as something which could be dissipated if the team was successful. The national newspapers confirmed the element of disorder, with a *Daily Sketch* headline in October 1920, being indicative: 'New Cross – Millwall Growls and Groans'.[22] The following month, the Emergency Committee of the FA met and concluded 'that missiles were thrown by a section of the spectators, and that there was a considerable amount of disorderly conduct, bad language and intimidation of the visiting players'.[23] In consequence, the Millwall ground was ordered to be closed. Commenting on this verdict, the *Brockley News and New Cross and Hatcham Review* stated:

> The tendency towards hooliganism among football crowds is becoming so marked that it is not to be wondered at that the FA took a very serious view of it. Since the Newport match there has been another angry demonstration at the Den, accompanied by stone throwing, and it is time something was done to eliminate it. It seems hard that the club has to accept punishment, and over 24,000 supporters be deprived of their afternoon's sport, because of the unruly conduct of a section of hooligans. Surely the great bulk of the orderly supporters can do something to assist the officials in stamping out this creeping paralysis. A supporters' club, pledged to help the officials in detecting and punishing the offenders is worth considering.[24]

The report, significantly, indicates not only a general trend of spectator misconduct at Millwall, but also the persistent presence of a 'small section of hooligans'. During a match between Millwall and Swindon in 1927 the referee was struck by a missile. The FA Disciplinary Committee, meeting in December 1927, concluded that 'Millwall FC be ordered to post notices on their ground warning spectators, and also required to offer a reward for information leading to the conviction of the offender, who, when ascertained they were to prosecute'. A subsequent analysis of the match reports in the local press revealed little apparent knowledge of, or concern about, the incident. The *Brockley News and New Cross and Hatcham Review* merely reported that the 'crowd grew very noisy',[25] and the *Kentish Mercury* failed to comment at all on crowd behaviour.[26] The lack of reference to the case in the press may be indicative either of the relatively minor nature of the incident which was regarded by the press as trivial or of the haphazard nature of the reporting in this period. That is, the reporters may simply not have known of the FA decision. Alternatively, it may have been a conscious policy on behalf of the local editors to avoid damaging reports concerning the club and its neighbourhood.

Whatever the explanation, by December of the same year, the writer of the Millwall programme felt it necessary to admonish the crowd for the barracking of players.[27] Clearly the official, if not the local media, considered the spectators at Millwall a 'cause for concern'. A similar interpretation can be drawn from an analysis of the reports of misconduct at a match between Millwall and Swansea in February 1933. While the minutes of the FA note the misconduct of spectators at the match, several local and national newspapers reports contain no reference to disorder. In the view of the FA, the misconduct was serious enough to warrant a caution and an order for a warning to be displayed around the ground, stating that further offences would result in the ground being closed.[28] Such a situation reflects the stage of the emergence of football spectating as a social problem. During this period, it was primarily the concern of the football authorities. Spectator misconduct, and particularly that of Millwall supporters, had not been elevated to a cause of national or wider political concern.

Further credence to this analysis can be gained from examining other incidents during the 1930s. For example, misconduct at the match between Millwall and Bradford in 1934 prompted the *Kentish Mercury* to state: 'Scenes at the Den. Millwall Supporters' Not so Bad as they are Painted'.[29] While claiming that 'nothing really serious occurred', the writer commented on the 'scare headlines' of the Sunday press. On the front page of *The People*, for example, the report began: 'We want the Ref. Crowd had paid, but fights were free' and then described the scene:

> When some of the crowd at the Second Division league match between Millwall and Bradford at New Cross yesterday didn't like the decisions of the referee they threw things at him. Then some of the players got out of control, and when free fights began to break out between various members of the teams a police officer dashed on to the field. He was followed a little later by a force of police but at the end of the game the crowd refused to leave the ground. Some of them began to demonstrate against the directors in the stand. They hung around the dressing rooms, shouting: 'We want the ref. We want the players'.[30]

After the referee reported the matter to the FA, the Emergency Committee (April 20th–May 28th 1934) convened and decided:

> In view of the fact that there had been enquiries on two previous occasions with regard to misconduct of spectators at the club's matches, and the club having been informed that any further offences would result in the ground being closed, the Commission decided that the ground of the club be closed for fourteen days.

Despite this, the Chairman of the club denied that anything had happened, 'save a little mild barracking'. He further noted:

There was some cat-calling outside the director's room, nothing else. It is untrue to say there was any interference by the police at any time. No missiles were thrown at the referee or the police and the crowd dispersed without intervention by the police. No complaint against players or crowd was made by any official of the match to the Millwall club.[31]

Some nine months later, however, the Den was again the scene of spectator misconduct. The referee sent a report to the FA which, in turn, fined Millwall £50. Examination of the local and national newspaper coverage again reveals variations in the style and content of reportage.[32] Similarly, in November 1938, the national press, in reviewing Millwall's home match against Southampton, again commented in critical fashion on the behaviour of the crowd. *The People* reported the misconduct under the headline: 'Fireworks at the Den. Millwall Crowd can't take it'.[33] A more detailed account was to be found in the *Daily Herald*:

> The behaviour of many of the spectators was most unsportsmanlike. Fireworks were thrown on the pitch to unsettle the players, and once in the second half, when a Southampton player was brought down unfairly and injured, hundreds clapped and cheered ... when the players were leaving the field fireworks were thrown amongst them.[34]

The FA Disciplinary Committee (6 December 1938–2 January 1939) fined the club £100 and warned 'that any further report of disturbances or unsatisfactory conduct by spectators will result in the closing of the ground for a considerable period'. Clearly, then, powerful groups outside the East End of London were beginning to define Millwall supporters as a problem. While there may have been some form of 'deamplification' at work in the local press, the FA authorities and the national press seized on examples of misconduct with some vigour. These sentiments were to find greater expression in the years after the Second World War.

Disorder after the Second World War: Amplification of a Fighting Tradition

Following another episode of misconduct at the Den in the match between Millwall and Barnsley in 1947, the FA (Disciplinary Committee, October–December 1947) were true to their warning of 1939 and closed the ground for seven days and fined the club £100. The reactions of some club officials and directors to the FA decision provide insights into their perception of who was responsible for the misconduct. The *Lewisham Borough News* quoted the club secretary stating that he 'condemned the action of the "hot-heads" among the supporters' and added that 'the club and spectators have to suffer the action of one or two stupid people who can't keep their tempers'.[35] Similarly, Mr Thorne, a Millwall director, argued that it was an atypical group of supporters, and not the club that was at the root of the problem:

> Many years ago – I think it was in 1921 – the Den was closed... but it must of necessity be an entirely new set of players, almost a new board of directors and an entirely new set of spectators. No, it is quite a coincidence that it should be Millwall again.[36]

On a factual basis, Mr Thorne was incorrect as the ground had also been closed in 1934. More pertinently, he believed that a 'new set of spectators' now followed the club. Although a new generation would have been attending the Den, it is likely that these new fans were located in the same social networks as the earlier generation. It was not, then, 'coincidence that it should be Millwall again'. The recurrence of spectator disorderliness at the Millwall ground was related to specific features of the social composition of the crowd and the structure of the community from which they were drawn.

Echoing the idea that the Millwall supporters were behaving in 'traditional fashion', A. A. Thomas, writing for the *Daily Worker,* commented as follows:

> There are several little outposts of bad sportsmanship still holding out in English football and the fining of Millwall and the closing of their ground for a week will act as a warning not only to the 'Tough' fans at the Den, but also to those at other grounds... It is unfortunate that the clubs themselves must bear the brunt of their unwelcome supporters' actions. Although they are nominally innocent, it is still their responsibility to see that their ground is kept free from these few roughs, who are hangovers from the days of cock-fighting and bear-baiting, and would be more at home attending bull fights than a game whose sportsmanship has made for Britain a reputation second to none.[37]

These comments stress the relative persistence, within specific communities, of the mores of nineteenth-century folk culture.[38] Such comments also reflect the ongoing attempts by the authorities and more established groups to control, regulate and supervise working-class leisure and colonize working-class culture. Interestingly, these comments appeared in a left-wing newspaper and not in the mainstream newspapers which would have been more likely, by and large, to reflect the 'hegemonic' values of British society.

Such 'hangovers from the days of cock-fighting and bear-baiting' are the possible link between those communities, which resisted colonization by the 'civilizing' actions of the state and groups such as the rational recreationalists, and the communities which in present-day Britain are termed 'rough' working class. The community from which Millwall drew such 'hangovers' may, in fact, be only one such example, for A. A. Thomas also refers to the existence of what he terms 'several little outposts of bad sportsmanship'. After the club was fined and its ground closed in 1947, the directors issued a list of 'Don't Do it Chums' advice in the club's programme in December 1947. The advice was addressed to the fathers in the crowd:

> Don't throw soil, cinders, clinkers, stones, bricks, bottles, cups, fireworks, or other kinds of explosives, apples, oranges etc. on the playing pitch during or after the match. If you do you are liable to eviction, prosecution and permanently denied admission to the Den. Don't forget there are ladies and children in your midst. Don't barrack, utter filthy abuse or cause physical violence to the referee or his linesmen inside or outside the Den. Don't assemble in small or large numbers in the streets adjacent to the Den. Don't barrack, utter filthy abuse or molest in any manner the visiting or Millwall players.[39]

The reference to spectators gathering in large numbers outside the ground highlights a form of behaviour which the club was aware of and concerned about, but which had not surfaced in the match reports of the local or national newspapers. Crowds outside the stadium were thus beginning to emerge as a 'new problem', alongside the now 'traditional' problems which largely occurred inside the ground. This new post-match problem was raised again in November 1949 following the match between Millwall and Exeter City. The FA Disciplinary Committee minutes of January 1950 noted that 'the referee and linesman reported that when fifty yards from the Millwall ground after the match, they were subjected to abuse and hostility by a crowd, numbering 150–200 people. The referee received a blow in the back and tea-cups were thrown at the three officials.' While the *Lewisham Borough News* noted that the referee required a police escort off the field, no details were given of the incidents which occurred after the match. The FA, however, was concerned and decided to close the Den for seven days and fine the club £100. They also expanded the club's responsibility for the conduct of its supporters, concluding 'that the Directors and permanent officials of the Millwall FC (including writers of programmes or magazines) should do their utmost to uphold the authority of the FA'. While the FA held the club responsible for its supporters as a whole, Millwall officials continued to place responsibility on the shoulders of a few, atypical individuals. Charles Hewitt, the Millwall manager, made his position apparent in the club's programme in January 1950:

> The findings and punishment meted out to the club have come as a great shock to the many thousands of loyal supporters who have always behaved in the manner expected of sportsmen and gentlemen, but it must be conceded that there are in our midst a few undesirables.[40]

Hewitt also expressed the opinion that if the misconduct did not cease then 'the best way to preserve the club would be to move – lock, stock and barrel – to another part of the Metropolis'. The manager's comments again emphasized the presence at matches of a 'few undesirables'. More importantly, he suggested that the real solution would be to move the club out of the district in which it was located. Thus, the connection is made by Hewitt between the 'undesirables' and the districts of New Cross, Lewisham and Deptford with their 'tough' reputation. Matches at the Den may have attracted members of the 'rough' working class more regularly and in greater numbers than was the case at other clubs. Such an analysis is supported by the Millwall manager's observation that the club would leave the district if the 'undesirables' continued to create disorder. The 'respectable' directors of Millwall may well have wished to distance themselves from people from 'rough' and violent roots, yet they also depended on such people for their attendance at the ground.

The Emergence of Millwall Fans on a National Stage

From the late nineteenth century to the early 1950s the forms of, and strategies for the control of, football hooligan violence developed through the interplay of national/local interests and authorities. In the late 1950s, Millwall appears to enjoy a relatively low-key phase – both in terms of forms of behaviour and the perception by outside observers of spectators at the Den. This phase comes to an end in September 1962.

Under the headline 'Bottle Thrown at Millwall. Police Step In', the *Daily Mirror* reported that: 'Police were called to stand behind the goal and there were no further incidents'.[41] While the club did not impose sanctions of any kind, the FA Disciplinary Committee (September 1962) decided 'that Millwall FC be ordered to post warning notices in prominent places at their ground for one month ... and to print in the official club programme ... a warning to their spectators similar to that contained in the warning notices'.

During the 1962–63 season, several cases of misconduct occurred at the Den and attracted the attention of the local and national press. The *Lewisham Borough News* reported on the game between Millwall and Wrexham, in February 1963, in the following way:

> A spectator tried to get on the pitch. One policeman who moved to stop him disappeared apparently into the crowd, but four other policemen took his place, and a man was taken from the ground. And there were shots of a different kind as the crowd left the ground – snowballs were thrown by them at the referee, who later left the ground under a police escort as a large crowd waited.[42]

Several other newspapers referred to the behaviour of the individual spectator involved and to the conduct of the crowd at the end of the match. However, a variety of interpretations were given to these actions. Thus while the *Lewisham Borough News* believed that the fan had been 'irritated beyond the point of endurance', *The Times* argued that the fan had 'Run Berserk'.[43] While the local newspaper still interpreted the actions of the spectator in traditional terms, that is, his actions were connected to events on the field of play, the national press were beginning to portray such behaviour in a more vivid and dramatic way, referring to individuals' psychological make-up. Spectator misconduct was being redefined. By April 1963, the *Kentish Mercury* was appealing to the fans to 'Keep Calm'. Significantly, their concern surrounded a local derby match between Millwall and Crystal Palace. The *Kentish Mercury* noted:

> Trouble flared again at the Den on Monday when Millwall fought out a full-blooded battle with Crystal Palace. And this time poor Millwall will suffer because of the behaviour of the fans... Moments of anger are becoming too common these days. Admittedly, they are caused by only a few fans who are unable to discipline themselves and enjoy a match without causing a disturbance.[44]

Local reports tended both to 'apologize' for the supporters' actions and celebrate their 'loyalty', 'authenticity' and 'manliness'. For example, during November 1963, at Brentford, again a local derby, fighting and missile throwing were reported to have occurred. During the same match, Alex Stepney, the Millwall goalkeeper, was attacked by Brentford supporters. The *Kentish Mercury* commented on the presence of a large number of Millwall supporters: 'Lucky for Alex Stepney that they did turn up as one of them came to his rescue when he was attacked. They're a loyal band.'[45] What interpretation can be placed on such 'loyalty'? While Brake refers to the 'symbolic importance of territory',[46] and Dunning *et al.* refer to the 'intense identification with the local turf' which the lower working class exhibit,[47] the former appears to rule out the possibility that such identification could be transferred to a sense of loyalty to representatives of their territory, that is, their football team. True, Brake refers to such symbolism as manifesting itself in 'aggressive support for local football' – in fact, the example he uses is Millwall – but the analysis is left there. Is it reasonable to suggest that such 'aggressive support' could be extended to the rescue of the Millwall goalkeeper and that such behaviour would be perceived by sympathetic 'outsiders' as an act of loyalty?

Several reports of spectator misconduct also stress the 'masculine' nature of the support offered by Millwall supporters. One writer argued, for example, that the fans have 'never believed soccer is a cissie's game'.[48] As noted, however, differences existed in the perception of the press and the club of what was permissible behaviour in public. In fact, a writer in the Millwall club programme in 1965 was forced to concede that those Millwall supporters involved in spectator disorder 'simply don't know what it means to behave in a civilised manner'.[49] However, the writer appears to fail to recognize that there exist, in English society, communities who share values which are, in specific ways, significantly different from those whom he assumes to be 'civilised'. If the writer had remarked that some supporters display a love of fighting and that this is a central source of meaning and gratification in their lives, he would not have been mistaken. But such values are not entirely absent in the 'respectable' society in which the writer is located. Whereas the aggressive masculinity of the 'rough' working class finds expression in public situations where a more regulated and controlled behaviour is expected, the aggressive masculinity of the 'respectables' manifests itself, by and large, in socially legitimate channels such as contact sports like rugby union.

Such violent, 'masculine' qualities appear to have been characteristic of spectating at the Den for a considerable period. But with the changing perception of fandom and spectator misconduct, such displays were increasingly seen as problematic. However, in direct contrast to such a perception, the *South East London Mercury* offered this comment on the Millwall crowd following another home match:

> At grounds that boast well-behaved spectators, we know that quite a few rocks and stones would have been thrown... The Lions have never lost the reputation of being ill-behaved for incidents that took place many years ago. We would go so far as to say that the New Cross crowd are as well-behaved as any in the country.[50]

The club Chairman, using the columns of the local newspaper commented: 'We must congratulate the New Cross crowd on the way they behaved. Only one person jumped over the "top" to have a crack at the villain of the peace, G. Kirby, the Walsall centre-forward'. Despite the discrepancies in newspaper coverage of the Millwall crowd, there seems to have been a general consensus regarding the existence of an 'unruly few'. The 1965–66 season closed with another case of misconduct being reported. Reinforcing the points made previously concerning the control of the excitement generated by the game, the *Daily Mirror* headline for the match between Millwall and Bournemouth on 13 April 1966 read: 'Stop the Brickbats – Or I Stop the Match. Ref. Warns "Lions" Fans as Promotion Fever Mounts'.

The image of Millwall spectators held by the media and other football supporters was clearly uppermost in the mind of this writer. As early as 1934, when the local newspaper complained of the national press coverage, Millwall supporters had gained a certain notoriety. By the 1960s, such a reputation was enhanced both by the nascent 'moral panic' concerning spectator misconduct in general, and by Millwall supporters' 'traditional' patterns of spectating at the Den and other grounds. National newspaper coverage did much to enhance this reputation. With reference to the national press coverage of misconduct at a match between Millwall and Plymouth Argyle, a *South East London Mercury* reporter defended Millwall fans:

> Suddenly, my colleagues on the National Press, who should know better, are stating that the Den should be closed for soccer, following incidents that took place away from Millwall's ground ... Because a few irresponsible hooligans had smashed up the Argyle coach, which was parked away from the Den, all the Millwall crowd are condemned.[51]

Two months later the match between Millwall and Huddersfield Town was marred by fighting between groups of rival supporters. The club officials and the local press feared that the FA – who had warned the club following the Plymouth Argyle match – would order the ground to be closed. Although the ground was not closed and no action was taken by the FA over an attack on a Wolverhampton Wanderers player during a match at the Den the following month, the local press maintained that the Millwall spectators and the club were being maligned in the national media. In April 1967, for example, the *South East London Mercury* argued: 'Once again the action of one spectator has brought Millwall into disrepute. It doesn't matter that heads were smashed at other grounds, the Lions have a bad name... They are "carrying the can" for soccer rowdies at most grounds'.

Similar misconduct marked the game against Aston Villa at the Den during the same month. Fights between fans, coupled with an attack on the referee, resulted in an official FA enquiry. The FA enquiry fined Millwall £1,000. The national press had, however, demanded more severe measures. Ken Jones, writing in the *Daily Mirror*, stated:

> I have every sympathy with Millwall. They do not encourage bad behaviour. They have made many attempts in the past to ensure that trouble does not happen. But it has happened again and again. Within the last twenty years the Den has twice been shut for a week, and on the last occasion the FA took into account five previous reports of misconduct by spectators. The record of their crowd is a bad one and Millwall must recognise the extent of it.[52]

Despite such commentaries by the national press, the local newspapers questioned the negative reputation of Millwall fans. The *South East London Mercury* commented:

> The image of a typical Millwall crowd as a horde of flatcapped beefy men hysterically waving their dockers' hooks does not exist. Again and again it is proved that when there is trouble it comes from teenagers. And they are not all home supporters either.[53]

This newspaper's ambiguous position concerning the 'alleged' assault was thus combined with an attempt to negate the 'image' of Millwall supporters presented in the national press. As such, it indicates that a sense of localism had not yet waned. In contrast, the *Daily Mail* was able to establish, from a 'police source' at Lewisham police station, that 'hooliganism is a great problem for us at Millwall. It has been for years.'[54] The national press were thus united in the view that action was essential. As *The People* simply but forcefully stated: 'Close the Den'.[55] A lull in the reporting of disorder involving Millwall fans appears between this latter incident, in 1967, and 1973. During September of that year, disorder at the match between Millwall and Aston Villa was, in contrast to the relative neglect of Millwall in the previous four seasons, given prominent attention in local and national newspapers. The *Birmingham Post* for example, labelled the misconduct, 'The Battle at the Den'.[56] A range of other incidents in the local and national press were recorded in this period. During 1976, however, incidents involving West Ham and Millwall supporters occurred away from the ground and resulted in the death, by stabbing, of a Millwall fan. Following the match between Millwall and Ipswich Town in 1978 the ground was closed yet again, this time for two weeks.

The reputation of Millwall supporters thus attracted nationwide attention. During the 1970s, their notoriety was such that they became the focus of a programme on BBC TV. The activities of 'F Troop', formed from the ranks of Millwall supporters, whose intention was to get involved in fighting, became known not only to their rival supporters but also to journalists and academics alike. *The Guardian* noted that Millwall fans were 'widely regarded as some of the worst in the country'.[57] Millwall fans were now being used as a 'social barometer' for the ills of football and society.

Making Sense of Millwall

By the 1960s the regular expression of such violence in the public context of soccer matches had come to be defined as a social problem of national proportions. Millwall supporters had become defined as the *enfants terribles* in this regard, so much so that the first governmental report into the phenomenon focused on Millwall supporters. The *Harrington Report* sought to substantiate the connections between the violence of the fans and the general level of violence in their community. Harrington noted:

> These Millwall youngsters are a strange mixture. They are tough but warm-hearted and reliable individually but they can turn into a hostile and threatening mob on the terraces... I believe much of this violence on the terraces is a reflection of the violent district in London's dockland in which they live. The general code of conduct seems to be 'if in doubt hit out'.[58]

Quoting one Millwall supporter, Harrington captured the essential nature of the relationship being examined: 'Fighting is a way of life – we are born into it'. Harrington concluded:

> In one dockland area notorious for serious outbreaks of hooliganism we found that fighting was regarded as a way of life the inhabitants were born to and the only

proper way of settling disputes. Here to avoid a challenge was unmanly; to remain passive was looked on as wrong. There was a suggestion that youths accepted without question a code about fighting handed down to them by their fathers.[59]

The existence of such a legacy, handed down from one generation to the next, is consistent with the persistent accounts of spectator misconduct involving Millwall supporters since the turn of the century. It is why Millwall supporters were seen to have been acting in 'traditional fashion' and why they were perceived to be 'hangovers from the days of cock-fighting and bear-baiting'. But the anxiety expressed about this dockland area in general, and Millwall in particular, despite demographic changes that have to varying degrees altered aspects of community life, has also resulted in the amplification, over time, of the threat posed by Millwall supporters. In the 1930s they were the subject of scare headlines in the national newspapers; in the 1960s and 1970s, they were branded the 'worst crowd in the country' (for further discussion see subsequent work by Robson).[60]

Reflecting on my Leicester days, two of the more enduring lessons from Eric were the need to avoid 'false dichotomies', and to view things processually. Looking back at the work on football hooliganism, and the debate that developed in the 1990s, I am struck by how those lessons were lost on a new generation of researchers. In addition, in fruitfully broadening out the research agenda to examine fandom as a whole, existing work on sport and the emotions[61] and Elias and Dunning's 'quest for excitement'[62] seem to have been overlooked by scholars studying fandom. Much can still be learned from this Leicester tradition, though it never claimed to be the final word.

In examining more recent manifestations of football hooliganism, the researcher is still faced with the twin themes that permeate the phenomenon: on the one hand, the social roots of such behaviour and, on the other, the perception by powerful outsiders of supporters in general, and Millwall fans in particular. The lasting legacy of the Leicester tradition, and Eric's mentorship, is a more comprehensive account of soccer hooliganism, and indeed sport violence more generally, that explores both dimensions in an interdependent manner.

Notes

[1]   Cohen, *Folk Devils and Moral Panics*; Pearson, *Hooligan*.
[2]   Vamplew, 'Ungentlemanly Conduct'.
[3]   Hall and Jefferson, *Resistance through Rituals*; Rude, *The Crowd in History*.
[4]   Samuel, *People's History and Socialist Theory*; Storch, *Popular Culture*.
[5]   Cohen, *Folk Devils and Moral Panics*; Pearson, *Hooligan*.
[6]   Maguire, 'The Emergence of Football Spectating as a Social Problem 1880–1985'.
[7]   Maguire and Young, *Theory, Sport & Society*.
[8]   Dunning, Murphy and Williams, *The Roots of Football Hooliganism*.
[9]   Robson, '*No One Likes Us*'.
[10] *The Hammers Gazette*, 11 Sept. 1909.
[11] Young, and Wilmott, *Family and Kinship in East London*.
[12] *Daily Chronicle*, 23 Sept. 1901.
[13] *FA Minutes, Emergency Committee*, 1 Aug.–31 Dec. 1901.

[14] *East Ham Echo*, 21 Sept. 1906.

[15] Dunning, Murphy and Williams, *The Roots of Football Hooliganism*.

[16] *Kentish Mercury*, 27 Sept. 1901.

[17] Maguire, 'The Limits of Decent Partisanship'.

[18] White, '"Campbell Bunk"'.

[19] Ibid. 17.

[20] Ibid. 24–5.

[21] *Lewisham Borough News*, 20 Oct. 1920.

[22] *Daily Sketch*, 18 Oct. 1920.

[23] Cited in *Birmingham Post*, 20 Nov. 1920.

[24] *Brockley News and New Cross and Hatcham Review*, 26 Nov. 1920.

[25] Ibid. 28 Oct. 1927.

[26] *Kentish Mercury*, 28 Oct. 1927.

[27] Cited in the *Leicester Mercury*, 21 Dec. 1927.

[28] *FA Emergency Committee Minutes*, 21 March–21 April 1933.

[29] *Kentish Mercury*, 29 March 1934.

[30] *The People*, 25 March 1934.

[31] *Daily Mail*, 27 April 1934.

[32] Maguire, 'The Limits of Decent Partisanship'.

[33] *The People*, 6 Nov. 1938.

[34] *Daily Herald*, 7 Nov. 1938.

[35] *Lewisham Borough News*, 9 Dec. 1947.

[36] *Kentish Mercury*, 12 Dec. 1947.

[37] *Daily Worker*, 8 Dec. 1947.

[38] J. Maguire, 'Images of Manliness and Competing Ways of Living in Late Victorian and Edwardian Britain', 265–87.

[39] Offical programme of Millwall FC December 1947, cited in *Daily Telegraph*, 1 Sept. 1974.

[40] Cited in *Lewisham Borough News*, 31 Jan. 1950.

[41] *Daily Mirror*, 7 Sept. 1962.

[42] *Lewisham Borough News*, 26 Feb. 1963.

[43] *The Times*, 26 Feb. 1963.

[44] *Kentish Mercury*, 5 April 1963.

[45] *Kentish Mercury*, 13 Nov. 1963.

[46] Brake, *The Sociology of Youth and Youth Subcultures*, 37.

[47] Dunning, Murphy and Williams, *The Roots of Football Hooliganism*.

[48] *Daily Mail*, 13 Dec. 1965.

[49] Cited in the *Birmingham Post*, 17 Dec. 1965.

[50] *South East London Mercury*, 17 Dec. 1965.

[51] Ibid., 19 Jan. 1967.

[52] *Daily Mirror*, 16 Oct. 1967.

[53] *South East London Mercury*, 19 Oct. 1967.

[54] *Daily Mail*, 16 Oct. 1967.

[55] *The People*, 15 Oct. 1967.

[56] *Birmingham Post*, 3 Sept. 1973.

[57] *The Guardian*, 8 Nov. 1979.

[58] Harrington, *A Preliminary Report on Soccer Hooliganism*, 26.

[59] Ibid. 26.

[60] Robson, '*No one likes us*'.

[61] Maguire, 'Towards a Sociological Theory of Sport and the Emotions'.

[62] Elias and Dunning, *Quest for Excitement*.

References

Brake, M. *The Sociology of Youth and Youth Subcultures*. London: Routledge and Kegan Paul, 1980.

Cohen, S. *Folk Devils and Moral Panics*. London: Robertson, 1972.

Dunning, E., P. Murphy, and J. Williams. *The Roots of Football Hooliganism: an Historical and Sociological Study*. London: Routledge and Kegan Paul, 1988.

Elias, N. and E. Dunning. *Quest for Excitement: Sport and Leisure in the Civilizing Process*. Oxford: Blackwell, 1986.

Hall, S. and T. Jefferson. *Resistance through Rituals*. London: Hutchinson, 1976.

Harrington, J. *A Preliminary Report on Soccer Hooliganism*. Bristol: HMSO, 1968.

Maguire, J. "The Limits of Decent Partisanship: A Sociogenetic Investigation of the Emergence of Football Spectating as a Social Problem." Unpublished Ph.D. diss., University of Leicester, 1985.

Maguire, J. "Images of Manliness and Competing Ways of Living in Late Victorian and Edwardian Britain." *British Journal of Sports History* 3, no. 3 (1986): 265–87.

Maguire, J. "The Emergence of Football Spectating as a Social Problem 1880–1985: A Figurational and Developmental Perspective." *Sociology of Sport Journal* 3, no. 3 (1986): 217–45.

Maguire, J. "Towards a Sociological Theory of Sport and the Emotions." In *Sport and Leisure in the Civilizing Process*, edited by E. Dunning and C. Rojek. London: Macmillan, 1992, pp. 96–120.

Maguire, J. and K. Young. *Theory, Sport & Society*. Oxford: Elsevier Press, 2002.

Pearson, G. *Hooligan. A History of Respectable Fears*. London: Macmillan, 1983.

Robson, G. '*No One Likes Us, We Don't Care': The Myth and Reality of Millwall Fandom*. London: Berg Press, 2000.

Rude, G. *The Crowd in History. A Study of Popular Disturbances in France and England*. New York: Wiley, 1964.

Samuel, R., ed. *People's History and Socialist Theory*. London: Routledge and Kegan Paul, 1981.

Storch, R., ed. *Popular Culture and Custom in Nineteenth Century England*. London: Croom Helm, 1982.

Vamplew, Wray. "Ungentlemanly Conduct: The Control of Soccer Crowd Behaviour in England 1888–1914." In *The Search for Wealth and Stability*, edited by T. Smout. London: Hutchinson, 1980.

White, J. ""Campbell Bunk": A Lumpen Community in London between the Wars." *History Workshop* 8 (Autumn 1979): 1–49.

Young, M. and P. Wilmott. *Family and Kinship in East London*. London: Routledge and Kegan Paul, 1957.

Sport and Gender Relations

Katie Liston

Eric Dunning is widely regarded as having made a substantial contribution to the emergence and development of the sociology of sport since the 1960s. He continues to contribute to this now vibrant discipline and has published extensively in this area across a wide range of topics including sport, violence and civilization; sportization and the emergence of a 'fair play' ideology; sport, alcohol and drugs; and sport and gender, amongst others. Throughout his work, Dunning uses the figurational perspective derived from the work of Norbert Elias and, since 1961, Dunning has developed this sociological framework in relation to aspects of the sport-gender nexus.[1] It is not possible here to discuss the entirety of his work in relation to sport-gender relations. For the purposes of this essay, I shall outline the relevance of his work on sport as a (former) male preserve and the ways in which he has (sometimes with others) expanded this thesis to look at aspects of the sociogenesis of females' increasing involvement in sport and its consequences. In particular, Dunning's work provides a foundation from which to address the ranking and self–conception of males and females, and the consequences of this for aspects of male and female habituses and behaviour. I shall then attempt to use aspects of Dunning's work as sensitizing concepts in order to examine aspects of changing gender relations in sports in modern Ireland. This essay therefore has two objectives: firstly, it is an attempt to outline and summarize the relevance of Dunning's work to our understanding of aspects of the sport-gender nexus in Western societies and, secondly, it is intended as a modest contribution towards 'a sociology of sport in the Republic of Ireland'. I shall firstly briefly outline the main characteristics of Dunning's (and Elias's) figurational approach to sociology and to the study of sport and gender. I shall then apply this perspective to a present-day phenomenon, that is, to females' increasing participation in traditional, male-associated, sports in Ireland since the 1970s. I shall also look at some of the consequences of this for the ranking and self-conception of males and females in sport.

A Figurational Sociological Approach to Sport and Gender

Dunning and Elias, and other figurational sociologists, have approached fundamental sociological issues such as the relationship between 'the individual' and 'society', or 'agency' and 'structure' by suggesting that these are false dichotomies. In highlighting these concepts as incongruent with the more complex and fluid realities of social relations between interdependent people, Elias (and Dunning) have argued that we need to move away from an image of humans as *Homo clausus* to one of *Homines aperti*. The difficulties associated with a *Homo clausus* position are more than adequately addressed elsewhere.[2] For the purposes of this discussion, it is simply necessary to remind readers that the *Homines aperti* position adopted by Dunning (and figurational sociologists generally) is an important starting point from which we can examine people 'in the round' and aspects of the sport-gender nexus in modern industrializing societies.[3] In other words, human beings are viewed by Elias and Dunning as 'open', interdependent people who form complex and fluid figurations with one another. Elias and Dunning put this as follows:

> Sociological theories often appear to start from the assumption that 'groups' or 'societies', and 'social phenomena' in general, are something abstracted from individual people, or at least they are not quite as 'real' as individuals, whatever that may mean ... If one watches a game of football one can understand that it is the fluctuating figuration of the players itself on which, at a given moment, the decisions and moves of individual players depend. In that respect concepts such as 'interaction' and its relatives are apt to mislead. *They appear to suggest that individuals without figurations form figurations with each other a posteriori.*[4] (emphasis added)

Dunning uses the Eliasian perspective to focus specifically on social relations *among and between* males and females in sport, and how changes in the structure of social relations between the sexes have impacted on males *and* females. In other words,

Dunning employs a central Eliasian principle, that of human interdependence, to argue that changes in the mutual balance of power between the sexes in a gynarchic direction[5] have enabling and constraining consequences for *both* males *and* females. For this reason, Dunning's earlier work (from 1961 to 1986) can be regarded as having made a contribution to our understanding of *gender relations*, notwithstanding his focus on one aspect of this – the experiences of males in sport.[6] I shall now outline the main contributions of his earlier work on the sport-gender nexus and the ways in which he has, more recently, elaborated on this to examine the sociogenesis and consequences of females' increasing participation in sport in the context of changes in the balance of gender power since the 1970s.

In general, it can be said that Dunning helps us to move towards a better understanding of why sport is becoming more important as a field for male dominance, both physical and symbolic, within the context of wider changes in power relations between men and women.[7] In 1973 Dunning, with Ken Sheard, argued that sport had become a key social activity for males in the preservation of stereotypical masculine behaviour, attributes and ideologies, particularly when females' increasing participation in sport was perceived by males as a threat to their dominance. They suggested that the egos of English male rugby players were threatened by growing female power (particularly by those females perceived as status equals) and that they strove to bolster their threatened egos through initiation ceremonies, male bonding rituals and the singing of songs that mocked females and male homosexuals. Dunning and Sheard attributed the rise and decline of a 'male preserve' in rugby football to the increasing power of women and suggested that the relationship between these two developments was 'curvi-linear', that is to say, 'that the same social process had different consequences at different stages'.[8] In 1986, Dunning argued that the increasing interdependence of males and females in sport was manifested in the ways in which males perceived females' increasing participation in male-dominated sports as a threat to their dominance and a challenge to their masculinity. The forms of resistance by males to female incursions into male-associated sports reflected the traditional importance of these sports to masculine habituses. He subsequently extended this argument to suggest there is strong reason to believe that, in industrial societies over the past 200 years, sport has become increasingly important in the process of identity-formation for males.[9] As the power relations between the sexes are equalizing over time – though not necessarily in 'a linear nor mono-directional way'[10] – and with the increasing participation of females in this formerly exclusive male preserve (particularly, though not exclusively, in sports such as rugby and soccer), sport has emerged as a 'battleground' over gender identities. Moreover, the shift in the balance of power between males and females has contributed to 'a weakening of the more extreme forms of patriarchy once characteristic of rugby clubs'.[11]

However, Dunning points out that shifts in power relations between the sexes since the 1960s have been, for the most part, relatively slight, particularly within public spheres. That is to say, there have been long-term gradual changes in a gynarchic direction but this is not to deny the continued dominance of andrarchy at cultural, institutional and ideological levels.[12] Dunning argued that the relatively recent (and slight) shift in the balance of power relations in favour of females (what he terms 'feminization') is largely a consequence of the decreasing importance of males' physical strength (for example, in relation to the increased use of technology in large-scale production and of farm machinery in agricultural work), increasing restrictions on violence, especially against females, and a lowering of thresholds towards the propensity for violence generally. In *Sport Matters*, he extends the Eliasian framework to explore the reasons for, and possible consequences of, females' increasing involvement in sport and, in particular, in traditional, male-associated, sports such as boxing, wrestling, soccer and rugby. This work could be seen as an extension of his previous work on gender relations to include the sociogenesis of females' participation (as athletes as well as spectators) in sport. In particular, his discussions of feminization processes (which he defined as 'an equalizing trend – to some degree a shift in the balance of power between the sexes in a gynarchic (matriarchal) direction'[13]) and generation-specific contexts of civilizing processes, have extended the figurational perspective to the study of gender relations, though it should be emphasized that our sociological understanding of this complex social phenomenon is by no means complete.

Over time, male and female athletes have become increasingly interdependent by virtue of what Dunning refers to as 'feminization' – the increasing opportunities for females to influence the self-regulation of others. By implication, this has impacted on the changing nature of power relations between the sexes. It is important to emphasize that, when we conceive of the relations between males and females in sports in terms of a figuration, 'the direction and the order followed by this formation and the transformation of ideas are not explained solely by the structure of one partner or the other but by the relation between the two'.[14] That is to say, the ways in which male and female athletes are 'bonded to each other makes them pursue the objectives and human requirements they actually do pursue'.[15] Feminization processes, therefore, have both constraining and enabling consequences for both males and females. For example, in the case of Ireland, some groups of males (particularly those involved in traditional, male-associated, sports such as Gaelic football, soccer and rugby) have perceived females' increasing involvement (as participants) in these sports since the 1970s as a threat. At the same time, the formal affiliation of women's sports organizations – for example, the Irish Women's Rugby Football Union (IWRFU) and the Women's Football Association of Ireland (WFAI) – to traditional male-governed organizations such as the Irish Rugby Football Union (IRFU) and the Football Association of Ireland (FAI), has (unintentionally) enabled males to be more involved in the provision for, and control of, women's sports as coaches, administrators, sponsors and match officials, amongst other roles. Historically, males have monopolized the organization and administration of contact and team sports in Ireland as well as females' access to these 'male preserves'. The relatively slight shift in the balance of power in favour of females has contributed to feelings of emancipation amongst some female athletes and also to feelings of resistance amongst some males (though this resistance is becoming weaker). That males have become increasingly aware of their female counterparts is an indication that the gradual shift in gender relations in the social field of male-associated sports has impacted on *both* males and females.

Towards a Figurational Sociology of Sport in the Republic of Ireland

It is not possible to discuss in detail the contributions that Elias and Dunning have made to our understanding of the emergence and development of sport as a social phenomenon.[16] However, I shall attempt to outline briefly the relevance of their work to the sociology of sport by employing aspects of their work as sensitizing concepts for the understanding of sport in Ireland. Dunning argues that the equalizing and civilizing concepts of 'fair play' are features of specifically 'modern' sports and therefore these characteristics are not necessarily as applicable to all sports, independently of time and place, as others imply.[17] Moreover, the balance between skill and strength that has characterized the development of sport forms over time has shifted towards skill in accordance with what Elias calls a 'civilizing process'. While females' participation in sport generally has increased substantially in the past 100 years, Dunning argues that sports have become one of the last bastions of male exclusiveness – a 'male preserve' – precisely because of this increasing female participation. This would also account for the persistence of cultural associations between sport and gender, for example, in the commonsense idea that 'rugby is a man's game'.

Historically, the emergence and development of modern forms of sport can be linked to changing ideas about physically active human bodies or, to be more precise, physically active male bodies. Elias and Dunning argue that the process of the emergence of modern sport is, itself, part of wider and long-term civilizing processes in which sport (as a social activity) generates and releases excitement and tension. This generation and release of emotions was crucial in industrializing societies such as Ireland that were characterized over time by increasing levels of restraint and a movement towards more orderly and more regulated behaviour, and less violence. As Elias argues, in societies undergoing a civilizing process, individuals acquire 'a reliable armour not too strong and not too weak, of individual self-restraint'.[18] For Elias and Dunning, sports provide opportunities for the arousal and dissipation of pleasurable excitement in highly routinized societies. They provide a 'safe' social enclave within which 'a controlled and enjoyable decontrolling of restraints on emotions is permitted'.[19] In this sense, it could be said that sport is a modern 'mock' battle, homologous with the 'real' battles that characterized warrior societies. In industrial societies 'the power of civilian relative to military elites is high'. Though violence and fighting have become less favoured relative to earlier forms of societies, the balance of power between the sexes tends to favour men 'to the extent that violence and fighting are endemic features of social life', and 'macho values tend to play a more important part in masculine identity under social conditions where fighting is frequent and the balance of power is skewed more heavily in favour of men'.[20] As Dunning has noted:

The balance of power between the sexes will also veer in favour of men to the degree that their chances for engaging in unified action are greater than those of women, and to the extent that men monopolize access to and control of the principal institutional determinants of life chances, especially in the economy and the state.[21]

While the physical differences between male and female bodies are well documented and important in this regard, the central question is not about these 'natural' differences but why some differences, and not others, become central to social processes that have contributed to the construction of women and women's sports as inferior. The power chances of women will tend to be increased (and they will have increased opportunities to challenge the stricter segregation of the sexes that generally characterizes andrarchal societies) when social relations become more pacified; that is, when the pressure for the self-restraint of violent actions becomes stronger than the impulse for violence.

Sport and Gender Relations in 'Modern' Ireland

In the late twentieth century, sociologists, historians and feminists highlighted the prevalence of patriarchal social relations in various social fields in Irish society. For example, Byrne and Leonard and O'Connor categorized Irish society as capitalist and patriarchal, while Curtin, Jackson and O'Connor argued that capitalism and patriarchy played a role in 'gender stratification' and the subordination of women.[22] To date, however, work of this kind has failed to acknowledge that women are sometimes more powerful than men, and that gender relations are much more complex than suggested by Curtin *et al.* and others. Sport has been omitted from sociological and feminist research in Ireland to date, both in terms of an analysis of sporting processes and their distinctive social dynamics, and also in relation to an analysis of part-connections in this regard including the complex social relations involved in the reproduction of class differentiations in sport, and aspects of the sport-gender nexus. These are glaring omissions when we consider the contributions that sport sociologists, notably Dunning but also others,[23] have made to a more adequate understanding of sport and the sport-gender nexus.

Perhaps it is not surprising that sport and leisure have been relatively free of critical sociological analysis, for sociologists in Ireland have not established themselves as significant commentators on how life in Ireland is changing.[24] Sport is an element of Irish life so pervasive that virtually no individual (irrespective of their like or dislike of sport) is untouched by it. The sociological study of sport can take us to the very heart of critical issues in the study of Irish culture and society as sport signifies a great deal about ourselves and therefore contributes to the ongoing production, reproduction and change of many aspects of social life. In a manner similar to Dunning's argument concerning sport in Britain,[25] we can say that Irish males, virtually independently of social class, are forced to develop an internalized adjustment to sport. We need only glance at the coverage given to sporting events in the print and visual media to appreciate the importance of sport to many people. The reception given to the Irish men's soccer team on their return from the 1990

World Cup, and the nationwide celebration of their qualification for the 2002 World Cup Finals, have been matched, if not surpassed, by subsequent outrage and national public debate during, and since, what has become known as 'the Roy Keane saga'.[26] Research shows that up to 74 per cent of Irish men and women regularly take part in sport as participants or spectators, and that sport plays a central role in aspects of the Irish economy such as employment, tourism, travel and the Irish economy.[27] Another example of the importance of sport is the 'household name' status accorded to successful sportsmen and women such as Sonia O'Sullivan, Michelle Smith (prior to her four-year suspension for a doping offence), Roy Keane and Brian O'Driscoll. The full significance of sport lies not in its prevalence however, but in the manner in which it imparts key social meanings about individual and group identity (for example, developments in sport can provide an index of global processes), as well as about ways of living. According to the Irish Government:

> Irish people love their sport and either play or follow a wide range of sporting activities ... The value of participation in sport and active leisure pursuits in the physical, psychological and social development of individuals is well documented and accepted.[28]

Not only is sport a popular activity, it is also deeply embedded in the social fabric of Irish society. The idea that sport is good for one's physical and mental health reflects an increasing awareness of health and lifestyle choices. Sport crystallizes collective identities, whether at parish, club, team, county, national or international level but, at the same time as it unites a group internally, it also divides them from others (the opposition or 'enemy').

Females' Motivations for Participation in Traditional Male-Associated Sports

Since the 1970s, females in Ireland have been relatively enabled to participate in traditional, male-associated, sports such as Gaelic football, soccer and rugby.[29] Approximately 80,000 females currently play Gaelic football while the numbers of females participating in soccer and rugby are substantially lower (6,500 and 900, respectively). Not surprisingly, perhaps, women's Gaelic football (known officially as Ladies Gaelic football) receives a higher profile than the other two codes of women's football in Ireland. The growing involvement of women in these sports raises a number of questions, one of which relates to females' motivations for participation in male preserves such as these. Dunning and Maguire have argued that aggressive masculinity and the subordination of females came to represent a process of male identity testing and formation that was particularly evident in sports. They also suggested that developments in technology (including the emergence of contraception) have led to a decrease in family size as well as the proportion of women's lives spent pregnant and nursing infants and that these processes have reduced the power chances derived by men from their physical strength and ability as hunters, fighters and more recently, athletes. In addition:

> the Western European 'civilizing process' has involved, on the normative level, an accumulation of controls and taboos, for example, against males striking females,

and, on the level of habitus and personality, a lowering of the 'threshold of repugnance' regarding violence and aggression.[30]

Dunning and Maguire (and Elias before them), emphasize the importance of long-term processes that have generated social conditions for change occurring on two levels: at the level of social structure, but also at an habitual or personality level where technological developments and changes in thresholds of repugnance (matched by internalization at an habitual level) have meant that power-ratios between men and women have shifted, relatively, in favour of the latter. Under these changing social conditions, the entry of females into former male preserves such as rugby, soccer and Gaelic football is more adequately understood within the context of a gradual (though by no means, linear) shift in the balance of power between males and females, in favour of the latter, which has been mirrored in other interrelated developments in Ireland since the 1970s. These developments have included: women's increasing access to the public domain (for example, their increasing participation in the labour force as full- and part-time employees and the removal of the marriage bar in the civil service); technological and medical advancements such as the invention of the tampon and the availability of contraceptives which have enabled women to postpone motherhood and remain involved in sports and physical activities whilst menstruating; women's (and men's) increasing access to education following the introduction of free second-level education in 1969; reform of the private sphere and the gradually decreasing size of Irish families; Ireland's entry into the European Community (now the European Union) in 1973; and the introduction of divorce. In contrast to this analysis, those explanations of females' entry and increasing participation in former male preserves which focus only on the intentions of certain social groups (for example, the female Gaelic footballers involved in establishing the Ladies Gaelic Football Association (LGFA) in 1974, or the female soccer players who established the Ladies – later the Womens – Football Association of Ireland in 1973) are unsatisfactory because they fail to take adequately into account the ways in which social change is not necessarily planned by a single individual or group of people or, equally, that males were also involved in the establishment of these organizations. Similarly, these one-sided explanations do not take adequate account of the fact that one of the consequences of increasing interdependence between people in modern industrializing societies such as Ireland, has been that social change often results not just from the *intended,* but also from the *unintended* consequences of purposeful human action. A key factor in a gradual inharmonious equalization of power relations between the sexes [31] has also undoubtedly been the declining power of the Catholic Church in Ireland in the past 20 years and a correlative increase in the power of media in Irleand.[32]

Males can often experience the civilizing process as 'emasculating' on the one hand and 'feminizing' on the other, as it tends to increase the relative power chances of women in an increasingly pacified society. According to Dunning and Maguire:

> Sport – along with such occupations as the military and the police – will come to represent an enclave for the legitimate expression of masculine aggression and for

the development and expression of more traditional masculine habituses involving the use and display of physical prowess and power. It will come, that is to say, to represent a primary vehicle for the 'masculinity-validating' experience and to be regarded as a bastion against 'feminization' and 'emasculation'. However, its status as such will be threatened to the extent that the growing power, and correlatively, self-confidence, assertiveness and independence of women allows them to mount a successful challenge against traditional andrarchal (patriarchal) ideas and institutions and to enter sport themselves.[33]

However, one criticism of Dunning and Maguire's work is that they tell us relatively little about women's motivations for entering the field of sports, and what they do tell us is not securely grounded empirically. While their analysis focuses centrally on broader social processes such as technological developments (including birth control and household technologies), lowering birth rates and family sizes, that have equalized male and female power relations, they go on to argue that:

women have *presumably* been motivated in this connection by such things as: (i) an interest in obtaining the sorts of 'mimetic', 'sociability' and 'motility' satisfactions that can be obtained from sports by men, together with the sorts of gains regarding self-concept, self-assurance and habitus (e.g. greater feelings of security in public spaces and greater ability to defend themselves against a physical attack) which can accrue in that connection; and (ii) a desire for equality with men as a result of frustrations experienced over the constraints and limitations traditionally placed on female roles.[34] (emphasis added)

More particularly, they write that:

the growing involvement of women in sport in and of itself represents an equalizing trend. Nevertheless, as we have seen, this growing female involvement in what started as an exclusive male preserve has tended to involve two specific sets of penalties for sportswomen which show that modern sport and modern society still remain predominantly andrarchic. On the one hand, the femininity of sportswomen tends to be compromised in the eyes of others, especially as a result of their participation in contact sports ... It tends to be compromised in their own eyes, too ... On the other hand, women face numerous obstacles with respect to participation in sport that are not experienced by males.[35]

My own data from interviews conducted as part of a doctoral research project,[36] suggest that Irish females' identification with sports was shaped by their relations with other people, particularly by relations with males, from a young age. The cohort of females were socialized into a network of social relations between the sexes that was (and is) undergoing change (for example, the gradual decline of the power of the Catholic Church over the means of orientation of males and females; the emergence of national organizations for women's sports such as the LGFA (1974), the WFAI (1973) and the IWRFU (1991); and the increasing entry of females into the public sphere generally as seen in the election of two female Irish Presidents in the past ten years) and a movement towards increasing self-restraint, particularly in relation to the use of, and propensity towards, violence. Partly through fears of feminization, sports such as Gaelic games, rugby and soccer became key social sites for the expression of more traditional forms of masculinity in Ireland. While advocates of women's rugby and soccer would largely characterize the recent affiliations with their male counterparts as progressive,[37] a more adequate sociological analysis of this development would point to a number of consequences arising from this development, most notably perhaps, the persistence of social barriers to the development of women's participation in traditional, male-associated, sports by virtue of the increasingly interdependent ties between males and females in sport. Moving closer together seems to create a different kind of resistance from that involved in more segregated sport forms, involving a movement from patronizing dismissals of women's sports to a heightening of resentment and sometimes fear, on the part of males. In the Irish case (as elsewhere), the emergence of joint (or affiliated) sports associations such as the Irish Hockey Union (and increased mixed sex participation in sports) is probably necessary to encourage changes in masculine habituses. One of the consequences, therefore, of changes in the social relations between males and females participating in sports such as Gaelic football, rugby and soccer is that the mutual balance of power between the sexes is moving from harmonious inequality towards inharmonious equality.[38]

In *Sport Matters* (1999), Dunning again questioned whether females were motivated to participate in sports for reasons similar to males. In interviews conducted for this study, females cited a number of motivations for their participation in male-associated sports. 'I play Gaelic 'cos I enjoy it, it's my outlet. I was always good at it' (Fiona). Similarly, Áine emphasized the stress-relieving benefits that she felt she gained from her involvement in sports. In her words:

> I adore being fit. I think I'm a bit obsessed about being fit, number one. It's a brilliant stress relief as well. I find you just go out and you do... you could be in the [worst] form ever . . . You don't feel like doing anything and you go out and you walk away and you feel so much better in yourself. And I suppose it gives you high energy levels and you know, it's like when I look at people in work and I can fit in so much and I'm always in good form and people are so stressed in there. But if I'm stressed I'll come out of the meeting and I'll just go into the pool for an hour and then I'll come out and I'll feel fantastic. And rather than take it out on everybody else and wreck my own head I'll just go out and plough through the pool and come back... So it's a mental thing as well, it's mental really.

Other interviewees stressed enjoyment, sociability and the feeling of being physically fit. While Mary's working role was intensive and demanding, she felt that 'once you get out you'd feel so much better for it. And you meet so many people. Particularly around Dublin there's a phenomenal amount of people that play'. Similarly Sue said:

> I feel good after it. I just enjoy doing it. Just fun, I really enjoy it. I like feeling fit. I feel good. It's a physical and an emotional thing. Something like squash is a great stress buster as well. I just go in and smack a ball and it's great because I work at home all day and depending on the research that I'm in and you're either stuck in a dusty library or you're in manuscripts somewhere or you're working at home stuck in front of the computer which is also in my bedroom so I spend three quarters of my life in my bedroom. So it's great to actually get out, it's important for me.

Helen emphasized the health and fitness benefits of her participation in sports generally as well as what she referred to as 'social aspects'. She continued as follows:

> I like the fact that you're actually fit. The feeling of being fit is just really good. I like that. I like the healthy aspect it gives you, I feel so much better myself. And I really like the social aspects, you develop a real camaraderie from training with a group of women for three or four times a week.

In contrast, Betty was more explicit about her competitive motivations and desire for achievement. In her words, she was always 'striving to be the best':

> I hate being a beginner at anything. It's like I have to be the best, it's terrible. I'm not the most talented athlete you'd ever meet in your life but I work incredibly hard... I train incredibly hard to try and achieve, to be better. And my motto is always 'the day that you think you are the best, you should give up because you should always strive to be the best every day'. Like every day that you train, you should learn something new or push yourself a little bit harder. I suppose it is. It's striving to be the best. It's competitiveness.
>
> Q: So you don't like losing?
>
> A: No, but I think I'm getting better at it because I play for Ireland.

These interview excerpts suggest that the motivations of females who compete at the elite levels have much in common with those of men. Moreover, it would appear that Dunning, as noted above, is correct to argue that women are motivated by the 'mimetic', 'sociability' and 'motility' satisfactions that can be obtained from sports, as well as gains regarding identity.[39]

Consequences for the Ranking and Self-conceptions of Males and Females

Despite the national and international achievements of this cohort of females,[40] their status as athletes remains low and relatively marginal. They have experienced what Dunning describes as powerful ideologies questioning their femininity and sexual orientation. One interviewee was implicitly aware that one of the reactions to her participation in camogie[41] was being perceived as 'more masculine' and 'butch' than her non-playing friends. When probed on whether she adapted her behaviour in any way as a result, she said:

> the only thing that I do change is whether I speak up, whether I don't speak up, whether I'm being myself or not, personality wise. But I don't change my appearance to look more feminine or less masculine or whatever. I look this way and that's the way I look. I don't think anybody goes out deliberately to look like 'I play camogie and I'm going to be seen as butch so I'm going to wear these clothes to look feminine'. I don't think people make that deliberate choice. I don't make those conscious choices. I don't know if anybody does. (Nicola)

While Nicola claimed that she did not consciously adapt her behaviour, Catherine claimed that her femininity was important to her in terms of portraying a feminine image of women's rugby. In her words:

It's the fact that I'm a woman and I'm feminine and that's the way I am and I want to look feminine and I would always try and portray the fact that people who you think wouldn't play rugby do play rugby. And people talk to me and say, 'Oh I would always imagine them to be butch' and I would say: 'there's a lot of extremely attractive women who play rugby'. There's one girl who won the Irish face of '94 who was a model. We've got models, we've got actresses, we've got singers. There's a variety of people who come together because they love the sport.

One of the consequences (for males and females) of females' increasing participation in traditional, male-associated, sport-games has been 'corresponding changes at an ideological and value level regarding what constitute socially acceptable 'feminine' habituses and behaviour'.[42] Dunning argues that many males feel threatened by the correlative growth of female power and, as noted earlier, in relatively pacified or 'civilized' societies, sport will be an area of social life where expressions of masculine aggression have a relatively high degree of legitimacy, and will thus come 'to represent a primary vehicle for the masculinity-validating experience'.[43]

Dunning also argues that in Britain the 'symbolic vilification' of women in sports contexts tended to take place 'behind closed doors in rugby union and more openly in soccer'.[44] A similar pattern can be seen in Ireland, and this is related to the status of the two sports and the social class differences of participants and spectators of these sports. While substantially fewer male and female players participate in rugby than in soccer, rugby union is a predominantly middle and upper-class sport. Soccer participants and spectators are predominantly drawn from working-class backgrounds. The profile of soccer in Ireland has also shifted in the past five years with the relatively recent success of the Irish men's rugby team. For example, the international men's recent successes in the Triple Crown, as well as the achievements of provincial rugby teams such as Munster and Leinster in the Heineken Cup and Celtic League,[45] have raised the profile of rugby vis-à-vis that of soccer. However, these changes in the status of rugby do not appear to have had a significant impact on the status of women's rugby. While the IWRFU has been formally affiliated to the IRFU since 2001,[46] the financial and organizational investment in the IWRFU has not changed substantially. While international female players' travelling, accommodation and kit expenses are now covered by budgetary allocations from the IRFU, the status of women's rugby remains marginal. However, the low and relatively marginal status of women's rugby has not seemed to deter some females from participating in this sport. For Sinéad, Catherine and Orla, their motivations for elite-level participation in rugby included: 'basically getting recognition for being a sportsperson whether you are male or female'; 'challenging the old boys' network'; and 'the enjoyment I get from challenging myself and keeping physically and mentally fit'. However, the profile of women's rugby has changed in the past 13 years since the IWRFU was established and there is anecdotal evidence (for example, female club representatives are invited to club banquets in addition to some female players receiving club awards) to suggest that females are becoming more involved in aspects of the rugby club culture in Ireland in addition to their increasing participation in the sport itself. In other words, there is limited anecdotal evidence to suggest that the symbolic vilification of female rugby players, which had previously taken place behind 'closed doors', is being challenged by women's increasing participation in more aspects of the rugby union culture. However, this is not to deny the ongoing importance of rugby to masculine habituses and behaviour and the curvi-linear relationship that seems to exist between, on the one hand, the use by males of sporting contexts (particularly rugby) as sites for the symbolic vilification of women, and on the other hand, the concomitant increase in females' participation in male-associated sports, including rugby.

Similar to the low profile of women's rugby in Ireland, the marginalization of women's soccer is also evident in that country. Dunning has drawn attention to the importance of national differences in relation to the growing involvement of women in sport and has suggested that the sporting participation of females may have been somewhat easier to accomplish in the US than Britain 'partly on account of a degree of male support'.[47] There may also be particular social factors which are relevant to the Irish situation. While an andrarchal social structure remains dominant in Ireland (as in the US and Britain generally), particularly in the social field of sports, the dominance of the Catholic Church, which is more specific to Ireland than to the US and Britain, and the impact of this on forms of sexual segregation in Ireland (though this is changing) also need to be taken into account in relation to the marginalization of women's sport. In relation to this process of marginalization, one interviewee argued that Irish women's football has 'been the poor relation of men's football for years'. She continued:

> I mean poor in terms of the financial and social investment in the game. Sure the prevailing attitude of men is that women can't play football anyway, they can't kick the ball long enough and they can't head the ball hard enough. (Moira)

Dunning also argues that males have reacted to females' increasing participation in what were formerly 'male preserves' (such as rugby and soccer) by vilifying females' participation and protecting their male status. 'It is also arguably the case that the use by males of sporting contexts as sites for the ritual and symbolic vilification and demeaning of females has grown as the power of women as increased.'[48] He suggests:

> Many men ... will feel their masculinity compromised, constrained and threatened, on the one hand by this civilizing process *per se* which they will experience as 'emasculating', and on the other by the correlative growth of female power. Assuming Elias's theory to be sound, it is this twin process which appears to lie at the roots of the fear of 'feminization' discussed by Messner (1987) and which, if I am right, is by no means confined to the USA.[49]

In this regard, the field of male-associated sports in Ireland has become one of the primary sites for the expression and reproduction of a particular masculine identity and the production and reproduction of traditional male habituses involving the use and display of physical prowess and power. Dunning also argues that one of the consequences of women's entry into, and increasing participation in these sports has been the impact on aspects of females' habituses and behaviour. Females who participate in some traditional, male-associated, sport-games in Ireland (as elsewhere) have been subject to stigmatization and labelling as 'butch', lesbian or overly-masculine. Debates about the appropriateness of females' dress (for example, wearing a skirt without under-shorts in camogie) and behaviour (for example, the prohibition on a shoulder-charge contact in Gaelic football) at Annual Congresses of respective women's sports organizations reflect the boundaries that males and females perceive to represent appropriate female behaviour. The self-images of female athletes have been influenced by these debates and broader social processes and it has become necessary for females participating in such sports to find ways of deflecting adverse criticism and of handling the psychic discomfort of guilt.[50]

Conclusion

Dunning's work, like that of Elias, is characterized by a consistent focus on social processes and developments as emanating from social relations between increasingly interdependent groups of people.[51] According to Elias and Dunning, it is the relations between people – the dynamics of 'groups-in-controlled-tension'[52] – that define the social field of sports. Using Dunning's work, we can understand the slight, and by no means linear, shift in power relations between males and females (in Ireland, as elsewhere) as a consequence of the increasing pacification of social relations between the sexes; that is, when the pressure for self-restraint of violent actions (generally, though by no means exclusively, associated with male behaviour) has become stronger than the impulse for violence. As a result we have, over time, seen a concomitant decrease in the segregation of the sexes and the increasing entry of Irish women into more spheres of public life, for example, in government and state organizations, the public sphere and public discourse generally. Females' increasing entry and participation in sport and physical activities, particularly traditional, male-associated, sports, is an important example of changing power relations between the sexes and this has been facilitated by civilizing processes in Ireland. It is appropriate to conclude this discussion using Dunning's own words:

> Sport groups are a type of social figurations and … their dynamics are best conceptualized as a tension-balance struck between the opposites in a whole complex of interdependent polarities … The immediate figuration formed by those who participate directly in and are present at a game forms part of a wider figuration that consists, on one level, of the club organizations that pick the teams and are responsible for such matters as the provision and maintenance of playing facilities and, on another, of the legislative and administrative bodies that formulate the rules, certify and appoint the controlling officials, and organize the overall competitive framework. In its turn this figuration forms part of the wider figuration constituted by members of the society as a whole and, in its turn, too, the societal figuration exits in an international framework.[53]

Modern sports appear to have a historically variable relative autonomy; that is to say, what happens in sport can be explained by looking at the changing balances of power between the groups involved in sports, the integration of sports in wider social figurations such as national societies, and the stage of development of wider social totalities. Using the figurational sociological perspective, Dunning's work offers a theoretically and empirically informed framework from which to investigate further aspects of: (i) the position of different sporting disciplines in the overall status hierarchy of sports; (ii) particular athletes' positions within sports; (iii) the consequences of social relations for the self-conceptions of masculine and feminine habituses; and (iv), the ways in which changes in the self-images and social make-up of male and female athletes go hand in hand with changes in the social structure of gender relations more generally.

Notes

[1] For example, Dunning and Sheard, 'The Rugby Football Club as a Type of Male Preserve'; Elias and Dunning, *Quest for Excitement*; Dunning and Maguire, 'Process-Sociological Notes on Sport, Gender Relations and Violence Control'; Dunning, *Sport Matters*.

[2] For example, see Elias, *The Society of Individuals*; Dunning, 'Figurational Sociology and the Sociology of Sport'; Dunning, 'Figurational Sociology and the Sociology of Sport: Some Concluding Remarks'; Dunning, *Sport Matters*.

[3] Dunning, 'The Development of Football as an Organised Game'; Dunning, 'Sport as a Male Preserve'; Dunning, 'Sport and Gender in a Patriarchal Society'; Dunning and Maguire, 'Process-Sociological Notes on Sport, Gender Relations and Violence Control'; Dunning, *Sport Matters*.

[4] Elias and Dunning, *Quest for Excitement*, 199–200.

[5] Elsewhere, it is suggested that changes in the mutual balance of power between males and females in a gynarchic direction are more adequately understood as a shift from 'harmonious inequality' towards inharmonious equality. See Liston, 'Playing the Masculine/Feminine Game'.

[6] Jennifer Hargreaves criticizes Dunning for an absence of focus on females' experiences in sport while Colwell suggests the existence of a male bias in his work. See Hargreaves, 'Sex, Gender and the Body in Sport and Leisure', and Colwell, 'Feminisms and Figurational Sociology'.

[7] For example, see Dunning and Sheard, 'The Rugby Football Club as a Type of Male Preserve'; Dunning, 'Sport as a Male Preserve'; Dunning, *Sport Matters*.

[8] Dunning and Sheard, 'The Rugby Football Club as a Type of Male Preserve', 18.

[9] Dunning and Maguire, 'Process-Sociological Notes on Sport, Gender Relations and Violence Control'; Dunning, *Sport Matters*.

[10] Brinkgreve, 'Elias on Gender Relations', 143.

[11] Dunning, 'Figurational Contributions to the Sociological Study of Sport', 233.

[12] Elias, 'The Changing Balance of Power Between the Sexes'.

[13] Dunning, *Sport Matters*, 237

[14] Elias, *The Society of Individuals*, 25.

[15] Mennell, *Norbert Elias*, 138.

[16] For example, see Elias and Dunning, *Quest for Excitement*.

[17] Dunning, 'The Dynamics of Modern Sport'.

[18] Elias, 'Introduction', 41.

[19] Elias and Dunning, 'Leisure in the Spare-Time Spectrum', 96.

[20] Dunning, 'Sport as a Male Preserve', 269.

[21] Ibid.

[22] Byrne and Leonard, *Women and Irish Society*; O'Connor, *Emerging Voices*; Curtin, Jackson and O'Connor, *Gender in Irish Society*.

[23] For example, see Birrell and Cole (eds) *Women, Sport and Culture* and Fasting and Sisjord, 'Sport and Society around the Globe'.

[24] The following outline is modelled on the Introduction in Dunning, *Sport Matters*.

[25] Dunning, *Sport Matters*, 222.

[26] Roy Keane left the Irish squad during the 2002 World Cup and announced his retirement from international soccer. He has subsequently declared himself available for international selection however.

[27] Department of Education, *A National Survey of Involvement in Sport*; Department of Education, *The Economic Impact of Sport*.

[28] Department of Education, *Targeting Sporting Change in Ireland*. This quotation is a good example of the uncritical acceptance of the dictum – sport is good.

[29] The Women's Football Association of Ireland, the Ladies' Gaelic Football Association of Ireland and the Irish Women's Rugby Football Union emerged in 1973, 1974 and 1991, respectively.

[30] Dunning and Maguire, 'Process-Sociological Notes on Sport, Gender Relations and Violence Control', 307.

[31] The concept of the 'inharmonious equalization of power relations' is adapted from Van Stolk and Wouters, 'Power Changes and Self-Respect'.

[32] Inglis, *Moral Monopoly*.

[33] Dunning, *Sport Matters*, 229. See also Dunning and Maguire, 'Process-Sociological Notes on Sport, Gender Relations and Violence Control'. We might also include firefighting here.

[34] Dunning, *Sport Matters*, 231. See also Dunning and Maguire, 'Process-Sociological Notes on Sport, Gender Relations and Violence Control'.

[35] Dunning and Maguire, 'Process-Sociological Notes on Sport, Gender Relations and Violence Control', 314.

[36] Between 1999 and 2002, 12 in-depth interviews were conducted with female athletes participating at national or international levels in traditional, male-associated, sport-games including Gaelic football, soccer, rugby and camogie. The names of interviewees have been changed to protect their anonymity. See Liston, *Playing the Masculine/Feminine Game* for further details.

[37] The IWRFU affiliated with the IRFU in 2001 while the WFAI affiliated with the FAI in 2002. To date, the LGAA has not affiliated with the GAA but a pilot scheme has been established (and extended) to examine barriers associated with this.

[38] My thanks to Dominic Malcolm for clarification of these points.

[39] Dunning, *Sport Matters*, 231.

[40] Eight of the 12 females had achieved international 'caps' while the remaining six were national title holders in their respective team sports.

[41] Camogie is the female equivalent of hurling.

[42] Dunning, *Sport Matters*, 226.

[43] Ibid., 229.

[44] Ibid., 234–5.

[45] The Heineken Cup is a competition for the leading club sides in England, France, Italy and Wales, and the leading regional sides from Ireland and Scotland. The Celtic League was established in 2001 for the leading club and regional sides from Ireland, Scotland and Wales.

[46] In 2002, 5 per cent of all Irish adult rugby players were female (815 of 17,000) and the IWRFU received 0.58 per cent of the domestic budget for the administration and organization of women's rugby (see Liston and Menzies [eds], *Women and Sport in Ireland*).

[47] Dunning, *Sport Matters*, 234.

[48] Ibid.

[49] Ibid., 229.

[50] This is adapted from Sheard, 'Aspects of Boxing in the Western "Civilizing Process"'.

[51] This contrasts with sociologists who write about social relations and 'discourses' as if they were 'outside' of, and unrelated to, people.
[52] Elias and Dunning, *Quest for Excitement*, 196.
[53] Dunning, 'The Dynamics of Modern Sport', 207.

References

Birrell, S. and C. Cole, eds. *Women, Sport and Culture*. Champaign, IL: Human Kinetics, 1994.

Brinkgreve, C. "Elias on Gender Relations: The Changing Balance of Power Between the by Sexes." In *The Sociology of Norbert Elias*, edited by S. Loyal and S. Quilley. Cambridge: Cambridge University Press, 2004.

Byrne, A. and M. Leonard. *Women and Irish Society: A Sociological Reader*. Belfast: Beyond the Pale Publications, 1997.

Colwell, S. "Feminisms and Figurational Sociology: Contributions to Understandings of Sport, Physical Education and Sex/Gender." *European Physical Education Review* 5, no. 3 (1999): 219–40.

Curtin, C., P. Jackson, and B. O'Connor. *Gender in Irish Society*. Galway: Galway University Press, 1987.

Department of Education. *The Economic Impact of Sport*. Dublin: Government Publications Office, 1994.

Department of Education. *A National Survey of Involvement in Sport and Physical Activity*. Dublin: Government Publications Office, 1996.

Department of Education. *Targeting Sporting Change in Ireland: Sport in Ireland, 1997–2006 and Beyond*. Dublin: Government Publications Office, 1997.

Dunning, E. "The Development of Football as an Organised Game." MA thesis, University of Leicester, 1961.

Dunning, E. "Figurational Sociology and the Sociology of Sport." In *Sport and Social Theory*, edited by C. R. Rees and A. Miracle. Champaign, IL: Human Kinetics, 1986: 29–56.

Dunning, E. "The Dynamics of Modern Sport: Notes on the Achievement-Striving and the Social Significance of Sport." In *Quest for Excitement: Sport and Leisure in the Civilizing Process*, edited by N. Elias and E. Dunning. Oxford: Basil Blackwell, 1986: 205–24.

Dunning, E. "Sport as a Male Preserve: Notes on the Social Sources of Masculine Identity and its Transformations." In *Quest for Excitement: Sport and Leisure in the Civilizing Process*, edited by N. Elias and E. Dunning. Oxford: Basil Blackwell, 1986: 267–84.

Dunning, E. "Sport and Gender in a Patriarchal Society." Paper presented at the World Congress of Sociology, Madrid, 1990.

Dunning, E. "Figurational Sociology and the Sociology of Sport: Some Concluding Remarks." In *Sport and Leisure in the Civilizing Process*, edited by E. Dunning and C. Rojek. Basingstoke: Macmillan, 1992: pp. 221–84.

Dunning, E. *Sport Matters: Sociological Studies of Sport, Violence and Civilization*. London: Routledge, 1999.

Dunning, E. "Figurational Contributions to the Sociological Study of Sport." In *Theory, Sport and Society*, edited by J. Maguire and K. Young. London: JAI, Elsevier Science, 2002.

Dunning, E. and J. Maguire. "Process-Sociological Notes on Sport, Gender Relations and Violence Control." *International Review for the Sociology of Sport* 31, no. 3 (1996): 295–317.

Dunning, E. and K. Sheard. "The Rugby Football Club as a Type of Male Preserve." *International Review of Sport Sociology* 5 (1973): 5–24.

Elias, N. "Introduction." In *Quest for Excitement: Sport and Leisure in the Civilizing Process*, edited by N. Elias and E. Dunning. Oxford: Basil Blackwell, 1986: 41.

Elias, N. "The Changing Balance of Power Between the Sexes – A Process-Sociological Study: The Example of the Ancient Roman State." *Theory, Culture and Society* 4 (1987): 287–316.

Elias, N. *The Society of Individuals*. Oxford: Basil Blackwell, 1991.

Elias, N. and E. Dunning. *Quest for Excitement: Sport and Leisure in the Civilizing Process*. Oxford: Basil Blackwell, 1986.

Elias, N. and E. Dunning. "Leisure in the Spare-Time Spectrum." In *Quest for Excitement: Sport and Leisure in the Civilizing Process*, edited by N. Elias and E. Dunning. Oxford: Basil Blackwell, 1986: 91–125.

Fasting, K. and M. Sisjord. "Sport and Society around the Globe: Nordic Countries." In *Handbook of Sports Studies*, edited by J. Coakley and E. Dunning. London: Sage, 2000: 551–3.

Hargreaves, J. "Sex, Gender and the Body in Sport and Leisure: Has There Been a Civilizing Process?" In *Sport and Leisure in the Civilizing Process*, edited by E. Dunning and C. Rojek. London: Macmillan, 1992: 161–83.

Inglis, T. *Moral Monopoly: The Rise and Fall of the Catholic Church in Modern Ireland*. Dublin: University College Press, 1998.

Liston, K. "Playing the Masculine/Feminine Game: A Sociological Analysis of the Social Fields of Sport and Gender in Ireland." Ph.D. diss., University College Dublin, 2004.

Liston, K. and G. Menzies, eds. *Women and Sport in Ireland: Report prepared for Dáil Joint Committee*. Dublin: Government Publications Office, 2004.

Mennell, S. *Norbert Elias: An Introduction*. Dublin: University College Dublin Press, 1992.

O'Connor, A. P. *Emerging Voices: Women in Contemporary Society*. Dublin: Institute of Public Administration, 1998.

Sheard, K. "Aspects of Boxing in the Western "Civilizing Process"." *International Review for the Sociology of Sport* 32, no. 1 (1997): 53.

Van Stolk, B. and C. Wouters. "Power Changes and Self-Respect: A Comparison of Two Cases of Established-Outsider Relations." *Theory, Culture and Society* 4, no. 4 (1987): 485.

The Gendering of Sports Injury: A Look at 'Progress' in Women's Sport through a Case Study of the Biomedical Discourse on the Injured Athletic Body

Nancy Theberge

In a 1988 review essay on women and sport, Susan Birrell wrote of the 'unfortunate neglect' among feminist sport scholars of Eric Dunning's contribution to the analysis of gender and sport. As she indicated, during the 1980s, when the key analytical and political task was to overcome the heritage of women's exclusion from sport and the absence of scholarly analysis of women's sport experiences, Dunning's work on gender and sport was neglected precisely because it was about men and the masculine preserve of sport.[1] In his more recent book, *Sport Matters*, Dunning extends his earlier consideration of the masculine preserve to a discussion of the implications of historical shifts in the balance of power between the genders for women's condition in and outside sport.[2] Historical shifts in gender relations are the point of departure in the present essay for an examination of sport, health and injury. The essay examines literature on sport injury with an eye toward understanding gendered constructions of the injured athletic body.

In *Sport Matters*, Dunning indicates that two of the main ways in which the theory of civilizing processes may be used for explorations of sport and gender are the analysis of: (i) the relative empowerment of females to enable them, at least in some measure, to challenge what started out as an exclusively male preserve; and (ii) corresponding changes at an ideological and value level regarding what constitutes socially acceptable feminine habituses and behaviour.[3] The analysis of health, injury and sport, with a specific focus on gender, allows for an assessment of some aspects of the meaning and dimensions of 'progress' in women's sport.

In her recent history of women's sport in Canada, Ann Hall writes of the remarkable changes that have occurred in women's sports in North America. She notes however that these changes have a 'dark side, especially at the highest levels'.[4] Among the problems that Hall cites are cheating, drug use, unhealthy practices and body abuse, and she locates these problems within a context of the growing marketing of women's team sports and the commodification of women athletes. This essay explores one aspect of health and sport, through an analysis of gendered understandings of sport injuries. The analysis allows for further exploration of the meaning and dimensions of 'progress', as evidenced by women's increasing incorporation into the world of sport and the values and ideologies surrounding this process.

Sport, Health and Gender

The subtitle of Birrell's review essay, 'From Women in Sport to Gender Relations', was a reference to the evolution of feminist analysis of sport in the decades preceding the essay's appearance in 1988. Since then, the study of gender and sport has matured considerably, such that by 1998, one of the leading textbooks in the sociology of sport identified gender as the most popular topic in the field in the 1990s.[5] Over the last two decades, analyses have moved from documenting and explaining patterns of gender inequality within sport to exploring how sport is implicated in the reproduction and challenging of gender relations and ideologies in the broader society.

One of the topical areas in the sociology of sport that also saw development in the 1990s was sport, health and injury, with some of the work in this area being done by Dunning's colleagues at Leicester who, like Dunning, have adopted a figurational approach.[6] The most developed work in this area has been on the normalization of injury and pain in sport. This research was initially focused mainly on male athletes and grounded in a gendered analysis that saw the routinization of injury and pain as a way for men to validate their masculine and athletic identities. [7] As research among women athletes appeared, it became clear that similar processes occur and that women's sport, like men's, is marked by the valorization of pain and injury.[8] This research provided compelling evidence of the incorporation of women into the dominant model of men's sport, in which athletes' bodies are subjected to rationalized processes of intervention in the interests of performance.

A corresponding development has been the increasing acceptance of women as athletes and women's sport as legitimate. For most of the last century, the dominant discourse surrounding women and sport was grounded in the 'myth of female frailty', the view that women were unsuited for vigorous physical activity, and a corresponding view that to the extent that women did engage in sport, it was a pale approximation of the 'real' sport played by men.[9] Increased participation and improved performances in recent decades have dramatically challenged historical ideas about the gendering of athleticism. This process is far from complete, however, and sport remains an arena for ideological struggle over constructions of gender. Documentation of this struggle is contained in a series of studies by the Amateur Athletic Foundation tracing media coverage of men's and women's sports over a decade. These studies show that despite some improvements, television coverage of women's sport is still marked by negative or ambivalent values about women and athleticism.[10]

The analysis provided here presents a further examination of gendered constructions of sport by examining constructions of the injured athletic body. It is of interest to know how two seemingly divergent processes – the incorporation of women into the dominant model of rationalized sport, where performance is emphasized, and gendered constructions of sport in which women historically have been constructed as inferior 'other' – converge in the case of gendered constructions of the injured athletic body. The analysis in this essay presents a further examination of gendered constructions of sport by examining constructions of the injured athletic body.

A Case Study of the Gendering of Sport Injuries

In the early 1980s, reports of an increase in knee injuries among women athletes began to appear in the sport medicine literature. A specific focus on knee injuries among women basketball players appeared in the middle of this decade and since then there has been accumulating epidemiological evidence of an increased incidence among women athletes of a specific injury to the knee, tears of the anterior cruciate ligament (ACL).[11] This increased incidence has been described as an 'epidemic'[12] and a 'plague'.[13] Moreover, as is frequently noted in the literature on this topic, rates of ACL tears are considerably higher among women than men, with estimates of the difference ranging from two to eight times greater.[14] In this respect, ACL injuries are a departure from the standard pattern of variations in sport injuries by sport, rather than gender.[15]

The 'epidemic' of ACL injuries among women athletes has been the focus of extensive interest in both the sport medicine community and the popular press. Within sport medicine, there have been numerous sessions at scientific meetings as well as symposia and retreats devoted exclusively to this topic.[16] While this is standard practice for prominent research topics, a more notable feature of interest in ACL injuries among women athletes has been the extensive coverage of the topic in the popular press. In 1995, the American weekly magazine, *Sports Illustrated*, published a story entitled 'Out of Joint' on the incidence of ACL injuries among women basketball players in the United States.[17] The article profiled several prominent players in leading collegiate athletic programmes who had sustained ACL injuries, some of which ended their season and damaged their teams' championship hopes, provided data on the higher incidence among women athletes and discussed various theories to explain why women are at greater risk. (More on the discussion of theories is provided below.) Similar discussions highlighting the gendered nature of the condition appeared in the *New York Times* in March 2001 and at about the same time in the *Chronicle of Higher Education*, a biweekly that provides coverage and commentary on issues in higher education.[18] In addition to these in-depth discussions in widely circulated and prominent media, additional accounts of ACL injuries in women athletes have appeared in a variety of other popular outlets over the last decade.

The extensive attention to ACL injuries in women athletes offers a case study in the construction of sports injuries as gendered. The discourse on this topic addresses a number of concerns. In addition to the perhaps most obvious question of why these injuries are occurring, additional questions are why is this of interest, what can and should be done and, perhaps most fundamentally as a sociological concern, what if anything does the occurrence of ACL injuries say about women's participation in sport and more specifically about the 'progress' that has occurred? Questions of meaning and significance have been at the heart of popular and scientific inquiry about women and sport since at least the late nineteenth century. Increased participation and improved performances have exposed the fallacy of 'the myth of female frailty' that dominated ideological constructions in the previous century, or at least would seem to have done so. This issue is at the heart of the research presented here.

A Lay Description of the ACL and the Understanding of Sports Injuries

The anterior cruciate ligament stabilizes the knee, a function that is particularly important in sports that require quick starts and stops, cutting and changing direction, such as basketball, soccer and skiing. Among the possible knee injuries that may occur in sport, the 'epidemic' reported in the literature involves tears to the ACL.

Epidemiological discussions of injuries commonly distinguish between risk factors, which predispose individuals to the occurrence of injury, and the precipitating mechanism or event that causes the injury. Risk factors are further distinguished as 'internal', which are understood to lie within the individual and 'external', which exist outside the individual. The important implication of the distinction between intrinsic and extrinsic factors concerns the possibility of manipulation or adaptation, in order to reduce risk. Internal factors, which are often understood as 'natural', cannot be changed, or changed only at great cost or difficulty. External factors typically are much more amenable to modification.

The literature on ACL injuries among women has focused on three theories of causation.[19] An anatomical theory is that women's wider hips and a lower centre of gravity place greater pressure on the knee, thus putting women at greater risk. A second theory is hormonal and suggests that the surge in oestrogen during a woman's menstrual cycle loosens the ligament and therefore makes it more likely to tear. This theory draws on the established fact that hormonal changes during pregnancy enable relaxation of the ligaments of the pelvis during childbirth. A third theory is neuromuscular, and considers the interplay between the neuromuscular system and movement to enhance body control; one focus of this is jumping, which has been heavily implicated in the incidence of ACL injuries. Common to all theories is an understanding that women more often perform certain physical tasks (the injury mechanism) in ways that increase the risk of injury to the ACL. What is at issue in the theories is the explanation for this. In layperson's terms the question is why some athletes (who more often are women) position their bodies in ways that increase the likelihood of injury. Anatomical and hormonal theories point to intrinsic factors, while neuromuscular theories pose an interplay between biological and anatomical factors and training to achieve muscular control.

Data and Analysis

The analysis presented here explores the discourse surrounding ACL injuries in order to examine gendered constructions of the injured athletic body. A web-based search, utilizing the search engine Medline, was conducted to identify sources on ACL injuries among women athletes. Of the articles identified, as many as possible were obtained. These were supplemented by other sources that came to the researcher's attention. The final sample included 49 articles, published between 1994 and 2002. While extensive effort was expended to locate as many articles as possible, there is no assumption here that the database is inclusive of all published literature. It is, however, thought to be sufficiently extensive to provide an adequate basis for examining key themes and constructions relevant to the interest in the gendering of athletic injuries.

The analysis was conducted in two stages. In the first stage, sources were examined to determine the relative coverage and emphasis on different topics and interpretations. A coding scheme was developed, based on a preliminary examination of the sources in order to become familiar with their contents. The sources were coded by two senior undergraduate kinesiology students with academic backgrounds in the relevant disciplines, including anatomy, physiology, biomechanics and sociology. The unit of analysis for the examination of the comparative coverage of themes was the individual article. An explanation of themes and the manner in which they were coded is presented in conjunction with the discussion of the data.

In the second stage of the analysis, sources which explored themes that emerged as particularly significant to the understanding of gendered constructions were examined in more detail. This analysis was completed by the author.

Descriptive Analysis of Article Contents

The majority of articles (65 per cent) drew on mixed gender samples to develop the discussion, although slightly more than a third (35 per cent) drew exclusively on women athletes. The levels of sport participation discussed ranged from elite to recreational, with no clear pattern.

One of the initial concerns that guided the analysis presented here was the determination of where discussions are presented. The interest here was to identify relevant populations interested in the apparent epidemic of knee injuries among women. The sources identified were classified as scientific (these were further distinguished as review or research pieces); clinical, involving the management and rehabilitation of ACL injuries; and popular, meaning they were directed at a general or lay readership rather than a scientific or professional audience. Twenty-nine articles (59 per cent) were scientific and, of these, 17 were review and 12 were research pieces. Thirteen (27 per cent) were popular and seven (14 per cent) were clinical. Here it is of interest to note that, on the basis of the sources identified in this project, attention in the popular press was greater than in the clinical literature. Explanations for this can only be speculated upon. Is it the case that the popular press has picked up on women's 'damaged bodies' to a greater extent than the relevant allied health professions have turned their attention to tending to these bodies? Another possibility is that the relative absence of clinical discussions reflects a typical lag between research on the risks and mechanisms of injuries and corresponding discussions on their management and rehabilitation.

Another preliminary concern was the basis of interest. Five concerns were identified, which are not mutually exclusive (that is, a given study or discussion could address more than one concern). In descending order of importance, the literature presented interest in ACL injuries in women athletes as: a scientific question (61 per cent), a health concern (51 per cent), a sport-related concern, for example, time lost from training and competing (49 per cent), a social issue, for example, as an indication of the 'costs' of advances in women's sport (16 per cent), and an economic concern, related to the costs of rehabilitation and long-term health effects (12 per cent). Thus, the bulk of the interest in this issue is based on the scientific, health and performance-related aspects of the injury.

A major focus of the research, and the basis for the qualitative analysis presented below, is the discussion of risk factors for ACL injuries. These data are presented in Table 1. Of particular interest here are the frequencies for the categories related to the three main theories discussed earlier: anatomic, hormonal and neuromuscular. There is extensive discussion of both anatomical and neuromuscular factors. These two are closely related in that discussions of neuromuscular processes typically involve discussions of anatomy, since these processes involve movement patterns of body parts (muscles). There is also considerable interest in hormonal influences, which sees the highest percentage among articles with this topic as a primary interest (14 per cent), while 49 per cent (14 plus 35) have at least some discussion of this topic.

Additional risk factors which were identified include strength or cardiovascular conditioning, with 31 per cent of sources having at least some discussion of this.

Table 1 Risk Factors

Causes / Focus	Primary Focus (%)	Some Discussion (%)	Mention Only (%)	No Mention (%)
Type of Activity	0%	18%	55%	27%
Manner of Participation	4%	24%	22%	49%
Anatomic	8%	65%	20%	6%
Hormonal	14%	35%	18%	33%
Conditioning	2%	29%	43%	27%
Neuromuscular	8%	63%	10%	18%

Table 2 Suggestions for Further Investigations

Suggestions for Further Investigations	% of Articles
Musculoskeletal	4%
Hormones	27%
Training	8%
Braces/Taping/Shoes	8%
General ACL	25%
Coaching	6%
Injuries General	2%
Prevention	8%
Mechanisms	4%
Sex Differences	6%
No Suggestion	33%

Two other types of external risk factors – type of activity (contact versus non-contact sports) and manner of participation (or 'style' of play) – figure less prominently in the articles' contents.

A related focus of interest is topics recommended for future research (Table 2). The most frequently mentioned is hormonal factors (27 per cent), followed by a category of 'general research into ACL injuries' (25 per cent). No other types of factors are mentioned in more than 8 per cent of the sources.

The descriptive content analysis indicates that by far the most commonly discussed risk factors are anatomical conditions and neuromuscular processes, which are associated with one another. Hormonal concerns also figure prominently in the discussions as both a risk factor and a topic recommended for future research. In light of these patterns, a further qualitative analysis was conducted to explore in more detail the discourses surrounding neuromuscular and hormonal factors related to the occurrence of ACL injuries among women athletes.

Neuromuscular Influences

A symposium at the annual meeting of the American College of Sport Medicine in May 2003, on 'Sports Injury Prevention in the New Millennium', included presentations on a number of major sport injuries (head and neck, ankle, hamstring, knee, groin). The presentation on knee injuries, by one of the leading researchers in the field, William Garrett, concentrated on ACL tears.[20]

In his preliminary overview remarks, Garrett noted that being female is a risk factor for the occurrence of ACL injuries; here he was repeating the accepted wisdom on this topic. In discussing explanations for the occurrence of ACL injuries, Garrett concentrated on neuromuscular approaches, specifically the position of the knee and muscle activation patterns which place the knee in the position of risk of injury. Importantly, with respect to gender, he observed that these patterns occur more frequently in women. The emphasis on motor control is significant because positioning of the knee and muscle activation are factors that are modifiable.

Having established the significance of neuromuscular processes in the etiology of ACL tears, Garrett went on to summarize the state of research on various prevention programmes that concentrate on neuromuscular strengthening and conditioning. His conclusion was that while there are some problems in the science underlying these studies, which generally are far from the randomized control trials that are the gold-standard of epidemiological research, the accumulating evidence is convincing in suggesting the probable effectiveness of prevention programmes.

In the conclusion to his talk, Garrett indicated that there are other risk factors related to ACL injuries in women athletes, some of which are difficult to control. He noted several topics mentioned prominently in the literature and discussed earlier in this article, including flexibility and joint laxity, hormonal influences and anatomical factors, and indicated that the literature on these factors is inconclusive.

Garrett's presentation is cited here because it is a succinct and recent 'state of the art' account of the issues surrounding neuromuscular risks and prevention strategies for ACL injuries, as they pertain to women. Elements of his discussion are found throughout the literature examined in this article. Several sources discuss the evidence that women more often perform movements in ways that put the knee at risk of injury. The *New York Times* article mentioned earlier quoted a leading researcher saying: 'we know how the ACL is injured. We can predict when it is going to be torn. The thing we don't know is why women are tending to get into that position so much more than men are'.[21] An article in the internet source CNN.com indicated, 'Nobody knows the causes of these bad habits'.[22]

The literature also stresses that a reason for the focus on the neuromuscular basis of the injuries is that these factors are modifiable or 'controllable'. The article in the *Chronicle of Higher Education,* mentioned earlier, reported that researchers have zeroed in on neuromuscular problems, 'because this is where we felt we could have the most impact'.[23] A review article in the *Journal of Sport Rehabilitation* noted that, 'looking at gender differences, we can target the areas that have the most potential for injury reduction in females'.[24] Following on from the emphasis on focusing on modifiable risk factors, several sources discussed research that demonstrates the probable effectiveness of neuromuscular training and conditioning programmes in reducing the risk of ACL injuries.[25]

Another aspect of the discourse on gendered movement patterns is worthy of note, though this cannot be discussed in detail here. In the face of a developing consensus that women more often engage in movement patterns that place them at risk of injury, there have been suggestions of the development of gender-specific training programmes. At issue here is the relevance of gender to physical performance and, where relevant, whether and how it should figure in the development of training programmes. The background to this question is the historical view of women's frailty, which dominated ideological constructions of women for most of the last century. Against this we have the contemporary incorporation of women into the rationalized model of modern sport, where specialized programmes reflect the application of scientific knowledge and the investment of resources. One discussion of this issue appeared in the *New York Times* article mentioned earlier, which quoted a medical researcher saying it was time to consider alternative training methods for women. The story then went on to state: 'This was not to suggest that women were lesser or deficient athletes'.[26] A key issue here is whether gender-specific programmes for women are driven by an ideology of pathology and deficiency or a recognition of difference without implying inferiority. This is one of the most important issues to be worked through in further considerations of medical constructions of the injured athletic body.

Hormonal Influences

The focus on hormones as a risk factor for ACL injuries among women athletes is of particular interest in the light of the well-established feminist critique of medical science as constructing women's bodies as more tied to nature, and the location of this in the reproductive role.[27] Whereas at the end of the nineteenth century, the participation of women in vigorous sporting activity was proscribed for fear of harm to women's reproductive systems, the connection between sport and reproduction takes a new face with the implication of hormones as a causal factor in the 'epidemic' of ACL injures. Accordingly, one of the interests in the qualitative analysis of these sources was to explore the discourse surrounding this association.

One of the striking features of this literature is the appearance of cautionary remarks in discussions of the association between hormones and the incidence of ACL injuries. A brief summary of relevant points from four research articles indicates the following: the discussion of the results of studies that found, respectively, a positive relationship between menstrual cycle phase and the incidence of ACL injury,[28] and a positive association between hormonal changes during pregnancy and laxity of the ACL joint,[29] both indicate that caution is required in the interpretation. Another study of hormonal changes associated with menstrual cycle and ligament laxity,[30] and one on menstrual cycle phase and the incidence of ACL injuries,[31] are more definitive in the presentation of the results, while noting that limitations such as sample size,[32] and continued uncertainty about the casual mechanisms that may be at play,[33] indicate a need for continued research.

Caution also is indicated in a web-based account of a session of the American Orthopaedic Society for Sports Medicine. The lead researcher on a study of the effects of hormones on ACL cellular metabolism is quoted as advising that, 'the clinical significance of our data must be taken with caution... whether this leads to risk of injury remains to be studied'. Another researcher, commenting on findings of an association between menstrual phase and injuries, warned that 'it is important not to rush to clinical judgments' and that the findings are 'cause for concern' and 'reason for further investigation'. A third researcher indicated the cause and effect of the relationship between hormones, hormone cycle and knee injuries has not been proven.[34]

Another web-based source provided an overview of various theories on the causes of ACL injuries in women athletes. At the outset of the article it is noted that there is no conclusive evidence as to why women are more susceptible to ACL injuries. The piece then goes on to review various theories and here it is notable that they are presented without additional commentary; that is, there is no further mention of the need for caution in making sense of the findings. This may have the effect of blunting the initial indication of inconclusive evidence.[35]

One newspaper source on hormonal research is titled, somewhat ominously, 'Hormones Linked to Female Knee Injuries'. The article introduces the topic by stating that researchers' 'suspicions women's hormones made them more susceptible to injuries' were confirmed by research. The piece then goes on to say, 'what this study means for how and when women should be active is not clear' and quotes the author of a study showing a relationship between menstrual cycle and injuries as 'warning against overreacting... This research does not justify pulling young ladies out of sports or putting young women on oral contraceptives in order to prevent ligament injuries. We don't have enough information yet to justify (these measures).' The article also notes that: 'It's important to remember this is only one study. More research needs to be conducted'.[36]

In summary, the literature on hormonal influences suggests that researchers take considerable care in discussing the possible association between hormones and injuries among women athletes. This is reflected in the various cautions and reservations expressed in the literature, both professional and popular. These no doubt are located at least in part in scientific norms of acknowledging methodological and other limitations of research studies. Perhaps more meaningful, with regard to the social construction of women's athletic injuries, is the acknowledgment by a lead researcher on this topic that the prescription of oral contraceptives is not warranted; what is notable here is the explicit acknowledgment of the clinical implications of hormonal theories of causation. It is perhaps also notable that this statement appeared in the same newspaper piece that also had the least nuanced reference to this research, in the headline 'Hormones Linked to Female Knee Injuries'. Moreover, while two sources that appeared in the popular press were the least circumspect in their discussion of this association, and the newspaper article in particular contained some passages which, taken alone, overstated and simplified the state of scientific thinking on the topic, each piece also exhibited a measure of balance and qualification in the discussion of this topic.

The caution attached to contemporary commentary on the hormonal basis of injuries to women athletes is in striking contrast to medical pronouncements on the dangers of women's sport participation that figured prominently in debates about this issue in the late nineteenth and early twentieth centuries. During that period, the medical wisdom of the day argued against strenuous physical activity for women on the basis that it was unhealthy for them. Notably, these claims were not supported by the limited scientific research then available.[37]

While the emphasis on caution in interpreting and reacting to the research on hormonal influences is encouraging, it is important also to question the persistence of interest in hormonal factors. It will be recalled that hormonal factors ranked first in the list of topics recommended for further research. Comparisons to the focus on neuromuscular processes are relevant. There is developing consensus in the literature that neuromuscular processes are central to the occurrence of ACL injuries. Moreover, and importantly, this approach is the basis for the development of prevention programmes. In contrast, the role of hormones as a risk factor is debated and, more importantly, were this link to be clearly established, the implications for prevention are problematic, as indicated in a prominent researcher's comment on the inadvisability of putting young women on oral contraceptives. Thus, while there may exist a scientific rationale for pursuing research into the hormonal basis of ACL injuries, the political and clinical implications of this are questionable.

Concluding Comments

It is important to emphasize that the analysis presented here is concerned with interpretations of ACL injuries and, as such, is a study of the social construction of medical knowledge. It takes as a point of departure that there is an accepted understanding in the sport medicine and sport communities that the rate of occurrence of ACL injuries among women is notable, indeed alarming. In fact, this is an issue in need of careful examination. What is needed to complete the investigation of this topic, and is not dealt with in the present investigation, is a critical analysis of the construction of ACL injuries as an 'epidemic'. The most commonly cited evidence on injury rates is taken from data compiled by the National Collegiate Athletic Association (NCAA), the governing body of university athletics in the United States. The NCAA maintains an Injury Surveillance System (ISS) that tracks injury trends on a yearly basis from a representative sample of NCAA member institutions. Rates are calculated by comparing the number of injuries in a specific category with the number of athletes at risk in that category. Sex-specific knee injuries were calculated for a five-year period, from 1989 to 1993, for two sports, basketball and soccer. These sports were chosen because they were the only two in the ISS that offered similar rules and playing conditions for both male and female competitors. Results showed knee injuries in soccer were 2.4 times higher for women than men, and in basketball, 4.1 times higher for women than men. An additional finding was that no other knee structure showed the distinct gender difference in injury that occurred with ACL tears, except torn cartilage injuries, which are associated with ACL tears. While the finding of higher rates among women than men in comparable sports, for certain types of injuries, is clearly of interest, it is notable that the authors of the article presenting this research indicate that 'it should be pointed out that even in the female group such an injury [ACL] is relatively infrequent in the college environment'.[38]

Another factor relevant to the interest in ACL tears is the physical damage incurred. A leading researcher on this subject, who is a physician, writes that 'reconstructive surgery repairs the knee but does not restore it to normal function'.[39] This same author, writing with a colleague, indicated elsewhere that although ACL injuries are not the most frequently-occurring sport injuries, they are the most devastating due to the cost of care and the amount of time lost from sport.[40] It should be noted that these concerns apply equally to men and women.

In summary, data suggest that in some sports, where the conditions of participation share some similar features, there are higher rates of ACL injuries among women than men. Moreover, the long-term costs of these injuries are considerable. These findings, however, do not address some important issues in the evaluation of injury incidence as epidemic. One of these is a comparison with other sports, and activities. It is of course impossible to obtain a meaningful comparison by gender for injuries sustained in sports in which one gender greatly predominates, such as American football, or where playing conditions are different for men and women, as in hockey, where intentional body checking, resulting in forceful collisions between players, is prohibited in the women's game but an established and often celebrated part of the men's game. The NCAA data, from which the most commonly cited indicators of comparative rates of ACL tears in women and men are obtained, also show that the sport with by far the highest injury rate is football.[41]

A critical analysis of the construction of an 'epidemic' of sport injuries would take into consideration not only rates and consequences but other factors, such as the populations at risk. One wonders if there would be as much interest in ACL injuries, and whether the incidence would be labelled as epidemic, were the gender ratios reversed, or other populations, say minority male athletes, determined to be at higher risk. And how much interest would there be if theories did not suggest a hormonal basis to the risk among women? To pose these questions is not to suggest that progress is diminished when attention is paid to the damage inflicted by sport injuries on athletes' bodies and the cost of this to health care systems. There is, however, much more to be worked through to understand how gender is implicated in the values and ideologies surrounding health, injury and sport.

An analysis of the construction of an 'epidemic' of injuries in women's sport would be part of a broader project to understand the gendered athletic body within biomedical discourse. Perhaps the most extensively discussed topic in this effort is the female athlete triad of osteoporosis, amenorrhea and eating disorders. An additional example is a piece that appeared in 2003 in the *New York Times* on burnout and injury among adolescent female distance runners.[42] Clearly there is a need for further analysis of the complexities of gendered constructions of the athletic body in order to assess the meanings and dimensions of 'progress' as women gain access to the masculine preserve of sport. In this regard, we continue to see the relevance of Eric Dunning's work on civilizing processes and gender relations.

Notes

In preparing this essay, I was assisted by several people. I thank Tanya Spitzig and Davor Cvijic for assistance with coding the journal articles, Davor Cvijic for helping me understand the biomedical discussions of sports injuries, and Andrew Parker for reacting to an earlier version of this paper. The research reported here was supported by a grant from the Social Sciences and Humanities Research Council of Canada.

[1] Birrell, 'Discourses on the Gender/Sport Relationship'. The works Birrell discusses are Dunning and Sheard, 'The Rugby Football Club as a Type of Male Preserve', and Dunning, 'Sport as a Male Preserve'.

[2] Dunning, *Sport Matters*. Dunning's writings on gender also have an historical link to my own work in this area. At the 1983 meetings of the North American Society for the Sociology of Sport (NASSS) in St Louis, Dunning and I were co-presenters in a keynote session on gender and sport. Dunning's presentation was the basis of his 1986 article, while my presentation appeared in revised form as Theberge, 'Towards a Feminist Alternative to Sport as a Male Preserve'. In addition to memories of this shared platform for presenting our work, each of us remembers this meeting fondly for a dinner we enjoyed along with other NASSS colleagues at a riverboat restaurant on the Mississippi.

[3] Dunning, *Sport Matters*, 226.

[4] Hall, *The Girl in the Game*, 189–90.

[5] Coakley, *Sport in Society*, 211.

[6] Waddington, *Sport, Health and Drugs*; Waddington, Roderick and Parker, *Managing Injuries in Professional Football*; Roderick, Waddington and Parker, 'Playing Hurt'; Roderick, 'The Sociology of Risk, Pain and Injury'; Malcolm and Sheard, '"Pain in the Assets"'; Malcolm, Sheard and Smith, 'Protected Research'.

[7] Young, 'Violence, Risk and Liability'; Young, White and McTeer, 'Body Talk'.

[8] Theberge, *Higher Goals*; Young and White, 'Sport, Physical Danger and Injury'; Pike and Maguire, 'Injury in Women's Sport'.

[9] Theberge, 'Women's Athletics and the Myth of Female Frailty'.

[10] Amateur Athletic Federation, *Gender in Televised Sports*.

[11] Arendt, 'Anterior Cruciate Ligament Injuries in Women'.

[12] Longman, 'Shooting Pains', 1.

[13] Woolston, 'Women Suffering Knee Injuries in Sports'.

[14] Longman, 'Shooting Pains'.

[15] Griffin, 'The Female Athlete'; Arendt and Dick, 'Knee Injury Patterns'.

[16] Examples include sessions on ACL injuries and women athletes at the 2001 and 2002 meetings of the American College of Sport Medicine, another titled 'ACL Research Retreat: the Gender Bias', 6–7 April 2001, held at the Kentucky Sports Medicine Clinic in Lexington, and a symposium on 'Facts and Fallacies of ACL Injuries in Women' at the 1999 Annual Meeting of the American Academy of Orthopaedic Surgeons.

[17] McCallum, 'Out of Joint'.

[18] Longman, 'Shooting Pains'; Jacobson, 'Why Do So Many Female Athletes Enter ACL Hell?'

[19] Jacobson, 'Why Do So Many Female Athletes Enter ACL Hell?'

[20] I attended this session at the American College of Sports Medicine Annual Meeting, 28–31 May 2003, San Francisco, CA. An audiotape of the session is available from Mobiltape Corporation, Valencia, CA. The account presented here is taken from my notes, which were then expanded and verified by listening to the tape.

[21] Longman, 'Shooting Pains', 3.

[22] Woolston, 'Women Suffering Knee Injuries in Sports'.

[23] Jacobson, 'Why Do So Many Female Athletes Enter ACL Hell?', 45.

[24] Ireland, Gaudette and Crook, 'ACL Injuries in the Female Athlete', 108.

[25] Arendt, 'Common Musculoskeletal Injuries in Women'; Longman, 'Shooting Pains'; Ireland, 'Anterior Cruciate Ligament Injury in Female Athletes'; Jacobson, 'Why Do So Many Female Athletes Enter ACL Hell?'

[26] Longman, 'Shooting Pains', 4.

[27] Davis, 'Embody-ing Theory'.

[28] Myklebust *et al.* 'A Prospective Cohort Study of Anterior Cruciate Ligament Injuries'.

[29] Charlton *et al.* 'Correlation of Estradiol in Pregnancy and Anterior Cruciate Ligament Laxity'.

[30] Heitz *et al.*, 'Hormonal Changes Throughout the Menstrual Cycle'.

[31] Wojtys *et al.*, 'The Effect of the Menstrual Cycle on Anterior Cruciate Ligament Injuries in Women'.

[32] Heitz, *et al.*, 'Hormonal Changes Throughout the Menstrual Cycle'.

[33] Wojtys *et al.*, 'The Effect of the Menstrual Cycle on Anterior Cruciate Ligament Injuries in Women'.

[34] Slack Incorporated, 'Hormones'.

[35] Doctor's Guide, 'Link Found Between Menstrual Cycle and Knee Injuries'.

[36] Liddane, 'Hormones Linked to Female Knee Injuries', F03.

[37] Theberge, 'Women's Athletics and the Myth of Female Frailty'.

[38] Arendt and Dick, 'Knee Injury Patterns Among Men and Women'. Another analysis of NCAA data showed similar patterns of higher rates among women in these sports. See National Collegiate Athletic Association, *NCAA Injury Surveillance System*, 700.

[39] Ireland, 'Anterior Cruciate Ligament Injury in Female Athletes', 153.

[40] Ireland, Gaudette and Crook, 'ACL Injuries in the Female Athlete'.

[41] See http://www1.ncaa.org/membership/ed_outreach/health-safety/iss for comparative data across 16 sports, for both practice and game times. Football ranks highest for injury incidence in both categories.

[42] Bloom, 'Among Runners, Elite Girls Face Burnout and Injury'.

References

Amateur Athletic Federation. *Gender in Televised Sports: 1989, 1993 and 1999*. Los Angeles: Amateur Athletic Foundation, 2000.

Arendt, E. "Common Musculoskeletal Injuries in Women." *The Physician and Sportsmedicine* 24 (July 1996): 39–47.

Arendt, E. "Anterior Cruciate Ligament Injuries in Women." *Sports Medicine and Arthroscopy Review* 5, no. 2 (1997): 149–55.

Arendt, E. and R. Dick. "Knee Injury Patterns Among Men and Women in Collegiate Basketball and Soccer." *American Journal of Sports Medicine* 23, no. 6 (1995): 694–770.

Birrell, S. "Discourses on the Gender/Sport Relationship: From Women in Sport to Gender Relations." *Exercise and Sport Sciences Review* 16 (1988): 459–502.

Bloom, M. "Among Runners, Elite Girls Face Burnout and Injury." *New York Times* (20 April 2003).

Charlton, W. P. H., L. M. Coslett-Charlton, and M. G. Ciccotti. "Correlation of Estradiol in Pregnancy and Anterior Cruciate Ligament Laxity." *Clinical Orthopaedics and Related Research* 387 (2001): 165–70.

Coakley, J. *Sport in Society: Issues and Controversies.*, 6th edn. New York: McGraw-Hill, 1999.

Davis, K. "Embody-ing Theory: Beyond Modernist and Postmodernist Readings of the Body." In *Embodied Practices: Feminist Perspectives on the Body*, edited by K. Davis. London: Sage, 1997.

Doctor's Guide. "Link Found Between Menstrual Cycle and Knee Injuries." *Doctor's Guide to Medical and Other News* (1999), http://www.pslgroup.com/dg/2D20A.htm.

Dunning, E. "Sport as a Male Preserve: Notes on the Social Sources of Masculine Identity and its Transformations." *Theory, Culture and Society* 3, no. 1 (1986): 79–90.

Dunning, E. *Sport Matters: Sociological Studies of Sport, Violence and Civilization.* London: Routledge, 1999.

Dunning, E. and K. Sheard. "The Rugby Football Club as a Type of Male Preserve." *International Review of Sport Sociology* 8, nos. 3–4 (1973): 5–24.

Griffin, L. Y. "The Female Athlete." In *Orthopaedic Sports Medicine*, edited by J. DeLee and D. Drez Jr,. Vol.1. (1994): 356–73.

Hall, M. Ann. *The Girl in the Game: A History of Women's Sport in Canada.* Toronto: Broadview, 2002.

Heitz, N. A., P. A. Eisenman, L. B. Beck, and J. A. Walker. "Hormonal Changes Throughout the Menstrual Cycle and Increased Anterior Cruciate Ligament Laxity in Females." *Journal of Athletic Training* 34, no. 2 (1999): 144–9.

Ireland, M. L. "Anterior Cruciate Ligament Injury in Female Athletes: Epidemiology." *Journal of Athletic Training* 34, no. 2 (1999): 150–4.

Ireland, M. L., M. Gaudette, and S. Crook. "ACL Injuries in the Female Athlete." *Journal of Sport Rehabilitation* 6, no. 2 (1997): 97–110.

Jacobson, J. "Why Do So Many Female Athletes Enter ACL Hell?" *Chronicle of Higher Education* 45 (9 March 2001): 45–6.

Liddane, L. "Hormones Linked to Female Knee Injuries." *The Toronto Star* (26 April 2002):, FO3.

Longman, J. "Shooting Pains: A Special Report; Knee Injuries Take a Toll on Many Female Athletes." *New York Times* (29 March 2001).

McCallum, J. "Out of Joint." *Sports Illustrated, 13 Feb.* (13 Feb. 1995): 44–8, 53.

Malcolm, D. and K. Sheard. ""Pain in the Assets": The Effects of Commercialization and Professionalization on the Management of Injury in English Rugby Union." *Sociology of Sport Journal* 19, no. 2 (2002): 149–69.

Malcolm, D., K. Sheard, and S. Smith. "Protected Research: Sports Medicine and Rugby Injuries." *Sport in Society* 7, no. 1 (2004): 97–110.

Myklebust, G., S. Maehlum, I. Holm, and R. Bahr. "A Prospective Cohort Study of Anterior Cruciate Ligament Injuries in Elite Norwegian Team Handball." *Scandinavian Journal of Medicine and Science in Sport* 8, no. 3 (1998): 149–53.

National Collegiate Athletic Association. *NCAA Injury Surveillance System 1990–1996.* Overland Park, KS: National Collegiate Athletic Association, 1996.

Pike, E. and J. Maguire. "Injury in Women's Sport: Classifying Key Elements of Risk Encounters." *Sociology of Sport Journal* 20, no. 3 (2003): 232–51.

Roderick, M. "The Sociology of Risk, Pain and Injury: A Comment on the Work of Howard L. Nixon II." *Sociology of Sport Journal* 11, no. 1 (1998): 175–94.

Roderick, M., I. Waddington, and G. Parker. "Playing Hurt: Managing Injuries in English Professional Soccer." *International Review for the Sociology of Sport* 35, no. 2 (2000): 165–80.

Slack Incorporated, "Hormones, Biomechanics are Possible Clues in Gender-Disparate Injury Rate." *Orthopedics Today*, (1997), http://www.slackline.com/ortoday/199709/hormone.asp.

Theberge, N. "Towards a Feminist Alternative to Sport as a Male Preserve." *Quest* 10, no. 2 (1985): 93–202.

Theberge, N. "Women's Athletics and the Myth of Female Frailty." In *Women: A Feminist Perspective*, edited by J. Freeman., 4th edn. Mountain View, CA: Mayfield, 1989.

Theberge, N. *Higher Goals: Women's Ice Hockey and the Politics of Gender.* Albany, New York: State University of New York Press, 2000.

Waddington, I. *Sport, Health and Drugs: A Critical Sociological Perspective.* London: E & FN Spon, 2000.

Waddington, I., M. Roderick, and G. Parker. *Managing Injuries in Professional Football: The Roles of the Club Doctor and Physiotherapist.* Leicester: Centre for Research into Sport and Society, 1999.

Wojtys, E. M., L. J. Huston, B. D. Mebourne, K. P. Spindler, and T. N. Lindenfeld. "The Effect of the Menstrual Cycle on Anterior Cruciate Ligament Injuries in Women as Determined by Hormone Levels." *The American Journal of Sports Medicine* 30, no. 2 (2002): 182–8.

Woolston, C. "Women Suffering Knee Injuries in Sports." CNN.com, 22 Feb. 2000.

Young, K. "Violence, Risk and Liability in Male Sports Culture." *Sociology of Sport Journal* 10, no. 4 (1993): 373–97.

Young, K. and P. White. "Sport, Physical Danger and Injury: The Experiences of Elite Women Athletes." *Journal of Sport and Social Issues* 19, no. 1 (1993): 45–61.

Young, K., P. White, and W. McTeer. "Body Talk: Male Athletes Reflect on Sport, Injury and Pain." *Sociology of Sport Journal* 11, no. 2 (1994): 175–94.

Physical Education and Figurational Sociology: An Appreciation of the Work of Eric Dunning

Ken Green

Introduction

Although I have subtitled this essay 'An Appreciation' it cannot, given the necessary limitations on space, do justice to the – as yet largely undiscovered – significance of figurational sociology in general, and the work of Eric Dunning in particular, for our understanding of physical education and sport in schools. Like others before me I have, over the course of two decades, moved from being a physical education teacher to becoming a self-styled sociologist of sport and physical education. In the process my perspective on physical education, and physical education *teaching* in particular, has become increasingly tied up with figurational sociology and the work of Eric Dunning and the 'Leicester School'. Before I say more, however, I want to begin with a few personal reflections upon my involvement with Eric and his work.

I first became aware of sociology of sport in the late 1970s. As a mature student with, to put it mildly, an undistinguished academic record I was studying physical education at the University of Birmingham. Underwhelmed by the subject matter of the traditional sub-disciplines of what is now called 'sports science' – namely, exercise physiology, sports psychology, biomechanics and so forth – I discovered a latent interest in philosophy and the social sciences. Even now, 25 years on, I can still vividly remember standing in front of the physical education and sports section of the university library shelves bemoaning the dearth of texts in the areas that interested me, before happening upon Eric's edited collection, *The Sociology of Sport,* published in 1971. As a young undergraduate it was something of a defining moment. Some people (sociologists as it turned out) evidently *were* reflecting critically upon those aspects of sport (such as what I perceived to be its increasingly competitive and 'violent' character) that had led me to turn my back on it in my late-teenage years. More subconsciously than consciously, I began the process of becoming a 'lay' sociologist of physical education and sport! The process became more deliberate when I moved from school teaching into lecturing and, in the 1990s, undertook postgraduate degrees at the Centre for Research into Sport and Society at Leicester University.

It was during this period that I first met Eric 'in the flesh', at a conference jointly hosted by the CRSS and the North-West Counties Physical Education Association (the parent body of the *European Physical Education Review*). The conference was attended by, and featured a number of, established 'social scientists' of physical education. What might loosely be termed the 'Socratic dialogues' that followed the conference papers featured, unsurprisingly, the 'grand old man' of sports sociology and his colleagues from the 'Leicester School' – Patrick Murphy, Ken Sheard and Ivan Waddington. As with *The Sociology of Sport,* a *leitmotif* of discussion and debate was Eric and colleagues' persistent questioning of taken-for-granted assumptions of many of the academics and teachers present – whether as presenters or delegates – regarding, amongst other things, the supposed intrinsic worth and purposes of physical education. Two decades on from *The Sociology of Sport,* and amidst a burgeoning sociology of physical education scene, there was evidently still a good deal of room for the more thoroughly sociological approach to the subject of physical education that Dunning and the 'Leicester School' were championing for the sociology of sport generally.

Ironically, given that the sociological study of sport has its roots in academic physical education, Dunning has very little to say explicitly about the subject. Nevertheless, his work seems to me to be significant for physical education in at least two ways. Firstly, at a general level, it draws our attention to the need for a more properly sociological perspective on an area – physical education and sport in schools generally – which is shot through with ideology and pseudo-sociology. Secondly, and more particularly, Dunning's commentaries on sport have particular resonance for a subject which many still refer to as '*sport* in schools'. I want to say a little more about these two themes, and the relationships between them, by commenting upon the ways in which I have found some of the key concepts associated with figurational sociology and the work of Eric Dunning to be of direct relevance to the sociology of physical education and my own research.

Dunning has noted that,

> (The sociology of sport) is largely the creation of physical educationalists, a group of specialists whose work, because of their practical involvement in the area, sometimes lacks, firstly, the degree of detachment that is necessary for fruitful sociological analysis, and secondly, what one might call an 'organic embeddedness' in central sociological concerns. That is, much of what they have written focuses mainly on problems specific to physical education, physical culture and sports and fails to bring out the wider social connections. Moreover it tends to be empiricist in character.[1]

The latter two observations seem to be especially true for the sociology of physical education. In particular, it is true that the early period of what we would now view as sociological research into physical education was, indeed, empiricist in character, focussing as it did upon the process of teaching physical education – the 'science' or study of teaching physical education or pedagogy as it is otherwise referred to – rather than other aspects of the subject, such as the ideologies and related discourses associated with health-related fitness and sport, in particular, and physical education in general. Over the course of the last two decades, however, there have been signs of change, albeit alongside a good measure of continuity. The work of some eminent sociologists of physical education in the 1980s,[2] 1990s[3] and the first decade of the twenty-first century,[4] reflects not only a growing concern with the 'wider social connections' of physical education, but also the liveliness of sociological research into physical education and sport in schools.

Despite the dynamism of the sociology of physical education in recent years, however, it remains the case that contemporary issues, such as 'quality' physical education, continuing professional development and health-related physical education, continue to be seen all too often as pedagogical issues requiring empirical study in search of practical strategies to bring about 'change', rather than as issues that would benefit from, indeed require, deeper and more fundamental sociological understanding. Recent research indicates, for example, that physical education teachers can sometimes be difficult to train or develop[5] not least because they are heavily socialized into sporting orientations,[6] are unreliable or unpredictable when implementing policy[7] and, indeed, have not changed the way they teach much over the years despite innovations in the curriculum.[8] These issues are still taken to be largely pedagogical concerns which are best approached by research oriented towards psycho-social explanations and strategies, rather than by genuinely sociological research which stresses the interconnected aspects of broader social phenomena; that is to say, interdependent people (physical education teachers) whose thoughts and behaviours are heavily circumscribed, not to say constrained, by their habituses (both individual and group) and by broader social networks with other teachers, governors, parents, the Department for Education and Skills, OFSTED (Office for Standards in Education) and so forth. In short, there remains an apparent reluctance on the part of would-be sociologists of physical education 'to commit themselves to a thoroughly sociological approach'.[9]

There are, of course, notable exceptions to the tendency towards pedagogically-oriented empiricism.[10] And yet, even within the growing body of (often ex-physical education teacher) academics adopting sociological perspectives on physical education, there remains a distinct tendency for such work to remain resistant to (perhaps because its authors are ignorant of) some of the theoretical and methodological issues that have been rehearsed in Dunning's ground-breaking sociology of sport for two decades or more.

Dunning goes to the heart of one of the central ways in which the sociology of physical education is 'resistant' to a more properly sociological approach when he comments that 'theoretical work . . . can be valueless, particularly to the extent that it is either oriented more towards ideological issues than towards adding to knowledge'.[11] As I have previously noted, Dunning has highlighted the degree to which the sociology of sport, as a specialism, 'developed mainly within physical education rather than the parent subject (sociology)'.[12] Although he adds, 'I do not mean this in an entirely negative sense', Dunning is clearly pointing up one of the problems which can arise when those studying their subject matter have their roots deeply embedded in what they are purporting to study in an 'objective' manner. In this regard, Dunning speculates on what the sociologies of medicine and law might have looked like had they been developed primarily by the practitioners themselves, that is to say, doctors and lawyers. This point about the emotional involvement with, and attachment to, their subject matter – whether as teachers, teacher-trainers or academics – is fundamental and lies at the heart of many of the issues and debates surrounding physical education as it has increasingly come under the sociological gaze over the last quarter of a century or so. It is, in my experience, precisely because many physical educationalists have a very strong emotional attachment to, and thus are very deeply involved with, their subject, that they have difficulty recognizing, let alone subjecting to critical scrutiny, many of the assumptions and premises upon which their work rests. This is so even when they appear to be constrained by the conventions of sociology as a discipline.

Whilst there may be no doubting the sincerity of those advocating on behalf of physical education, the impact of this apparently unrecognized involvement with our subject matter has, I would argue, resulted in a tendency among physical educationalists towards partiality and even bias in our study of physical education, without our necessarily realizing it or intending it to be so. This is reflected particularly in the commonplace tendency for physical educationalists to reify their subject, that is to treat a process – physical education – which is, in fact, nothing more nor less than the (recurring) *practices* of physical education teachers, as a thing in its own right, as if physical education were not only a set of traditions but that these traditions have become, as it were, ossified into something of which teachers and academics see themselves being the guardians. One might say that this is simply a manner of speaking, the way in which physical educationalists talk about what it is they do and, of course, it may well on occasions be just that. However, one cannot escape the impression that many physical educationalists (including those who might reasonably be expected to be constrained towards more 'objective' or detached positions, namely, academics) display a tendency to talk of physical education as if it has a readily identifiable core or essence – something it is 'at heart' and must always be if it is to be worthy of the name. As McNamee has observed repeatedly, those who tend to concentrate their efforts upon identifying a supposed essence to the subject frequently appear to be taking the supposed intrinsic worth of their subject for granted.[13] This tendency toward reification is, in no small measure, a consequence of physical educationalists' close involvement with, and a deep-seated attachment to, their subject matter.[14]

I was reminded of these impressions and, indeed, the manner in which Dunning's application of Eliasian sociology to the world of sport (and, by implication, sport in schools) goes to the heart of sociological research into physical education at two international conferences in 2004. The first was a conference on the sociology of sport where I found myself involved in a debate, in the course of which a fellow delegate asserted that, as a sociologist of sport, I was surely compelled to advocate an essentialist view of the inherent worth of physical education and sport and, because I did not do so, I could be considered to have 'no values' worth speaking of. In response, I found myself arguing, in effect, about the nature of ideology and the notion of involvement-detachment.

The second conference – the 2004 Pre-Olympic Conference – included the strongest presence of sociologists, and for that matter social scientists, of sport and physical education that many delegates could recall at this particular international gathering of sports scientists. However, the papers presented by many sociologists at that conference indicate that Dunning's observations regarding the significance of involvement-detachment for researching sport, and sport in schools, are as pertinent as ever to the study of physical education. If the Pre-Olympic Conference demonstrated one thing it was that, even among highly-regarded social scientists of physical education, there can be an alarming tendency towards the kinds of uncritical advocacy, and even proselytizing, that are symptomatic of a strongly-felt, emotional attachment to physical education and sport sciences. Amade-Escot,[15] for example, talked of the 'essential criteria and nature of "quality physical education"', whilst MacDonald considered access to the curriculum knowledge and skills known as physical education to be a 'right' and spoke of the 'urgency' needed in order 'to advocate (and) vigorously promote clear outcomes for PE'.[16] MacDonald concluded that armed with the 'right' purposes, 'physical education will better be able tell the community what it stands for and why it has a rightful place in the curriculum'. In discussion surrounding developments since the Post-Berlin World Summit on Physical Education, Talbot commented that the papers presented demonstrated that 'we've not articulated the case for PE properly'.[17] At the same time, another eminent physical education academic responded by saying that it was a matter of 'articulating the *right* message in the *right* way' (original emphasis).[18] We were also told by another speaker that, 'The purpose of the World Summit on PE was primarily political' and that 'we need . . . a new discourse that embraces ideology' because 'the PE profession needs to realise that they are part of a global industry with an important "political" product to sell to governments'.[19] For his part, when reporting research exploring 'sport in education', Bailey spoke of projects that aim 'to gather and present evidence to policy makers regarding the benefits to schools of good quality PE and sport' and, in doing so, 'draw together persuasive data'.[20] True believers indeed!

Lest one conclude that such examples of involvement with the research topic may be more prevalent in oral presentations and subsequent discussion at conferences, numerous examples of similar presumptions can be found in the academic literature. Penney and Chandler, for example, take the role of their subject for granted when they comment thus: 'we regard substantial change within the subject as a matter of necessity if it is to have educational worth in the 21st century' and add that 'we stress the need to a view of (physical) education ... as a *force for future changes*' (original emphasis).[21] Armour and Jones are typical of many who assert 'the unique educational potential of (physical education)'[22] (see, for example, the studies in the 'life-worlds' or 'narratives' of physical educationalists of Armour[23] and Dowling-Naess[24]). Armour and Jones talk of getting 'our message across',[25] argue the need to 'return to the central activities of physical education' and exhort teachers 'to believe in ourselves' and 'trust their instincts'. 'Surely the way forwards', they add, 'is to provide proof ... of the broad educational potential of sporting activities'.[26] In short, value orientations evidently continue to suffuse what are presented, implicitly or explicitly, as broadly social scientific, and often avowedly sociological, studies of physical education. As Dunning observes of no less a figure than Karl Marx, so we might also say of the sociology of physical education: 'idealism continues to vitiate (our) analyses'.[27] Whilst sociologists cannot say what physical education teachers *ought* to be doing, they can analyse and seek to understand why they *do* what they do and why they *think* what they think. At the same time, sociologists are in a position to throw light upon the prominent ideologies within the subject-community and beyond, and the relationship between these and the 'philosophies' (in the aphoristic sense) held by physical educationalists at all levels of the subject-community.

At this point I want to recap what I see as the significance of Dunning's utilization of key sensitizing concepts in figurational sociology, such as involvement-detachment and habitus, by briefly outlining how I have sought to make use of these in my own research. At the heart of my research in recent years has been an attempt to make sense of the relationship between physical education teachers' 'philosophies' and practices and the ideologies underpinning these. I have sought, amongst other things, to identify and examine what teachers themselves, rather than academics or teacher trainers, think and do in the name of physical education. I have done so in an attempt to construct a more systematic understanding of physical education teachers' views of their subject, 'in the belief that greater understanding will enhance our capacity to exercise control'[28] over an important aspect of young people's educational experiences. In order to achieve this, I attempted to explore physical education teachers' habituses as part of their lived reality; that is to say, the various predispositions that suffuse their personal and professional lives, as well as the inevitable constraints provided by the particular circumstances they experience. In (figurational) sociological terms, these predispositions and contextual constraints can be viewed as aspects of people's networks of interdependency or figurations. Taking a figurational approach to making (sociological) sense of the ideological themes permeating physical education teachers' 'philosophies' necessitated a shift of focus away from what has hitherto been an undue concentration on the justificatory ideas – the academic philosophies of physical education – towards a closer examination of the networks of relationships in which physical education teachers, as practitioners, were enmeshed and which formed the essential context for understanding their everyday 'philosophies'.

It was apparent from my research that physical education teachers tended not to have anything that could justifiably be called a 'philosophy', in the sense of an integrated, coherent set of ideas. Confusion and/or contradiction frequently characterized their commentaries. In setting out their thoughts about physical education, teachers typically articulated a kind of check-list of preferences revolving around words and phrases like 'enjoyment', 'health', 'skills' and 'sport for all'. What they exhibited were commitments to particular ideologies, such as health promotion and sports performance and, frequently, a medley of ideologies to suit particular practical situations. If one were to be kind, one might describe these views in terms of what Reid refers to as 'value pluralism' – a multiplicity of justifications for physical education based on a plurality of values such as health, sports performance and character-development.[29] However, in reality, physical education teachers' views were a pastiche of differing 'philosophies' or, rather, ideologies (for example, regarding participation in lessons, health, personal and social education, school teams, sports performance and sporting skills) that were not always, or at least not easily, reconcilable. Rather than representing a plurality of values, physical education teachers seized upon things for justification; that is to say, they sought *ex post-facto* justifications for the things they did and the things they preferred or felt constrained to do.

The 'philosophies' of physical education teachers are not, then, philosophical as such. Rather they are, more usually, an amalgam of beliefs, values and attitudes – of ideologies – that emerge from a figuration of the teachers' personal and sporting biographies and their working context. What Reid refers to as 'metatheoretical uncertainty' to describe the 'plurality' of competing 'philosophies' among physical education teachers,[30] would – from a figurational sociological perspective – be better described as a fusion of prior values, beliefs and commitments, more-or-less permeated and amended in accordance with experience and more-or-less adapted to fit the practical constraints of the day-to-day job of teaching. The ways in which the teachers in the study thought about physical education had been shaped by their past experiences and had become bound up with the job itself. As such, theirs tended to be *practical* 'philosophies'. Accordingly, an abiding theme of my research has been the claim that in order to make sense of physical education teachers' 'philosophies', one must recognize that people can only be understood – or, to couch the point in Eliasian terms, physical education teachers only emerge as people – when their views are seen in the context of their time and related to the framework of their period.[31]

In this vein, teachers' thoughts on physical education need to be viewed as aspects of their networks of social relationships, past and present. The figurations of which individuals are a part have immense significance for their nascent identities: 'People model their ideas about all their experiences chiefly on their experiences within their own groups.'[32] And, because personal and collective identities are particularly important in the world of sport,[33] and because sport lies at the heart of physical education, the networks of physical educationalists (whether teachers or academics) can be said to be of particular significance for a sociological attempt to construct an adequate explanation of their 'philosophies'. It was Elias's contention that each person develops their own individual and unique habitus as well as a series of social habituses – such as gender habituses – which are shared with others who have been habituated through similar experiences.[34] In this regard, Elias often spoke of social habitus to refer to the 'level of personality characteristics which individuals share in common with fellow members of their social groups'.[35] Physical education teachers' thoughts, as well as their proffered practices, are characterized by degrees of involvement and detachment, not least in terms of the ties that bind them to particular we-groups – ranging from school physical education departments (at the professional level) to particular sporting communities, such as sports clubs, or sporting forms. As a result, teachers are more-or-less susceptible to the compulsion of the figuration of which they are a part.

My research also demonstrated the need to appreciate the manner in which physical education teachers' work is circumscribed by wider social processes (such as the medicalization of life and the professionalization of work). Whether they realize it or not, whether they like it or not, physical education teachers are caught up in broader unplanned social processes, such as the medicalization of life, over which they have little control but which may constrain their work in important ways. More directly, they are heavily immersed in wider professional processes, such as the academicization of (nominally) practical subjects such as physical education. The upshot of these processes is that physical education teachers frequently feel themselves compelled to do things – such as develop health-related education and examinations in physical education – and have to find some way (frequently retrospectively) to justify their actions. In this regard, physical education teachers' 'philosophies' are better viewed, it is argued, as *justificatory ideologies*.

Of course, aspects of physical education teachers' 'philosophies' may, to a greater or lesser extent, be related to factual knowledge of a broadly scientific, even philosophical, kind. More often, however, they tend to be an amalgam of values, beliefs and pragmatism and, thus, frequently share one thing in common: a tendency to rely on theoretical knowledge as a 'prop' for a preferred way of seeing the world. Consequently, it is argued that much of the 'knowledge' that constitutes physical education teachers' 'philosophies' is, in fact, ideological and, as such, is more-or-less mythical. Ideologies, as Dunning says of theories in general, 'become fashionable for a greater or lesser period of time for extra-scientific reasons',[36] and, as Elias has noted, frequently this leads to an 'uncritical submission to the authority and prestige of the dominant standards'.[37] In physical education such dominant tendencies are perhaps most evident in the form of the widespread reification of 'traditional physical education' with competitive team games at its core. As de Swaan notes in relation to religion,[38] so we might also note in relation to physical education that there are ideologies which are inherited and used by practitioners to orientate themselves to their professional situations. Particular ideologies endure in the physical education subject-community partly because people believe in the ideas contained within them (for example, the health benefits of sport) and partly because they assume that other people believe them too. These beliefs are most likely to take root, we might add, when and where physical education teachers need 'props' on which to support their preferred views and practices – particularly when the beliefs are more-or-less in tune with teachers' intuitions. Physical education teachers, like others – de Swaan points to priests in this regard – tend to follow the ideology that is available to them whilst adapting it to incorporate their own preferences and practices.

Much of the 'knowledge' incorporated into, and thus constituent of, physical education teachers' 'philosophies' is, in fact, ideological; that is to say, it is by degrees more-or-less mythical, more-or-less false, more-or-less distorted. Whilst in the late twentieth century ideologies *per se* may be said to 'have absorbed a good deal of factual. . . knowledge'[39] they are, nonetheless, best viewed as located along a continuum between involvement and detachment.[40] From this perspective, Dunning observes that whilst ideologies 'differ in their degrees of reality-congruence. . . they always. . . contain a mythical component',[41] making them what Elias termed 'an amalgam of realistic observations and collective fantasies'.[42] From such a perspective, it is clear that when physical education teachers reveal their thoughts on the purposes of their subject, these thoughts 'bear the stamp of higher. . . (or) lesser detachment or involvement'[43] and, in the process, reveal varying degrees of 'reality-congruence'. Thus, involvement-detachment is a particularly useful way of making sense of, and explaining, the continuum of more-or-less mythical or reality-congruent, more-or-less involved or detached, knowledge[44] reflected in the 'philosophies' and practices of physical education teachers, teacher-trainers and academics and the ideologies underpinning these.

With regard to the process of conducting research (particularly qualitative research) into physical education, issues of involvement-detachment are particularly pertinent, for much research into the subject still tends to involve (ex-) physical educationalists investigating the beliefs and practices of other physical educationalists and sports scientists. It is self-evident to sociologists that perceptions regarding the usefulness and nature of research problems are inevitably grounded in values and beliefs acquired by the researcher during his/her life-course. This remains, however, a particular problem when researching physical education, given the particularly deep attachments to sport and physical activity physical educationalists (including the researchers) are likely to have developed and the resultant bonds with the subject that this is likely to have encouraged. It is worth remembering that, as Dunning reminds us, it is not possible to obtain complete detachment. It is, therefore, more accurate to say that movement of this kind – along the involvement-detachment continuum towards a greater degree of detachment and towards a blend of the two most likely to generate reality congruent data – is a desirable feature of any systematic study and particularly sociological studies of physical education.

At the same time, however, it is crucial when studying physical education to appreciate that *complete* detachment on the part of the researcher is neither achievable nor, for that matter, desirable. One of the benefits of possessing 'insider' knowledge and experience can be a deepened appreciation of relevant issues as well as a heightened sensitivity towards the perceptions of those under scrutiny. This is particularly true with physical education. 'Insider knowledge' may range from relatively straightforward matters – including the meaning and significance of what might be termed 'insider language' or terminology (for example, 'health-related exercise' or 'games for understanding') – to more fluid and complex balances between involvement and detachment[45] that enable the researcher to be on his or her 'guard' for fluctuating responses – from both the interviewer and interviewee – to topics and questions to which they may have more or less emotional orientations, such as the relatively marginal professional status of their subject, the place of games in the physical education curriculum, the relative value of extra-curricular inter-school team sport and their role in the identification of 'gifted and talented' young sports men and women. All in all, the process of considering the issue of involvement-detachment holds out the promise to the researcher of gaining greater control over his/her emotional involvement which might, in turn, be expected to lead to the development of a more realistic or adequate analysis of the processes of physical education.

Conclusion

Eric Dunning is fond of describing himself as working in the shadows of Norbert Elias's work. Eric's modesty runs the risk, however, of vastly undervaluing his own contribution to sociology of sport. His contribution to the area has been such that he could properly lay claim to be a founding father of the sub-discipline of sports sociology. Whilst it is true that Dunning's work draws upon Elias's theory, such a statement underplays the extent to which his own work develops Eliasian sociology through the medium of sport. I would go one step further. My involvement in physical education – firstly as a teacher, then as an academic – has brought home to me two things. Firstly, the persistence amongst physical educationalists (as well, one might add, as the sports lobby, the media and government) of a tendency towards holding a one-sided, uncritical perception of sport as an unambiguously 'good', 'wholesome' and 'healthy' – in both a physical and moral sense – activity that is reflective of the nineteenth-century public school *mens sana in corpore sano* ethos.[46] And secondly, the need for a more properly sociological understanding of the process that is physical education, research into which remains, to a significant degree, dominated by feelings and imaginings.

In conclusion, it is unlikely that those of us researching or studying physical education, whether as students, teachers or academics, can hope or expect to make much headway towards a more properly sociological, and more adequate, understanding of this significant aspect of the schooling process without learning the lessons that are there for all of us to see in Eric Dunning's sociology of sport.

Notes

I'd also like to take this opportunity to offer my sincere thanks to Ivan Waddington not only for his invaluable comments on this and many other papers but also for the academic and professional support and guidance he has provided over the years, as both a teacher and a colleague.

[1] Dunning, *Sport Matters*, 12.
[2] See, for example, Colquhoun and Kirk, 'Investigating the Problematic Relationship Between Health and Physical Education'; Dewar and Lawson, 'The Subjective Warrant and Recruitment into Physical Education'; Evans and Davies, 'Sociology, Schooling and Physical Education'; Evans and Williams, 'Moving Up and Getting Out'; Lawson, 'Toward a Model of Teacher Socialization in Physical Education'; Lawson, 'Occupational Socialization, Cultural Studies and the Physical Education Curriculum'; Schempp, 'Apprenticeship-of-Observation and the Development of Physical Education Teachers'; Templin and Schempp, *Socialisation into Physical Education*.
[3] See, for example, Chen and Ennis, 'Teaching Value-Laden Curricula in Physical Education'; Colquhoun, 'Health Based Physical Education'; Colquhoun, 'Technocratic Rationality'; Evans, 'Defining A Subject'; Evans, 'A Short Paper About People, Power and Educational Reform'; Evans, Davies, and Penney, 'Teachers, Teaching and the Social Construction of Gender'; Fejgin, 'The Academicization of Physical Education Teacher Training'; Kirk, *Defining Physical Education*; Kirk, *Schooling Bodies*; Penney and Evans, *Politics, Policy and Practice in Physical Education*; Placek *et al.* 'Teaching Recruits' Physical Education Backgrounds and Beliefs About Purposes for their Subject Matter'; Scraton, *Shaping up to Womanhood*; Tinning, 'Problem-Setting and Ideology'.
[4] See, for example, Curtner-Smith, 'The Occupational Socialization of a First-Year Physical Education Teacher'; Curtner-Smith and Meek, 'Teachers' Value-Orientations'; Evans, 'Making a Difference?'; Evans, Davies and Wright, *Body, Knowledge and Control*; Gard and Wright, 'Managing Uncertainty'.
[5] Armour, 'Learning from Each Other'.
[6] Lawson, 'Toward a Model of Teacher Socialization'; Lawson, 'Occupational Socialization'.
[7] Curtner-Smith, 'The More Things Change, the More They Stay the Same'.
[8] Capel, 'Teachers, Teaching and Pedagogy in Physical Education'.
[9] Green, 'Understanding Physical Education Teachers' Lives', 260.
[10] Evans, 'Defining A Subject'; Evans, 'Making a Difference?'; Evans, Davies and Wright, *Body, Knowledge and Control*; Gard and Wright, 'Managing Uncertainty'; Kirk, *Defining Physical Education*; Kirk, *Schooling Bodies*; Kirk and Tinning, *Physical Education, Curriculum and Culture*; Shilling, 'The Body, Schooling and Social Inequalities'.
[11] Dunning, *Sport Matters*, 12–13.
[12] Ibid.
[13] McNamee, 'Philosophy and Physical Education'; McNamee, 'The Nature and Values of Physical Education'.
[14] Green, *Physical Education Teachers on Physical Education*.
[15] Amade-Escot, 'The Three Cornerstones'.
[16] Macdonald, 'Physical Education's Challenge'.
[17] Talbot, Oral response.
[18] Hardman, Oral response.
[19] Van Deventer, 'Post-Berlin Summit Developments'.
[20] Bailey, 'Sport in Education'.
[21] Penney and Chandler, 'Physical Education: What Future(s)?', 85.
[22] Armour and Jones, *Physical Education Teachers' Lives and Careers*. 140.
[23] Armour, 'Developing a Personal Philosophy'.

[24] Dowling-Naess, 'Sharing Stories'; Dowling-Naess, 'Narratives About Young Men and Masculinities in Organised Sport'.
[25] Armour and Jones, *Physical Education Teachers' Lives and Careers*, 107.
[26] Ibid., 139.
[27] Dunning, 'Figurational Sociology and the Sociology of Sport'.
[28] Dunning, *Sport Matters*, 240.
[29] Reid, 'Value Pluralism and Physical Education'.
[30] Reid, 'Folk Psychology', 103.
[31] Elias, *Mozart*.
[32] Elias, *What is Sociology?*
[33] Dunning, 'On Problems of the Emotions in Sport and Leisure'.
[34] Dunning, 'Figurational Contributions to the Sociological Study of Sport'.
[35] Mennell, *Norbert Elias*, 30.
[36] Dunning, 'Figurational Sociology and the Sociology of Sport', 187.
[37] Elias, cited in Mennell and Goudsblom, *Norbert Elias*, 231.
[38] de Swaan, *Human Societies*.
[39] Elias,cited in Mennell and Goudsblom, *Norbert Elias*, 32.
[40] Ibid.
[41] Dunning, 'Figurational Sociology and the Sociology of Sport', 178.
[42] Elias, cited in Mennell and Goudsblom, 227.
[43] Ibid., 218.
[44] Elias, 'Problems of Involvement and Detachment'; Elias, *What is Sociology?*
[45] Dunning, 'Figurational Sociology and the Sociology of Sport', 178.
[46] Dunning and Waddington, 'Sport as a Drug and Drugs in Sport'.

References

Amade-Escot, C. "The Three Cornerstones of Quality Physical Education." Paper presented at the Pre-Olympic Conference, Thessaloniki, Greece 6–11 Aug. 2004.
Armour, K. "Developing a Personal Philosophy on the Nature and Purpose of Physical Education: Life History Reflections of Physical Education Teachers at City Limits High School." *European Physical Education Review* 3, no. 1 (1997): 68–82.
Armour, K. "Learning from Each Other: Compensatory Professional Development in Physical Education." Paper presented at the 2004 Pre-Olympic Conference, Thessaloniki, Greece, Aug. 2004. 6–11.
Armour, K. and R. Jones. *Physical Education Teachers' Lives and Careers: PE, Sport and Educational Status*. Basingstoke: The Falmer Press, 1998.
Bailey, R. "Sport in Education. Project Overview and Main Findings." Paper presented at the 2004 Pre-Olympic Conference, Thessaloniki, Greece, 6–11 Aug. 2004.
Capel, S. "Teachers, Teaching and Pedagogy in Physical Education." In *Physical Education: Essential Issues*, edited by K. Green and K. Hardman. London: Sage, 2004, pp. 111–27.
Chen, A. and C. Ennis. "Teaching Value-Laden Curricula in Physical Education." *Journal of Teaching in Physical Education* 15, no. 3 (1996): 338–54.
Colquhoun, D. "Health Based Physical Education: The Ideology of Healthism and Victim Blaming." *Physical Education Review* 14, no. 1 (1991): 5–13.
Colquhoun, D. "Technocratic Rationality and the Medicalisation of the Physical Education Curriculum." *Physical Education Review* 15, no. 1 (1992): 5–12.
Colquhoun, D. and D. Kirk. "Investigating the Problematic Relationship Between Health and Physical Education: An Australian Study." *Physical Education Review* 10, no. 2 (1987): 100–9.

Curtner-Smith, M. "The More Things Change, the More They Stay the Same: Factors Influencing Teachers' Interpretations and Delivery of the National Curriculum Physical Education." *Sport, Education and Society* 4, no. 1 (1999): 75–97.

Curtner-Smith, M. "The Occupational Socialization of a First-Year Physical Education Teacher with a Teaching Orientation." *Sport, Education and Society* 6, no. 1 (2001): 81–105.

Curtner-Smith, M. and G. Meek. "Teachers' Value-Orientations and their Compatibility with the National Curriculum for Physical Education." *European Physical Education Review* 6, no. 1 (2000): 27–45.

de Swaan, A. *Human Societies: An Introduction*. Cambridge: Polity Press, 2001.

Dewar, A. M. and H. A. Lawson. "The Subjective Warrant and Recruitment into Physical Education." *Quest* 30, no. 1 (1984): 15–25.

Dowling-Naess, F. "Narratives About Young Men and Masculinities in Organised Sport in Norway." *Sport, Education and Society* 6, no. 2 (2001): 125–42.

Dowling-Naess, F. "Sharing Stories about the Dialectics of Self and Structure in Teacher Socialization: Revisiting a Norwegian Physical Educator's Life History." *European Physical Education Review* 7, no. 1 (2001): 44–60.

Dunning, E. "Figurational Sociology and the Sociology of Sport." *Theories of Sport*. Leicester: MSc Sociology of Sport course module, Centre for Research into Sport and Society, University of Leicester, 1992.

Dunning, E. "Figurational Sociology and the Sociology of Sport: Some Concluding Remarks." In *Sport and Leisure in the Civilizing Process: Critique and Counter-Critique*, edited by E. Dunning and C. Rojek. Basingstoke: MacMillan, 1992, pp. 221–84.

Dunning, E. "On Problems of the Emotions in Sport and Leisure: Critical and Counter-Critical Comments on the Conventional and Figurational Sociologies of Sport and Leisure." *Leisure Studies* 15, no. 3 (1996): 188.

Dunning, E. *Sport Matters. Sociological Studies of Sport, Violence and Civilization*. London: Routledge, 1999.

Dunning, E. "Figurational Contributions to the Sociological Study of Sport." In *Theory, Sport and Society*, edited by J. Maguire and K. Young. Oxford: Elsevier Science, 2002, pp. 211–38.

Dunning, E. and I. Waddington. "Sport as a Drug and Drugs in Sport: Some Exploratory Comments." *International Review for the Sociology of Sport* 38, no. 3 (2003): 351–68.

Elias, N. "Problems of Involvement and Detachment." *British Journal of Sociology* 7, no. 2 (1956): 226–52.

———. *What is Sociology?* London: Hutchinson, 1978.

———. *Mozart. Portrait of a Genius*. Cambridge: Polity Press, 1993.

Evans, J. "Defining A Subject: The Rise and Rise of the New PE?" *British Journal of Sociology of Education* 11, no. 2 (1990): 155–69.

Evans, J. "A Short Paper About People, Power and Educational Reform. Authority and Representation in Ethnographic Research. Subjectivity, Ideology and Educational Reform: The Case of Physical Education." In *Research in Physical Education and Sport*, edited by A. C. Sparkes. London: The Falmer Press, 1992, pp. 231–47.

Evans, J. "Making a Difference? Education and "Ability" in Physical Education." *European Physical Education Review* 10, no. 1 (2004): 95–108.

Evans, J. and B. Davies. "Sociology, Schooling and Physical Education." In *Physical Education, Sport and Schooling. Studies in the Sociology of Physical Education*, edited by J. Evans. Lewes: The Falmer Press, 1986, pp. 11–17.

Evans, J. and T. Williams. "Moving Up and Getting Out: The Classed and Gendered Opportunities of Physical Education Teachers." In *Socialization into Physical Education: Learning to Teach*, edited by T. Templin and P. Schempp. Indianapolis: Benchmark Press, 1989, pp. 235–51.

Evans, J., B. Davies, and D. Penney. "Teachers, Teaching and the Social Construction of Gender." *Sport, Education and Society* 1, no. 2 (1996): 165–84.

Evans, J., Davies, B. and Wright, J., eds. *Body, Knowledge and Control*. London: Routledge, 2003.

Fejgin, N. "The Academicization of Physical Education Teacher Training: A Discourse Analysis Case Study." *International Review for the Sociology of Sport* 30, no. 2 (1995): 179–90.

Gard, M. and J. Wright. "Managing Uncertainty: Obesity Discourse and Physical Education in a Risk Society." *Studies in Philosophy and Education* 20, no. 4 (2001): 535–49.

Green, K. "Understanding Physical Education Teachers' Lives, "Philosophies" and Practices: The Benefits of a Sociological Approach." *European Journal of Physical Education* 5, no. 2 (2000): 260.

———. *Physical Education Teachers on Physical Education. A Sociological Perspective on Philosophies and Ideologies*. Chester: Chester Academic Press, 2003.

Hardman, K. Oral response to papers presented on the theme 'Post-Berlin Summit Developments in School Physical Education', at the Pre-Olympic Conference, Thessaloniki, Greece, 6–11 Aug. 2004.

Kirk, D. *Defining Physical Education*. London: The Falmer Press, 1992.

Kirk, D. *Schooling Bodies. School Practice and Public Discourse 1880–1950*. London: Leicester University Press, 1998.

Kirk, D. and R. Tinning, eds. *Physical Education, Curriculum and Culture: Critical Issues in the Contemporary Crisis*. London: The Falmer Press, 1990.

Lawson, H.A. "Toward a Model of Teacher Socialization in Physical Education: The Subjective Warrant, Recruitment and Teacher Education." *Journal of Teaching in Physical Education* 2, no. 1 (1983): 3–16.

Lawson, H.A. "Occupational Socialization, Cultural Studies and the Physical Education Curriculum." *Journal of Teaching in Physical Education* 7, no. 3 (1988): 265–88.

Macdonald, D. "Physical Education's Challenge: Choosing The Right Purposes." Paper Presented at the Pre-Olympic Conference, Thessaloniki, Greece, 6–11 Aug. (2004).

McNamee, M. "Philosophy and Physical Education: Analysis, Epistemology and Axiology." *European Physical Education Review* 4, no. 1 (1998): 75–91.

McNamee, M. "The Nature and Values of Physical Education." In *Physical Education: Essential Issues*, edited by K. Green and K. Hardman. London: Sage, 2004: 1–20.

Mennell, S. *Norbert Elias. An Introduction*. Dublin: University Of Dublin Press, 1992.

Mennell, S. and J. Goudsblom, eds. *Norbert Elias. On Civilization, Power and Knowledge*. Chicago: University of Chicago Press, 1998.

Penney, D. and T. Chandler. "Physical Education: What Future(s)?" *Sport, Education and Society* 5, no. 1 (2000): 71–87.

———. and J. Evans. *Politics, Policy and Practice in Physical Education*. London: E & FN Spon, 1999.

Placek, J., P. Dodds, S. Doolittle, P. Portman, T. Ratliffe, and K. Pinkham. "Teaching Recruits' Physical Education Backgrounds and Beliefs About Purposes for their Subject Matter." *Journal of Teaching in Physical Education* 14, no. 3 (1995): 246–61.

Reid, A. "Value Pluralism and Physical Education." *European Physical Education Review* 3, no. 1 (1997): 6–20.

Reid, A. "Folk Psychology Neuroscience and Explanation in Physical Education." *European Physical Education Review* 5, no. 2 (1999): 101–20.

Schempp, P. G. "Apprenticeship-of-Observation and the Development of Physical Education Teachers." In *Socialisation into Physical Education: Learning to Teach*, edited by T. J. Templin and P. G. Schempp. Indiana: Benchmark Press, 1989, pp. 13–37.

Scraton, S. *Shaping up to Womanhood. Gender and Girls' Physical Education*. Buckingham: Open University Press, 1992.

Shilling, C. "The Body, Schooling and Social Inequalities: Physical Capital and the Politics of Physical Education." In *Physical Education: A Reader*, edited by K. Green and K. Hardman. Aachen: Meyer and Mayer, 1998, pp. 243–71.

Talbot, M. Oral response to papers presented on the theme, 'Post-Berlin Summit Developments in School Physical Education'. Pre-Olympic Conference, Thessaloniki, Greece. 6–11 Aug. 2004

Templin, T. J. and P. G. Schempp, eds. *Socialisation into Physical Education: Learning to Teach.* Indiana: Benchmark Press, 1989.

Tinning, R. "Problem-Setting and Ideology in Health Based Physical Education: An Australian Perspective." *Physical Education Review* 14, no. 1 (1991): 40–9.

Van Deventer, K. J. "Post-Berlin Summit Developments in School Physical Education – A South African Perspective." Paper presented at the Pre-Olympic Conference, Thessaloniki, Greece, 6–11 Aug. 2004.

Illusio in Sport

Alain Garrigou

Is the sociology of sport and leisure becoming a sociology of labour? Whilst the sub-discipline is becoming increasingly mainstream, the very nature of sport is itself changing rapidly. It may, therefore, be time to take a radical point of view: are we right to refer to an activity as a sport when it has more similarities with work than it does with other leisure activities? These developments in sport should not, however, reduce the importance of its sociological study. On the contrary, to some extent the success of the sub-discipline may reflect and depend on the existence of these changes. In a paper originally published in 1972, Eric Dunning noted that, until that time, the study of sport as a pastime tended to reduce sport to merely an 'adjunct of work'.[1] In this paper, and in a later paper published in their joint names, Elias and Dunning argued the case for a new understanding of sport which went beyond the simple work-leisure dichotomy, and which located sport within a broader, all encompassing spectrum of leisure, spare-time and work. The value of this approach has become more apparent as sport has become increasingly professionalized. Whilst the professionalization of sport has changed the link between sport and work, the concepts and the way of thinking developed by Elias and Dunning enable sport to remain comprehensible despite its recent and radical change.

As a particular kind of work, sport needs to be observed in its many and varied aspects. Not only do we need to focus on those athletes who, by embracing professionalization, emerge as champions, but also on the many technicians, physicians and coaches who work 'behind the scenes' to generate the performances necessary for high level competition. We need to focus also on the growing significance of the economic aspects of sports performance, the transformation of the 'raw material' of athletic ability by a specialized industry, and the changing organizational structure of commercial sporting bodies, with management and ownership structures that integrate sport more and more into the realms of the capitalist economy. Moreover, it might be argued that even amateur sport as a pastime has developed in ways which mean that it has become less of a leisure activity and more of a complement to work, for example when it is consciously played as a means of improving one's capacities to 'perform' in one's job. The so-called 'fitness industry' is probably the best example of this development. It should also be noted that in sport, as in other social activities, the social uses and meanings ascribed by individuals generate a variety of practices; indeed, it may be that the increasing differentiation in the social uses and meanings of sport and physical activity is an increasingly important aspect of sport in modern societies.

If we consider the 'spare-time spectrum', it is clear that, for some people, sport is not leisure but work. For some participants sport, therefore, has become very distinct from leisure. For those for whom sport becomes work, the mechanisms which generate tension-excitement, as identified by Elias and Dunning, may not apply.[2] For others, sport may belong to what Elias and Dunning referred to as 'intermediary spare-time activities mainly serving recurrent needs for orientation and/or self-fulfilment and self-expansion';[3] that is to say, some aspects of sport have become analytically distinct from leisure activities. This raises a number of important questions: if sport has shifted within the spare-time spectrum, has people's interest in sport also modified? What kinds of excitement can sport provide if it becomes increasingly like a form of work? The future of sport, I would argue, is greatly dependent on the social functions it performs, and on how these functions change over time.

Most of those who study sport – and Eric Dunning for one – do so partly because they enjoy sport on a social level, in their spare-time or leisure. Even at this level, however, the increasing competitiveness of sporting activities identified by Elias and Dunning has long been evident. It might be argued that this increasing competitiveness, and in particular the development of a 'win at all costs' mentality, poses a threat to sport as a valued social activity, and one response to this threat seems to have been to try to preserve a core of traditional sporting values, even though it must be recognized that, in their current form, it is unlikely that such values will flourish. However, the future of sport is less clear if changes lead to the destruction of the *illusio* by which players and spectators are involved and which sustains their interest.

According to the concept derived from Johan Huizinga[4] and developed by Pierre Bourdieu, *illusio* refers to one's interest in the game in a general sense and not in a specific economic sense. More precisely, Huizinga used the word *illusio* to mean 'to enter into the game'. Whilst Huizinga may have extended the use of the word to encompass the 'universe of deep seriousness', he did not systematically explore a sociology of involvement in the way that Bourdieu has done. For Bourdieu, '*Illusio* is the opposite of ataraxy: it means to be involved, taken in the game'. Moreover, for Bourdieu, to be involved, to be interested in the game, 'is to admit a special social game has sense, its stakes are important and worthy of being pursued'.[5] Bourdieu pointed out that every social field generates its own interest – for instance, in literature in the nineteenth century, when the principle of pure art was expressly built up partly in opposition to economic interests.[6] Nevertheless, there continues to be a special enigma in a game or sport. The *illusio* of sport is so special because of sport's 'unreal' or fictitious nature. We can better understand this special *illusio* if we analyze how it works in practice and, when sport ceases to be leisure and becomes a form of work, how *illusio* no longer functions, or at least how it changes significantly.

During the 2002 Tour de France, Lance Armstrong, winner of three previous tours and once again the rider holding the leader's yellow jersey, complained about the roadside spectators who, throughout the Tour, had shouted accusations of doping at him. Nobody was obliged to attend the race, he argued, their attendance and emotional involvement were voluntary. The insults, he seemed to believe, addressed the whole race and perhaps even the whole of cycling, but he did not feel that they were especially directed at him. Most importantly, however, his reaction to these incidents highlights the logical inconsistency of people who, whilst clearly interested in the 'show', and thus clearly influenced by the illusion of the sport, also believed that if the sport was not, to some extent, fixed, then it was certainly not being conducted in the way that it was purported to be.

Sport, like every social field, generates its own *illusio* but this level of interest rests on sport being a 'real' game, not a metaphor or a window onto another social milieu. In this sense, the sportive illusion is paradoxical because it is a belief based on the idea that sport is played for its own sake rather than for material rewards, that sport represents freedom and fun, that it is an essentially superficial activity played for pleasure, for beauty and so on. In a world of self-interest, sport is unusual in that its significance is singular and not related to external goals or benefits. One might say that we take part in sport simply for sport's sake.

For some people standing outside a game, not involved in its proceedings and/or unfamiliar with its rules and customs, sport can be incomprehensible. This might be described as a complete absence of *illusio*, and in such a situation the game, and participants' and spectators' enthusiasm for it, looks quite odd. People who do not understand or who do not like football, for example, may describe it as just 22 people fighting over a pig's bladder! For those who have an emotional commitment to a sports event, the interest is nevertheless bounded in a particular way. People cannot afford to disregard many other important aspects of their lives, for example work, money and perhaps even politics. Even if no *illusio* is constant, sport *illusio* is very special because, unlike most other social situations, sport is a social sphere in which we can display ecstatic and vociferous emotions; we can laugh in the stands and return to more normal modes of emotional expression as soon as the referee's whistle signals the end of the contest. Moreover, we can assume that the 'show', the score and the shouts of the fans have no 'real' or lasting importance. The common expression, 'it's only a game', highlights this split in consciousness and the divide between sport and the 'real' world. Elias and Dunning argued that this characteristic of leisure activities is what makes them so socially significant in modern societies; that is to say leisure pursuits, and sports in particular, provide opportunities for a 'controlled de-controlling of emotional controls'.[7]

People who devote themselves to sport are sometimes perceived as taking their passion and interest to extremes. Indeed, if a person spends what is considered by most other people to be too great a proportion of their life in a sportive *illusio*, they may be suspected of having pathological problems. This does not only apply to the sometimes addictive practice of gambling but, more generally, to the world of sporting contests. In this context, it should be noted that the term 'fan' derives from the word fanatic, which itself has connotations of emotional extremism. In Bali, Clifford Geertz noticed how discredited 'serious gamblers' were compared to those involved in the 'deep play' in cockfights.[8] Whilst this illusion of sport may arouse a common involvement amongst participants, it is an involvement which is both confined and delimited. As Huizinga pointed out, 'The player can abandon himself body and soul to the game, and the consciousness of its being "merely" a game can be thrust into the background'.[9] However, as we might say after particularly enjoying ourselves, a moment comes when it is necessary to 'come back down to earth' – that is to say, to resume living in the 'real world' – because, Huizinga argued:

> The play-mood is *labile* [unstable] in its very nature. At any moment 'ordinary life' may reassert its rights, either by an impact from without, which interrupts the game, or by an offence against the rules, or else from within, by a collapse of play spirit, a sobering, a disenchantment.[10]

However, the involvement of professional men and women in sport alters the dynamics of this process. For the professional athlete, sport can hardly be differentiated from work since it is work, and consequently their commitment to participation changes. Who can separate their interest in the financial side of a competition and their interest in winning for its own sake? It has often been noticed that the behaviour expressed by sportsmen and women in victory and defeat – whether of happiness or sadness – varies little between professionals and amateurs. Of course there is no incompatibility between different kinds of incentives, sportive as well as social; one can aim both for victory for the sake of playing the game whilst also being aware of the financial rewards associated with a victory earned in the course of one's work. In practice these motives are closely intertwined.

However, this linkage between sporting and financial rewards tends to break down when supporters condemn the 'abuse' of money in sport. Some may announce, for instance, that they will no longer pay high and rising entrance fees to attend events. In many cases this threat is not carried out. Nevertheless, some resentment remains against athletes who are perceived to be 'too well paid', particularly if these sportsmen and women go on to give the impression of workers who are not trying their hardest or producing their best performance. Usually, however, winning is enough to sweep away every reproach; *illusio* is maintained.

The presence of *illusio*, however, is rather more endangered by the illicit use of drugs in sport. If some athletes take drugs and others don't, the competition is unfair. Yet it may be argued that if everybody takes drugs, the contest is transformed from a test of sporting ability to a test of technological sophistication (and few would be interested to see which chemical laboratory, or which physician, was the best). Consequently, either the contest is no longer fair (as in a situation where doping is widespread though not universal, a situation that many suspect exists today), or it is no longer a sporting contest. But can the situation ever be as clear-cut as this suggests?

In 1998, when the Festina affair (trapped with drugs in a police control, the trainer confessed a general use of doping) initiated great public suspicion about the sport of professional cycling, the central questioned posed was whether it was merely the few who were cheats or, alternatively, whether the culture of doping in cycling was inherent to the sport. These two positions are radically different in terms of their implications for cheating. For example if, as some writers have argued,[11] almost everyone was taking illegal performance enhancing drugs, could their actions really be described as cheating? For business interests such as sponsors and media companies, a different question was raised: should their companies continue to associate their trademark with a sport so heavily scrutinized and so apparently corrupted and with a race which was widely perceived by the public to be closely associated with drug use? Behind the scenes, long discussions were held on this subject. For strategic reasons, companies initially adopted a cautious approach. These businesses could not protest too loudly about the state of the sport, for to plead total ignorance of doping in the sport either lacked credibility, or made the company look naive. It may also have been construed as irresponsible to withdraw support suddenly, without taking sufficient care of their former partners (for example, giving the cycling teams sufficient time to search for new sponsors). But some companies did give warnings, if no actual ultimatums. These companies stated in no uncertain terms that cycling must become clean, or at least clean up its reputation. And for their partners, the cycling teams, it was obvious that, in order to continue receiving financial support, they needed to return to what was perceived to be the old order; that is to say, to return cycling to more closely match the traditional definition of sport. Indeed, it became clear that a ramification of this doping scandal was that the economy of the whole of professional cycling became endangered, as the following comment from an advertising executive shows: 'The trademark (of the company) waited to see if cycling would be able to contain doping and to take measures against previous doping use… 1998 has been a breaking point with previous (practice).'[12] But the scandal of 1998 opened up the question of the *illusio* of cycling and its appeal to the public: would people maintain their former level of interest in the show if nothing is done to address the scandal? If new scandals occur, would spectators continue to believe in the validity of the sport? Cycling has survived but, nevertheless, some races and events find financial support from commercial backers difficult to obtain. The *Tour du Midi Libre*, a French cycle race with a long history, has been cancelled due to a lack of money, while in Spain, two of the more famous teams, Banesto and Once, have withdrawn from the sport.

The reaction of the media to such scandals further reveals the interweaving of sporting and economic interests. Some sports correspondents took great care to avoid issues concerning doping, perhaps in an attempt to protect their sources of information (and therefore their jobs) by remaining friendly with the cycling authorities. Their motivations for pursuing this line might have been because they valued their personal relationships with cycling personnel or - perhaps less likely - simply because they did not believe the stories to be true. However, despite the 'de-amplification' of the story by this section of the media, the doping affairs were too prominent, and too scandalous, for journalists to ignore them completely. Consequently, in the Tours de France hit by doping scandals, a division a labour between the media departments was agreed upon: the sports journalists solely covered the 'sporting' exploits of the cyclists, whilst the news or current affairs departments were involved in providing a more detailed picture of the history and structure of the sport, and the 'external' issues then affecting it. In July 2000 for instance, the reporters of a French TV Channel (FR3) filmed footage of a car from the US Postal team whose driver was attempting to dispose of a bag full of pharmaceutical goods, including phials of Actogevin (a medicine made with extracts of blood, and possessing similar properties to erythropoietin or EPO). This drug was little known at the time, and not prohibited but, perhaps surprisingly, the President of the television channel reacted by questioning the actions of the journalist responsible. The TV channel is one of the main supporters of the Tour de France and there was a clear conflict of interests between the value of an exclusive story, and the Channel's longer-term interest in attracting viewers to their programmes covering the cycling action on the Tour.

In their work, professional athletes cannot adopt the attitude that 'it is only a game.' Sometimes, as a metaphor, they may use these words, but only as a metaphor. The phrase echoes the very reverse idea; that is, it appears to function as a way of compensating for loss or disappointment in relation to something which clearly is *not* 'just a game'. As a consolation in defeat, professional athletes may refer to the recurrent definition of competition by which a given result is never definitive or vital; there is, after all, 'always tomorrow/next week/next year'. Consequently, professional sportspeople operate with an *illusio* involving a double standard; the idea that 'it is only a game' is used to soften the disappointment of defeat in relation to something which is *not* 'just a game' but is also a job – and a special kind of job. For instance, they are probably more or less aware of the possible consequences of being caught taking illegal drugs. Doping threatens both the athlete's social *raison d'être* as well as their income. However, athletes tend to hide this unpleasant fact from themselves. Because of the conditions of their 'workplace', if they want to continue participating in the sport, they essentially have no choice but to accept these conditions. Such questions concerning the consequences of using illegal substances are, therefore, irrelevant. That athletes collectively share this vision is important, for this sub-cultural rationalization helps to overcome the emotional anguish that such a paradoxical situation would otherwise entail. Risks to health are discounted and, if they are real, they concern the distant rather than immediate future. The immorality of breaching the principle of 'fair play' is obviated if it is believed that everybody is acting the same way. The topic of cheating cannot be openly discussed in the athlete's social circle. If doubts arise about the fairness and legitimacy of their activities, they are promptly erased by the requirements of the jobs, requirements of both a professional and a sporting nature. Take, for example, this report from *Le Monde*, "'Without this stuff", defended a previous professional, "I would have remained an average racer. In my time, no one could succeed without doping; it was a rule in the pack. Everybody had to manage. If the racer had no success, the team did not keep him."[13] Whilst some participants complain, and a few of them even embark on a moral crusade against doping, most of them simply accept it and live their sporting career like any other professional in a demanding profession.

The changes in sport in recent years (most notably professionalization and commercialization) have led to a situation where emerging elite performers have increasingly been recruited from the lower social classes who are happy to serve the kind of demanding apprenticeship required. For the higher and middle classes, the chances of success look so small that young talent is often diverted to other career paths which may be no less prestigious, but are likely to have higher rates of success and be more secure. More broadly, in Western nations statistics also show a decrease in the number of sportsmen entering into a range of sports, and especially sports which have been most affected by doping scandals. Correlatively, new champions come from poor countries. This is particularly the case in those sports where the investment of training and effort poses the greatest risks to long-term health. The risks which emerging athletes must assess can be measured either in terms of the amount of work necessary to achieve success, by the conditions in which success might be gained, or by the dangers to health that are inherent to some sports, but not to others (for example, rock climbing as opposed to basketball). Moreover, doping scandals have meant that particular sports, or at least the highest levels of those sports, become stigmatized. Thus many cyclists may, at one time or another, hear allegations and suspicions about their own drug use. Gossip normally focuses on the winners of races and championships and particularly those who come to dominate their sports. Lance Armstrong is a case in point. Consequently, the very role models who formerly attracted new people into the sport may now lead young people to reject sporting careers due to the fear that any success would lead to accusations of doping. This process is compounded by the increasing number of alternative or rival occupational opportunities which have developed as a consequence of the economic growth of the sports sector.

These changes have led sport towards a kind of social reproduction. It is very clear that the decision to invest time and effort in developing a sporting career depends on the broader social context in which that person finds him or herself. A positive decision is more probable in a family which is already involved in, or has a tradition of, sports-work. Even when public scandals produce suspicion about the validity of a competition, professionals are so greatly indebted to the sport that gave them their dream and their successes that they cannot stop having faith in it. For example, they may either believe that the situation and the problems have changed, or that their involvement in the sport will enable changes to be made for the better. The public suspicion of their sport cannot kill the expectations they have for their children, as indicated by the following quotation from a racing cyclist who has been involved in doping and has even been punished: 'I try to watch over his (my son's) entourage as he may make the same mistakes as me if he has the luck to become professional.'[14]

This double standard is not simply a personal characteristic of the people who come to work in sport, but an institutional mind-set which has grown up in the age of professional sport. Despite the many allegations that contests are not fair, and the questioning of officials' values and actions more generally, contemporary sport continues to survive partly because of the lasting hope that things will be better in the future. Even if today a sport cannot claim to be above suspicion, the improvements which may come, it is held, will redeem sport to the degree that it can continue to survive. At the same time, if sports administrators express alarm, thus suggesting the existence of a collective problem, they run the risk of reducing their sport to a minority activity of a few individuals. For instance, after the emergence of doping scandals related to the 2003 World Championships, the President of the International Amateur Athletic Federation, Lamine Diack stated: 'we must reduce this business to its real dimension. In 2002, we made 3,018 controls and found only 85 positive cases. 99 per cent of the athletes are thus clean. Against the cheaters, we'll try to make new arrangements.'[15] The message is clear. There is no alarm if doping concerns so few athletes. However, the problem is made worse because we, the public, cannot have confidence in the doping statistics. The recent scandal over THG (tetrahydrogestrinone) illustrates a well known, but often forgotten fact: tests only find the things for which they look. Consequently, the results of which Diack speaks are not an accurate assessment of doping. Whilst some may be aware of the intellectual inconsistency of Diack's argument, others may be more swayed by the practical nature of this approach which gives sport the best chance of avoiding a great crisis. More accurately than any institutional speeches could portray, the policies adopted by sports governing bodies, such as the creation of WADA (World Anti-Doping Agency), portray a new awareness of the dangers which such drug scandals pose to the long term future of sports and, more particularly, to *illusio* in sport.

Notes

[1] 'Leisure in the Spare-time Spectrum' originally appeared in Albonico and Pfister-Binz, *Sociology of Sport*. A revised version of the paper appears under the duel authorship of Elias and Dunning in *Quest for Excitement*.

[2] The paper, 'Quest for Excitement in Unexciting Societies' was originally presented at the 1967 Annual Conference of the British Sociological Association, held in London. A revised version subsequently appeared in Elias and Dunning, *Quest for Excitement*, 63–90

[3] Elias and Dunning, 'Leisure in the Spare-time Spectrum', 97.

[4] Huizinga, *Homo Ludens*.

[5] Bourdieu and Wacquant, *Réponses*, 92 (author's translation).

[6] Bourdieu, *Les règles de l'art*.

[7] Elias and Dunning, *Quest for Excitement*, 115.

[8] Geertz, 'Deep Play' and *The Interpretation of Cultures*.

[9] Huizinga, *Homo Ludens*, 40 (author's translation).

[10] Ibid.

[11] See for instance, Waddington, *Sport, Health and Drugs*.

[12] *Le Monde*, 29 July 2003 (author's translation).

[13] *Le Monde*, 11–12 May 2003 (author's translation).

[14] Ibid. (author's translation).

[15] *Le Monde*, 6 Nov. 2003 (author's translation).

References

Bourdieu, Pierre. *Les règles de l'art. Genèse et structure du champ littéraire*. Paris: Seuil, 1992.

Bourdieu, P. and L. Wacquant. *Réponses*. Paris: Seuil, 1992.

Elias, Norbert. "Leisure in the Spare-time Spectrum." In *Sociology of Sport: Theoretical Foundations and Research Methods*, edited by R. Albonico and K. Pfister-Binz. Basle: Magglinger Symposium, 1972.

Elias, N. and E. Dunning. *Quest for Excitement: Sport and Leisure in the Civilizing Process*. Oxford: Blackwell, 1986.

Geertz, Clifford. "Deep Play: Notes on the Balinese Cockfight." *Daedalus*, 101 (1972): 1–37.

Geertz, Clifford. *The Interpretation of Cultures*. New York: Basic Books, 1973.

Huizinga, Johan. *Homo Ludens*. Paris: Gallimard, 1951.

Waddington, Ivan. *Sport, Health and Drugs: A Critical Sociological Perspective*. London: Routledge, 2000.

Sports Celebrity and the Civilizing Process

Chris Rojek

'Sociologist of sport' is too limiting. There can be little doubt that Eric Dunning's work in the sociology of sport is seminal. From the late 1950s, his role in persuading fellow academics to take sport seriously qualifies him to be regarded as one of the founding fathers of the subject. In addition he developed novel approaches to the study of the rise of team games like rugby football and soccer, the dynamics of football hooliganism and sport in the Western civilizing process. However, Dunning's work is part of a much broader effort to re-orientate sociology, subjectivity and society to attain a *scientific* understanding of human relations. Together with Johan Goudsblom and Stephen Mennell, Dunning is the senior advocate of the figurational/process approach to sociology pioneered by Norbert Elias.

It is important to grasp the bold scale of ambition of this enterprise. Dunning and his associates muster a good deal of intellectual force in their analysis of sport, society and civilization. Theirs is a holistic approach to the phenomenon of sports which, paradoxically, recognizes the 'partiality' of their own perspective in the sense of acknowledging that their work should be judged as no more than an early stage in the scientific understanding of the sports process. Because Elias's approach makes a virtue of synthesis – from the classical tradition of sociology and comparative, historical and empirical research – it is quite difficult to situate in the history of ideas. Ultimately, it is best understood as a contribution of *scientific humanism*. Elias needed no lessons on the critique of scientism. His writings on science demonstrate the relationship between ideology, science and the reproduction of balance of power relationships between dominant established groups and the rest of society.[1] As a student in Heidelberg and Frankfurt, Elias's intellectual *milieu* was shaped by the liberal, tolerant sociological tradition exemplified above all by the work of Alfred Weber and Karl Mannheim.[2] At its heart was the commitment to put science to the service of human development by demystifying the power of ideology, domination and myth. From an early age, Elias treated science as humanity's best hope for achieving a better future. However, he was arguably more realistic than others in his *milieu* in regarding the goal of accumulating a comprehensive fund of scientific knowledge about society as a long-term task of inter-generational labour. Be that as it may, the humanistic goal of constructing a fund of scientific knowledge that permits purposeful human action to be based on more reality-congruent foundations is one of the hallmarks of process/figurational sociology.

One aspect of Elias's approach is the high value placed upon *testing* propositions by historical and empirical research. From the start, Elias was hugely impatient with idealist philosophy. He held that it was becalmed in the sultry, lotus latitudes of speculation. In his view, it engendered two forms of intellectual impoverishment.

The first of these is to be found in its tendency to conduct debate and research entirely at the level of ideas and propositions. Although these ideas purport to reflect the real world, Elias held that they reify human life. His concept of *zustandsreduktion* means the reduction of everything that is observed and experienced as a process to a static condition. Idealist philosophy is iconic in figurational/process sociology in producing this effect. It obstructs our capacity to orientate our concepts and actions with how things actually are in the world. To this extent it seriously distorts human understanding.

Secondly, its complacent, ultimately imperious refusal to adhere to any responsibility to produce *scientifically* testable knowledge was held to be untenable. Elias believed that sociology should aspire to produce a scientific approach to the study of society. Of course, he recognized that social groups wield science as power. His discussion of established-outsider relationships and his writing on involvement and detachment is, in part, an attempt to contribute to the sociology of this phenomenon.[3] Nonetheless, his commitment to examine social data using a combination of a long-term developmental perspective and comparative analysis showed that social science can produce relatively detached knowledge which is not subject to the charge of social relativism. The figurational/process approach then, is committed to engineering *detachment* from the idealized concepts and idioms of thought and behaviour that predominate in Western society.

All of these features are also prominent in Dunning's work. It is perhaps necessary to insist that an appreciation of Dunning's attachment to the figurational/process approach is indispensable in understanding his contribution to the study of sport. Sport studies is a highly inter-disciplinary field. However, Dunning's involvement in it has always been not merely in the role of a sociologist, but of a sociologist deeply committed to the perspective of a particular school of thought. As a graduate in the late 1950s and early 1960s, his keen interest in sport, especially soccer and cricket, made research into the sociology of sport a natural choice for him. At the same time it should be recognized that an academic interest in questions of culture and consumption was very unfashionable at the time. The institutions and experience of sport and leisure were viewed as subordinate to work. The latter was widely referred to in the sociological literature as 'the central life interest'. Dunning chose to pursue his vocation in the academic sociology of the day in a field that was widely considered to be peripheral, even 'trivial', by the upper echelons within the sociological community. Dunning's contribution will not be correctly assessed unless it is recognized that, from the first, his sociological interest in the field is to test and elaborate the figurational/process perspective. The latter is, in all respects, prior. In some ways he treats sport as a case study in which Elias's arguments are both tested and elaborated. As with Elias, this sense of participation in a preliminary phase of long-term inter-generational labour has bred a degree of single-mindedness in his work. Elias always insisted that his prime responsibility lay in pushing ahead with his work through historical and empirical research. With one or two exceptions,[4] he regarded critical commentary on rival social theories to be a sociological sideshow. This has also been Dunning's position.[5]

Sport and Social Integration

Although Dunning is perhaps best known for his work on football hooliganism and crowd violence, he constantly returns to the functions of sport in social integration. He defines sport as 'a form of non-scripted, largely non-verbal theatre and emotional arousal'.[6] He postulates that sport performs a number of functions of social integration in industrial society. The most important of these are:

(1) *Identity Formation:* sport provides a variety of contest settings in which self-conceptions are articulated and developed and rankings between individuals are established.

(2) *Collective definition:* sport is important in the identification of individuals with collectivities. In process/figurational terminology, sport is one means through which individuals negotiate a balance between autonomy and dependence in the 'We-I balance'.[7]

(3) *Generation and peaceful discharge of aggressive emotions.* It should be noted that this is *not* simple cathartic theory. Sport is one of the 'spectrum' of spare-time activities that enable both the generation and the relatively peaceful discharge

of aggressive emotions. Sports spectatorship is a type of *mimetic leisure,* which enables people to express particular levels of emotional arousal in controlled settings.[8]

(4) *De-routinization:* a long tradition in sociological debate proposes that everyday life is subject to processes of routinization that, at the subjective level of meaning, are experienced as depersonalizing and alienating.[9] Sport and other forms of mimetic leisure allow people to achieve a balance of contrast and variation in their lives and, as such, are release mechanisms for feelings of frustration and inauthenticity.

Dunning approaches the question of social integration at the level of social bonding. Thus, among his examples of the bonds achieved by sports participation and spectatorship in the 'We-I balance' are closer identification between the individual and the city and nation through contest events in national leagues and global competitions such as the Olympics and the World Cups in soccer, cricket and rugby. As with the wider civilizing process, this identification and interweaving of affect and interests is analyzed as an unplanned, unintended process. Needless to say, attributing social bonding at the level of theory is very different from proposing that integration is always realized at the level of practice. The pronounced stress that the figurational/process approach places on the concept of *balance* between autonomy and dependence, arousal and routine, is designed to highlight the conditional nature of integration. A logical possibility in any relationship of balance is that equilibrium may be disrupted by events. Indeed, this emerged as one of the defining themes in Dunning's work with his associates in Leicester on football hooliganism and crowd violence.[10] This research also identified a propensity to soccer hooliganism in the pattern of male aggressiveness found, in the English case at least, in the 'rougher' sections of the working class. Nevertheless, the emphasis upon balance is crucial and is often glossed over in secondary evaluations of the perspective. The perspective has no truck with polarized zero-sum approaches to power and identity. Instead it holds that individuals are always enmeshed with others in complex balance of power relationships which substantiate the notions of both 'individual' and 'society' in social consciousness. Enmeshment is understood to involve social bonding which is both constraining and enabling, as is logically the case with any balance of power relationship.

There are good reasons for this pronounced interest in social bonding and balance. Dunning followed Elias in holding that the idealist tradition contributed to the domination of what Elias called the *Homo clausus* model in debate and research on human relations.[11] The essential feature of this model is the privileging of individual autonomy so that social explanation follows from the decisions and actions of the individual rather than the historical and social context in which the individual is situated. In the terminology of the figurational/process perspective, *Homo clausus* is the parent of a 'we-less I' approach to social and historical investigation.[12] The stress on social *figurations,* and the consistent attempt to reconcile the behaviour of individuals in terms of the chains of interdependence that substantiate both the concept and experience of figurations, can be interpreted as a reaction to the *Homo clausus* model.

It also further illustrates the humanism of the figurational/process approach in as much as the concept of figuration automatically privileges interdependence and, inferentially at least, care for the other, over the notion of personal autonomy.

Viewed critically, it might be said that in some respects it is an *over-reaction*. The notion of the individual is presented as a product of a specific historical process involving a complex of chains of interdependence. The accent is upon elucidating the pattern of historical bonding and social interweaving that elicits the notion of individuality. However, an analysis of the biographies of particular individuals and their historical significance is arguably under-stated. True, Elias wrote at some length about Mozart and Hitler.[13] However, in each case the emphasis in his analysis is upon the social struggles for power and the nature of the historical causal chains that explain the situation and action of the individual.

The issue is even more acute if one considers the figurational/process perspective on the individual as a system of representation possessing general cultural significance. Again it is necessary to add a caveat. Elias's analysis of court society provides a rich analysis of the processes of idealization and denigration that characterized the power structure of absolutism.[14] His thoughts on the role of gesture, winks, nods, hugs, asides and other symbolic expressions in the repertoire of courtly preferment and disfavour in some ways anticipate Erving Goffman's sociology of face-work in urban-industrial society.[15] Arguably, Elias's work is more profound in bypassing the macro-micro divide that haunted American sociology of Goffman's day, instead treating the individual and society as a continuum. Be that as it may, the relative neglect in the figurational/process approach of the problem of the idealization of particular individuals in modern society is something that I wish to address in the rest of this essay. Before doing so, it is necessary to provide more clarification of the characteristic approach to questions of social bonding and individualism in modern society. A pivotal concept in this respect is Elias's notion of functional democratization.

Sport and Functional Democratization

One of the keys in privileging interdependence over autonomy in figurational/process sociology is the concept of functional democratization. Functional democratization refers to the historical tendency for individuals to become more interdependent as specialization in the division of labour and the institutions of normative coercion increases. By the latter term, which is not taken from the figurational/process perspective but from the sociology of Bryan Turner,[16] I mean schools, universities, hospitals, the police, the judiciary, welfare and health organizations, voluntary, labour and professional associations – in short, the network of institutions that emerged in the course of industrial society dedicated to the task of influencing and, when necessary, coercing behaviour into routine, predictable patterns of 'normality'. Functional specialization in the division of labour possesses an elective affinity with democratization because as individuals became more functionally specialized in work their reliance upon each other increased. The development of the division of labour and the gradual replacement of the absolutist state with multi-party states altered 'We-I' balances in fundamental ways. In particular, they weakened the hereditary principle of authority and challenged it with the meritocratic ideal. Accordingly, distinction, honour and power no longer derive primarily from bloodline, but from achievement. Let me elucidate this argument in relation to the figurational/process theory of functional democratization.

According to Elias and his followers, in all societies individuals have been caught up and supported in figurations of greater or lesser complexity. Even in societies that are less developed on economic, social, political and cultural levels, the chains of interdependence that connect people together have always been multiform and complex. The term 'less developed' societies is used here descriptively, not judgementally. It seeks to make the point that the connections between individuals that obtained, for example, seven hundred years ago can be shown by comparative and historical analysis to be unequivocally less complex and less multiform than are the connections between people today. Indeed, Elias's theory of the civilizing process is partly intended to demonstrate that the pattern and connectivity of chains of interdependence have undergone significant demonstrable historical transform-ations.[17] For example, the history of manners reveals an unanticipated, unplanned process in which interpersonal behaviour gradually became more restrained and the notion of sensitivity to others became normalized.

So it is with functional democratization. As the chains of interdependence connecting individuals multiplied, the chances of one individual or one group of individuals being able to satisfy the bulk of their needs by their own resources diminished. With the rise of the money economy, greater numbers of individuals began to devote their labour power to specialized functions in the division of labour and use surplus income to pay for goods and services that they could no longer supply for themselves. Similarly, as the institutions of normative coercion crystallized, the power ratios between individuals changed. As individuals became more dependent upon one another for the satisfaction of their physical and social needs the drive to recognize mutuality, acknowledge reciprocity and extend standards of tolerance to others was enhanced. The physical control of illegitimate behaviour was 'exported' to specialized institutions of normative coercion. Elias's theory emphasizes that functional democratization was instrumental in generating a *milieu* in which formal equality could be more readily acknowledged. Yet, although it recognizes the creation of new opportunities for social mobility and domination, and also for the idealization of particular individuals, his account tends to assign priority to the long-term levelling trend in balance of power relationships. Of course balance is always involved. For example, Elias maintains that the increasing division of functions solidified the concept of the individual as well as subjecting all individuals to new standards of behaviour that emerged in an unplanned and unintended way.[18] The threshold of shame and embarrassment in respect of aggression and incivility are examples that he explored more systematically elsewhere.[19] Although there are strong pressures to demarcate and elevate the individual from the rest of society, they are balanced by countervailing pressures to recognize mutuality, reciprocity and interdependence. Elias demonstrates that the long-term tendency is for the balance of power between first, the absolutist court and the society of commoners and later, the dominant industrial class and the rising working class, to diminish.[20] Of course, as with the general civilizing process, there are historical counter-reactions to this trend along many fronts. To take one example, his book on the Germans indicates that the Nazi Party was effective in introducing new status and racial divisions which suspended the *milieu* of formal equality and the meritocratic ideal.[21] It also suggests that in particular circumstances the demarcation between individual and society can sway from functional interdependence and reciprocity to authoritarian absolutism based around the cult of personality. However, for Elias, the long-term trend remains unambiguous. Functional democratization increases the general social consciousness of interdependence and bolsters the authority of the meritocratic ideal over the hereditary principle in the distribution of distinction, honour and economic resources.

It might be ventured that the corollary to all of this is the establishment of an achievement culture fastened to the meritocratic ideal, as opposed to the hereditary principle. All human groups require a basis for social integration and the distribution of resources. In tribal and traditional society this is supplied by the hereditary principle, which allocates status and economic capital on sponsorship criteria. Although sponsorship criteria persist in modern society, notably in respect of formal distinctions of ascribed celebrity and, more generally, in the terrain of cultural capital, the meritocratic ideal is ascendant. The meritocratic ideal is the corollary of democratic multi-party systems and enjoins that, formally speaking, status is achieved through participation in a contest system of reward.

The education system is one of the paradigmatic examples of this. In education, the individual participates in formalized knowledge contests designed to articulate and evaluate personal intelligence and self-discipline. In higher education this is conducted through the essay, the seminar presentation, the dissertation and the examination, and codified through the degree classification system in which personal merit is professionally assessed. The result is that some individuals leave university with higher degree classifications than others. This socially approved ranking system serves to differentiate individuals and, as such, should be regarded as an important institutional component in the process of individualization in contemporary society.

The employment system is another example. The meritocratic ideal is directly articulated through the ideology of equal opportunities. The employment interview is formally constituted as a level-playing field in which hereditary and other inegalitarian influences are present only in the cultural capital of the individual, that is, in terms of what they bear as a result of their habitus. By definition, it is also a contest situation in which all applicants accept that only one person will be offered the job.

In societies based around the meritocratic ideal, sport is also one of the paradigmatic institutions that articulate and elaborate the meritocratic ideal and reinforce achievement culture. In sport the value of individual discipline, training, teamwork, endurance, determination and ambition is potently stressed. The sporting contest is the arena in which these competing values are tested and collectively recognized. Moreover, because the basis of all sports is the body, sport presents a universal focus for what might be called the narrativization of achievement culture. Since embodiment is the prerequisite for participation in sport, it follows that it offers a universal focus for identity-formation and status ranking. As Dunning puts it:

> Modern sports are more than just contests to see who can run fastest, jump highest or score the highest number of runs, points or goals; they also involve forms of identity testing which, because the people involved have learned of the social value attached to sport, are crucial for the self-concepts of these individuals and their rank ordering as members of a group.[22]

Sport is presented as a social institution which increases the functionality of individuals by increasing their capacities and skills and also helps to integrate society by enlarging 'We-I' identification.

The Problems of Egoism and Commodification

However, neither Dunning nor Elias focused in any detail on the relationship between functional democratization, egoism and commodification.[23] The questions of egoism and commodification were logically consistent with the theory of the civilizing process but, as with the problem of the cultural articulation of some individuals as a system of representation possessing general cultural significance, they remain underdeveloped research areas in the figurational/process approach. Durkheim's study of *Suicide* supplies the classic statement of egoism in relation to the division of labour. While his work does not address the relationship between sport and industrial civilization, he does comment on the relationship between egoism and fantasy formation in egoistic individuals:

> Feeling ... that a constant passage from one egoistic pleasure to another is a poor method of escaping themselves and that fugitive joys, even though constantly renewed, could never quiet their unrest, they seek some durable object to which to attach themselves permanently and which shall give meaning to their lives. Since they are contended with nothing real, however, they can find satisfaction only in creating out of whole cloth some ideal reality to play this role. So in thought they create an imaginary being whose slaves they become and to which they devote themselves the more exclusively the more they are detached from everything else, themselves included. To it they assign all the attachment to existence which they ascribe to themselves, since all else is valueless in their eyes.[24]

In the terminology of figurational/process sociology, Durkheim's proposition might be expressed thus: egoism tilts the We-I balance in a direction which threatens personal wellbeing and social order. Durkheim's analysis suggests that the tendency towards egoism is generally distributed in society by the division of labour. It may become problematic when external conditions such as war, economic slump or political scandal, dictate. For Durkheim, egoism is a general tendency in the division of labour. It is not, however, a general problem either at the level of individual behaviour or social order. It only becomes so when certain external conditions obtain.

Durkheim, like Elias and Dunning, does not address the question of the relationship between commodification and egoism in detail. In the area of sports studies the question has been addressed by writers including Paul Hoch,[25] Gary Whannel,[26] Ellis Cashmore[27] and Doug Kellner.[28] Although there are important differences between their approaches, these commentators treat the sports celebrity as an idealized system of representation which is assembled by cultural intermediaries to generate social impact and pecuniary gain. For Cashmore and Kellner, the sports celebrity is, first and foremost, a product of the combination between the corporation and the media and must be approached as an example of commodification. They argue that corporations and the media package celebrities in idealized forms in order to maximize social impact and revenue. Kellner, drawing on the work of the situationist theorist Guy DeBord and the Frankfurt tradition of criticism, suggests that the sports celebrity is increasingly presented as an exalted participant in spectacular events.[29] David Beckham, Lennox Lewis, Tiger Woods, Anna Kournikova, the Williams sisters and Michael Schumacher have been elevated above the realm of mere contestants in sport to become global, fantasy sporting ideals, heroic players in all-encompassing sporting spectacles. To paraphrase Durkheim, they are portrayed as 'ideal objects' to which audiences 'assign the ultimate attachment to existence' since 'all else is valueless in their eyes'. According to Kellner, the form of the sporting spectacle accentuates the superior physical and gaming skills of sports celebrities and reinforces general fatalism by reducing the audience to spectators. The virtuosity of the player is portrayed as widening the gap between performer and public, thereby reinforcing the exalted status of the sports celebrity. On this reading, sports celebrities exert a disempowering effect in popular culture by emphasizing the gulf between the celebrity and the fan.

Cashmore, Whannel and Kellner emphasize the centrality of sports celebrity in contemporary popular culture. Celebrities are the idealized objects of popular fantasy, *par excellence.* There are several reasons for this. Four should be mentioned here.

Firstly, the growth of satellite television since the 1980s has enhanced the profile of sport in broadcasting schedules. The sponsorship deals associated with BSkyB's broadcasting of soccer in the UK and the ESPN cable channel's transmission of basketball in the USA have made both sports ubiquitous on television. Live matches are supplemented by a variety of commentary and analysis broadcasts consisting of sports news digests, interviews and previews. Only pop music and news, through channels like MTV, and the 24-hour news services provided by CNN and the BBC, rival the ascendance of sports in TV culture.

Secondly, over the last 25 years, the cultural *cachet* of sports has benefited from the increased concern with health and fitness in popular culture, itself the consequence of increased medical knowledge. If the healthy body is now widely desired and valued as an object of esteem in popular culture, the sports celebrity is the embodiment of this social category.

Thirdly, sports stars have been adopted as powerful symbolic tokens to negotiate the so-called crisis in masculinity. This argument is most closely associated with Whannel. He contends that in the 1990s sports celebrities acquired what might be called enhanced powers of moral regulation. Of course, these powers are powers of example rather than direct control. Whannel relates their growth to the increased prominence of sport in the media. In functional terms he argues that the influence of the sports celebrity has increased, while other figureheads and role models, from the social institutions of the family, the school and religion, have declined in power.[30]

Fourthly, the pre-eminence of sport in popular culture has reinforced the economic power of the sector. Sponsorship and prize money have increased. This translates into the modernization of stadia and ground facilities. It is also reflected in the salary structure of top sports players which now rivals Hollywood scales of reward.

The Elevation of the Sports Celebrity

Sports celebrities are now at the vanguard of popular culture. In his classic, and still very useful study of the Western power elite, C. Wright Mills examined the importance of interlocking circles in the domination of urban-industrial society.[31] Presciently, he identified the entertainment elite as growing in power and pointed to the interrelationships and mergers between it and the business, political and military elites. But he never seriously entertained the notion of an elite in sport that might move freely between all of these circles and enjoy a coveted status in its own right.

Yet this is exactly what has come to pass in celebrity culture, with top sports stars moving freely between elite circles in television, pop music, business and fashion. One sign of this is the growth of increasingly close relationships between sports players and representatives from other elite circles. In the 1950s, marriages and romances between sports celebrities and celebrities in other areas of society were infrequent. The unions between Billy Wright and Joy Beverley in England and Joe Di Maggio and Marilyn Monroe in the USA were exceptions to the rule. Arguably, with hindsight, they were harbingers of scene-changing developments in celebrity culture. Certainly, there was no parallel to the expanse of recent and current personal relationships between top sports stars and representatives from other areas of the celebritariat: John McEnroe and Tatum O'Neal, Jamie and Louise Redknapp (née Nurding), Andre Agassi and Brooke Shields, David and Victoria Beckham (née Adams), Fabian Barthez and Linda Evangilista, Kenny and Gaby Logan (née Yorath) and Jacques Villeneuve and Danni Minogue. And in terms of news coverage, advertising, political endorsement and product placement, there is a wealth of evidence to suggest that sports celebrity now permeates popular culture.

The elevation of the sports celebrity in popular culture over the last two years has been nothing short of astonishing. As Dunning and Sheard argue in what is perhaps the classic statement, the nineteenth-century roots of sports players and amateurs lay in close ties between participants and communities.[32] Participants represented communities as members of teams. Symbolically speaking, rugby, soccer and cricket teams embodied urban and suburban populations. Initially, with one or two notable exceptions, such as the cricketer W.G. Grace, spectators related to the team rather than the player. Team sports in industrial society were influenced by the ideology of muscular Christianity, which was based upon strong principles of social inclusion between players and spectators. Even when the spurt towards professionalization occurred in the twentieth century and players began to be recognized and rewarded for their 'star' quality, ties between sports celebrities and communities were cogently stressed. In soccer, stars like Stanley Matthews, Nat Lofthouse, Tom Finney, Johnny Haynes, Wilf Mannion and Stan Mortensen did not merely *play* for, respectively, Stoke City, Bolton Wanderers, Preston North End, Fulham, Middlesborough and Blackpool. They were the *apotheosis* of the culture of their cities, symbolizing not only the heart and soul of the spectators who watched them but the spirit of the associated community. Perhaps their wages were higher than most of the people who watched them from the terraces, and they certainly relished the superior status of achieved celebrity. Notwithstanding this, there was no sense of a lifestyle chasm between them and spectators, no implication that both followed the same game but lived in entirely different economic and cultural worlds.

Now, in an era where the salaries of top players are not measured in thousands but millions, and where politicians compete with each other to be photographed in the presence of the cream of the sporting crop, the situation has been transformed. Elevation is the process by which individuals of accomplishment are raised from the ranks of ordinary men and women into the echelons of achieved celebrity culture. The process usually involves dedicated teams of cultural intermediaries, who protect the financial interests of the player and seek to establish a monopoly position over the celebrity's image as a system of representation.[33] Sports celebrities like David Beckham, Roy Keane, Michael Jordan and the Williams sisters are aware of their advertising and merchandizing potential as brands and endeavour to legally codify their image rights.

As the income and cultural power of sports celebrities have increased, so the strength of ties with city and regional communities has attenuated. Soccer stars like Eric Cantona, Gianfranco Zola, Patrick Viera, Thierry Henri and Nicholas Anelka epitomize the disembedded social actors beloved by theorists of later modernity and globalization.[34] They are cosmopolitan flexible accumulators who exchange bonds of city, region and even nation, to participate at the highest levels in their chosen sport and, of course, for the highest salaries. They also bear the classic traits of the *nouveaux riches,* in being financially and culturally displaced from the working-class cultures from whose ranks they usually emerge and in lacking the cultural capital to become fully integrated into established dominant strata. In respect of the latter, the situation may be changing dramatically. I have already noted the increasing mobility of sports celebrities into personal relationships with representatives from other elite circles. The sheer scale of wealth enjoyed by top sports stars breaks down cultural barriers and, to some degree, overcomes problems of cultural capital. In addition, in late twentieth-century Western popular culture there is reason to believe that an important shift in glamour and influence has occurred between groups whose power derives from cultural distinction (novelists, playwrights, scientists, politicians, academics) towards idealized cultural bearers of 'the healthy/fit body', as embodied by fashion models and sports celebrities.

There is an immediate wholesomeness and allure about the image of the sports celebrity that is very piquantly expressed in popular culture. Film and rock stars like Marilyn Monroe, Elvis Presley, Jimi Hendrix, Brian Jones, Jim Morrison, River Phoenix and Kurt Cobain are portrayed as casualties of permissive society. They have emerged as case studies of the neurosis of celebrity culture with its inflated reward structure and moral licence. Sports celebrities have not avoided this stereotypical moral reaction. For example, in the UK there is a long tradition of soccer stars confessing to battles with either drink or drugs: Jimmy Greaves, George Best, Paul Gascoigne and Paul Merson. However, the pronounced image of the sports celebrity is that of the strenuously disciplined and achieved healthy body. Sports stars are presented as models of achieved celebrity, in as much as their fame is portrayed as a reflection of talent, training and determination.

Needless to say, despite their differences, Hoch, Cashmore, Whannel and Kellner staunchly eschew naturalistic explanations of sports celebrity. Instead they propose a hierarchical relationship between the corporation (the agent of commodification), celebrity (the idealized object) and the spectator (the commodified subject). The inference is that social integration is galvanized around the commodification process which, in effect, operates as a system of control and manipulation. Cultural intermediaries assemble the sports celebrity as a system of representation that is designed to make spectators consume commodities. This, of course, goes well beyond the range of products that bear the brand of the sports celebrity. It includes the various exercises in product endorsement performed by celebrities, from selling mobile phones to Apple laptops. This approach does not deny the role of talent, training and determination in projecting the sports celebrity into popular culture. However, it contends that the role of the corporation and its associated cultural intermediaries is of axial importance. Thus, Cashmore's analysis of *Beckham Inc* cogently stresses the prior and dominant relationship of *Manchester United Inc*. But is this a sufficient explanation of the process of elevation and, in particular, of the social psychology of fans?

Invasive Egoism

There is perhaps little point in gainsaying the proposition that commodification is a significant element in sports celebrity culture. It is no less than one would expect of the elevation of the sports star in culture, society and economy. The evidence of extensive commodification in sport is compelling, so much so that it is legitimate to refer to 'the sports industry', much as the Frankfurt School referred to 'the culture industry'.[35] Of course, the caveat should be added that the concept of the sports industry carries none of the closure and 'one-dimensionality' associated with the Frankfurt School in its heyday. Notwithstanding this, the sports industry unquestionably idealizes images of sports celebrities so that they become general objects of glamour and fantasy in popular culture.

But what does it mean to construct or participate in a culture dedicated to the idealization of particular individuals as a system of representation which is designed to have general social and economic influence? The commodification thesis tends to supply a 'top-down' model of idealization. An alliance between the celebrity corporation and the media is presented as the crucible in the idealization process. The sports celebrity and the fan are portrayed as reacting programmatically to the triggers implanted by the corporation and the media in the system of representation which culturally articulate the celebrity as an idealized figure in popular culture. However, this obscures the character of the 'We-I' balance in contemporary society which, it might be held, is strongly conducive to the construction of idealized celebrities.

Let me make the following case. In building an idealized object and supporting imaginary relationships between the object and the spectator, the sports industry contributes to what might be called invasive egoism. That is, a syndrome in which the fan retreats into an inner world in which, echoing Durkheim again, the attractions of the 'world outside' are insubstantial. It is relevant here to recall, as Dunning reminds us, that the etymological root of 'fan' is *fanatic,* a term which conveys an intense, in some cases, overwhelming emotional attachment to an external object.[36] For the fanatical 'fan', the attachment to an external celebrity is both a mark of individual distinction and a furlough from the routines of everyday life. The centre of life becomes the vicarious, imaginary relations between the fan and the idealized object. These imaginary relations become substitutes for real relations at home or work which may be experienced as unsatisfactory. Through vicarious identification with the sports celebrity, fans may compensate for emotional deprivation or a lack of achievement in personal life. Elias and Dunning suggested that sport has a mimetic function in the civilizing process.[37] That is, it allows for the arousal of powerful emotions which are generally controlled and inhibited by the functional requirements of urban-industrial society. Sports spectatorship acts as an escape valve for pent-up emotions, permitting tension-release and the 'acting out' of aggression. However, this discussion of mimetic leisure did not extend to consider the fantasy content of sports celebrity, the incitement of fantasy by the media or the development of psychological dependency ties in the fan around imaginary relations.

By following this logic a number of possibilities present themselves. Among the most intriguing is to posit an alternative approach to questions of hooliganism and crowd violence in sport. That is, an approach which places more weight upon the place of idealization processes, fantasy objects and imaginary relations in promoting violent conduct.

Imaginary relations and fantasies around sports celebrities have always been present. However, in contemporary society several conditions are in place that increase their presence in popular culture. The ubiquity of the media immediately comes to mind. But its cultural influence is itself a reflection of a transition from strongly to weakly integrated communities. This has been a longstanding theme in the sociology of industrial society as is evidenced in the distinctions made by Sir Henry Maine between 'status' and 'contract', Ferdinand Tonnies's 'Gemeinschaft versus Gesellschaft', Emile Durkheim's 'mechanical' versus 'organic' solidarity and David Riesman's 'inner' and 'outer' directed personalities.[38] More recently, David Putnam enjoyed major public success with his thesis that civil engagement has declined in everyday life and been replaced by privatized, fragmentary, contingent relations.[39] The burden of all of these arguments is that levels of social isolation and mobility have increased, making individuals unusually susceptible for support to the imaginary relations associated with the media. There is some evidence that this condition is favourable to the development of fanatical forms of behaviour.

For example, in celebrity culture at large we know that the incidence of stalking, kidnapping and assassination has increased over the last 25 years. The murderers of John Lennon in 1980, Rebecca Schaeffer, the star of the US TV sitcom *My Sister Sam*, who was murdered in 1989, and the BBC TV presenter Jill Dando, who was murdered in 1999, were all stalkers. In 1996 a man who had been stalking Madonna for a number of years was sentenced to 10 years in prison. One year later, a stalker who had been harassing the film director, Stephen Spielberg, was sentenced to 25 years in prison.

There is some evidence to suggest that sports celebrities are now becoming targets. In 1993, at the quarter-final stage of a tennis tournament in Hamburg, Monica Seles was stabbed by Gunther Parche who had formed an obsessive, imaginary relationship with Steffi Graff and sought to eliminate the chief rival to Graff's championship hopes. Seles retired from tennis for over two years. In 2000 Dubravka Rajevic was found guilty of stalking the tennis star Martina Hingis. In 2003, five men were charged with a kidnap attempt on Victoria Beckham and her son, Brooklyn. The data are hardly enough to support conclusive propositions. Yet inferentially they suggest that the price of elevation is that sports celebrities are at greater risk from stalking and harassment than was the case a quarter of a century ago.

Conclusion

I have argued that the influence of the sports celebrity is a neglected feature of the figurational/process approach. Functional democratization produces a 'We-I' balance from which, in conditions of media saturation, commodification, mobility and social isolation, syndromes of invasive egoism are, in an unplanned, unintended way, engendered. In these conditions, which I believe are close to Durkheim's category of 'high moral density', idealized systems of representation built around individuals who are acknowledged to be role models occupy a necessary place. Of course, these figures exemplify the process of commodification. However, I prefer to advance their role in moral regulation. Celebrities, I propose, offer parables to modern men and women of how to live their lives.[40] These parables have increased in significance as traditional structures of influence such as the family and organized religion have declined. There is no doubt that the corporation and media can shape these parables for their own ends. The sociology of media amplification and moral panics tends to confirm this. However, the cultural articulation of celebrity systems of representation and the repertoire of parables that they express are also functional corollaries of functional democratization and the civilizing process. A worthwhile goal of the figurational/ process perspective is the elucidation of this relationship, especially in the area of sports celebrity.

Notes

[1] Elias, 'Theory of Science and History of Science: Comments on a Recent Discussion'; 'The Sciences: Towards a Theory'; 'Scientific Establishments'.

[2] Alfred Weber occupied a chair of Sociology in Heidelberg where Elias studied. Karl Mannheim was part of the younger generation of lecturers in Heidelberg. When Mannheim accepted the chair of sociology at Frankfurt University he appointed Elias as his academic assistant.

[3] Elias and Scotson, *The Established and the Outsiders*; Elias, *Involvement and Detachment*.

[4] Elias's attack on Parsons is a case in point. See Elias, *The Civilizing Process Vol. 1*.

[5] See Dunning, 'Figurational Sociology and the Sociology of Sport', 221–84 for one of his most detailed 'exceptions to the rule'.

[6] Dunning, *Sport Matters*, 3.

[7] Elias, *The Society of Individuals*.

[8] Elias and Dunning, *Quest for Excitement*.

[9] George Ritzer, drawing on the Weberian tradition, has modernized the rationalization thesis in intriguing ways in his theory of the *McDonaldization* of society. See in particular, Ritzer, *The McDonaldization of Society*.

[10] See, in particular, Dunning, Murphy and Williams, *The Roots of Football Hooliganism*; Murphy, Williams and Dunning, *Football on Trial*.

[11] Elias, *The Civilizing Process Vol. 2*.

[12] Elias, *The Society of Individuals*.

[13] Elias, *Mozart*; Elias, *The Germans*.

[14] Elias, *The Court Society*.

[15] Goffman, *Interaction Ritual*; Goffman, *Frame Analysis*.

[16] Turner and Rojek, *Society & Culture*.

[17] Elias, *The Civilizing Process*.

[18] Elias, *The Society of Individuals*.

[19] Especially in Elias, *The Civilizing Process*.

[20] Ibid.

[21] Elias, *The Germans*.

[22] Dunning, *Sport Matters*, 5.

[23] It should perhaps be noted that the relationship between functional democratization, egoism and commodification is a *latent* feature of the theory of the civilizing process.

[24] Durkheim, *Suicide*, 289.

[25] Hoch, *Rip Off the Big Game*.

[26] Whannel, *Media Sports Stars*.

[27] Cashmore, *Beckham*.

[28] Kellner, *Media Spectacle*.

[29] DeBord, *The Society of the Spectacle*.

[30] Whannel, *Media Sports Stars*, 213.

[31] Wright Mills, *The Power Elite*.

[32] Dunning and Sheard, *Barbarians, Gentlemen and Players*.

[33] Rojek, *Celebrity*.

[34] Harvey, *The Condition of Postmodernity*; Giddens, *The Consequences of Modernity*; Beck, *Individualization*.

[35] Adorno and Horkheimer, *The Dialectics of Enlightenment*; Marcuse, *One Dimensional Man*.

[36] Dunning, *Sport Matters*, 6.

[37] Elias and Dunning, *Quest for Excitement*.

[38] David Riesman's classic, *The Lonely Crowd*, outlines a sophisticated reading of social transformations in the dynamics of personality and is one of the first convincing investigations of the relationship between personality formation and the media.

[39] Putnam, *Bowling Alone*.

[40] I hold that in societies of high moral density, the requirement for moral parables reflects occupational and geographical mobility and de-differentiation. One way of studying how sports celebrities function to provide parables for modern life is *via* the obituaries of sporting heroes. For example, when the British motorcycle star Barry Sheene died in 2003, the obituaries were to some extent morally ambivalent about his life. On the one hand they praised his heroism, determination and professionalism. On the other hand, they suggested that his taste for the high life in some way contributed to his premature death and, as such, offered a role model that was not to be emulated.

References

Adorno, T. and M. Horkheimer. *The Dialectics of Enlightenment*. Translation from 1947 original. London: Verso, 1986.

Beck, Ulrich. *Individualization*. London: Sage, 2001.

Cashmore, Ellis. *Beckham*. Cambridge: Polity Press, 2002.

DeBord, G. *The Society of the Spectacle*. Detroit: Black and Red, 1967.

Dunning, E. "Figurational Sociology and the Sociology of Sport: Some Concluding Remarks." In *Sport and Leisure in the Civilizing Process: Critique and Counter-Critique*, edited by E. Dunning and C. Rojek. Basingstoke and London: Macmillan, 1992.

Dunning, E. *Sport Matters: Sociological Studies of Sport, Violence and Civilization*. London: Routledge, 1999.

Dunning, E. and Rojek, C., eds. *Sport and Leisure in the Civilizing Process: Critique and Counter-Critique*. Basingstoke and London: Macmillan, 1992.

Dunning, E. and K. Sheard. *Barbarians, Gentlemen and Players: A Study of the Development of Rugby Football*. 2nd edn. London: Routledge, 2005.

Dunning, E., P. Murphy, and J. Williams. *The Roots of Football Hooliganism. An Historical and Sociological Study*. London: Routledge and Kegan Paul, 1988.

Durkheim, Emile. *Suicide*. Glencoe, IL: Free Press, 1951.

Elias, N. "Theory of Science and History of Science: Comments on a Recent Discussion." *Economy and Society* 1, no. 2 (1972): 117–33.

Elias, N. "The Sciences: Towards a Theory." In *Social Process of Scientific Development*, edited by R. Whitley. London: Routledge and Kegan Paul, 1974: 21–42.

Elias, N. *The Civilizing Process Vol. 1: The History of Manners*. Oxford: Blackwell, 1978.

Elias, N. *The Civilizing Process Vol. 2: State Formation and Civilization*. Oxford: Blackwell, 1982.

Elias, N. "Scientific Establishments." In *Scientific Establishments and Hierarchies*, edited by N. Elias, R. Whitley, and H. Martins. Dordrecht: Reidel, 1982: 3–69.

Elias, N. *The Court Society*. Oxford: Blackwell, 1983.

Elias, N. *Involvement and Detachment*. Oxford: Blackwell, 1987.

Elias, N. *The Society of Individuals*. Oxford: Basil Blackwell, 1991.

Elias, N. *Mozart: Portrait of a Genius*. Cambridge: Polity Press, 1993.

Elias, N. *Studien über die Deutschen*. Frankfurt: Suhrkamp Verlag, 1989. Published in English as *The Germans*, translated by E. Dunning and S. Mennell. Cambridge: Polity Press, 1996.

Elias, N. *The Civilizing Process*. Revised edn. Oxford: Blackwell, 2000.

Elias, N. and E. Dunning. *Quest for Excitement: Sport and Leisure in the Civilising Process*. Oxford: Blackwell, 1986.

Elias, N. and J.L. Scotson. *The Established and the Outsiders*. 2nd edn. London: Sage, 1994.

Giddens, Anthony. *The Consequences of Modernity*. Cambridge: Polity, 1990.

Goffman, Erving. *Interaction Ritual*. New York: Pantheon, 1967.

Goffman, Erving. *Frame Analysis*. New York: Harper and Row, 1974.

Harvey, D. *The Condition of Postmodernity*. Oxford: Blackwell, 1989.

Hoch, Paul. *Rip Off the Big Game*. New York: Anchor, 1972.

Kellner, David. *Media Spectacle*. London: Routledge, 2003.

Marcuse, H. *One Dimensional Man*. London: Abacus, 1964.

Murphy, P., J. Williams, and E. Dunning. *Football on Trial*. London: Routledge, 1990.

Putnam, David. *Bowling Alone*. New York: Touchstone, 2000.

Riesman, David. *The Lonely Crowd*. New York: Doubleday, 1950.

Ritzer, George. *The McDonaldization of Society: An Investigation into the Changing Character of Contemporary Social Life*. Thousand Oaks, CA and London: Pine Forge Press, 1993.

Rojek, Chris. *Celebrity*. London: Reaktion, 2001.

Turner, B. and C. Rojek. *Society & Culture: Principles of Scarcity and Solidarity*. London: Sage, 2001.

Whannel, Garry. *Media Sports Stars*. London: Routledge, 2002.

Wright Mills, Charles. *The Power Elite*. New York: Oxford University Press, 1956.

INDEX